Spatial Choice and Spatial Behavior

SPATIAL CHOICE
AND SPATIAL BEHAVIOR

Geographic Essays on the
Analysis of Preferences and Perceptions

Edited by

REGINALD G. GOLLEDGE
and
GERARD RUSHTON

OHIO STATE UNIVERSITY PRESS: COLUMBUS

Library of Congress Cataloging in Publication Data

Main entry under title:

Spatial choice and spatial behavior.

  Includes index.
  1. Geographical perception—Addresses, essays, lectures. 2. Choice (Psychology)—
Addresses, essays, lectures. 3. Cities and towns—Addresses, essays, lectures. I. Golledge,
Reginald G., 1937– II. Rushton, Gerard. [DNLM: 1. Spatial behavior—Essays. 2. Space
perception—Essays. BF469 S738]
G71.5.S67   910   76–889
ISBN 0-8142-0241-1

CONTENTS

INTRODUCTION

Social scientists in the nineteenth century widely recognized the pivotal role of human perceptions and preferences in their philosophies and their theories. Because their art of empirical investigation was relatively poorly developed in comparison with the natural sciences, they were forced to deal abstractly with concepts such as human values, wants, needs, and choices. Operationalizing these concepts has taken the best part of this century, and still there is conflict over their meaning, significance, and implication.

An increasing concern for operationalized concepts encouraged twentieth-century geographers to concentrate on directly measurable things such as locations, distributions, and interactions. As the level of empirical information concerning spatial patterns of human activities and spatial manifestations of human decisions increased, so too did a desire for adequate explanations and understanding of such information. Having achieved a certain facility for describing the spatial properties of inanimate phenomena (such as physical and economic landscapes), geographers turned to analyzing the reasons for the spatial existence of these phenomena. Questions asked included: Can patterns of spatial organization be understood in terms of a logic of individual decision-making? Can "optimal" patterns of spatial organization be constructed that maximize a set of "internally felt" preferences? Can strategies be identified that, if followed, would lead to spatial organizational patterns consistent with individual preferences? They soon realized that analysis of these questions required operational versions of the abstract concepts of human thought and action found so freely in nineteenth-century literature. Perhaps even more important, however, has been a renewed interest in the role of human behavioral processes in our explanations of spatial phenomena. The essays presented in this book provide examples of the diversity of opinions currently held regarding the potential role of the processes of perception and preference in explaining sensate spatial behavior.

Much past geographical research supports the contention that information about man's external environment is filtered and distorted in the minds of people and thus decisions should be studied in relation to "imaged" rather than "objective" worlds. Pursuit of this train of thought has focused some studies in "behavioral" geography on the perceived components of environments (or the "cognized" environment). The argument set forth to justify this emphasis is that, if we can understand *how* human minds process information from external environments and if we can determine *what* they process and use, then we can investigate how and why choices concerning those environments are made. Questions that are raised by this argument include: Does *what* is extracted from the environment depend on the type of exposure to it? Are there rules that guide the filtering process such that common decisions can be made by many humans? Are these rules capable of generalization across different environments, or are they place specific? If the acquisition of environmental knowledge is a learning process, which are the positive and which are the negative signals that affect the chance of an environmental element being noticed and used or eliminated from consideration? In short, the questions investigated revolve around the extraction and use of spatial information from external environments.

Although it is of considerable importance to understand cognized environments as well as external ones, this understanding adds little useful knowledge unless we comprehend *how* man uses his cognized environment. To understand this, geographers have focused on the spatial component in decision-making processes. Several essays in this book illustrate this concern. In particular they examine questions such as: When people make choices, what hypothetical ordering of attributes of choice phenomena is most consistent with the attributes of events actually chosen? How is this ordering accomplished? Is there some functional ordering of attribute combinations that can be estimated by an objective function? What is the nature of this function? Should the estimating function be based on actual or perceived attribute characteristics? Obviously, this last question is closely linked to the cognitive questions previously identified.

The success of research into the spatial significance of perception and preference is necessarily tied to the joint problems of concept identification and measurement. Not only do we need to know which variables are relevant but we also need to develop appropriate methods for *measuring* them. A particular problem faced by geographers is to develop measurements that are independent of the context of place—for if this cannot be achieved, how can we evaluate the effects of place? Other problems requiring solution include: the examination of sequential decisions and their consistency or variability in differential spatial contexts, the validation of results obtained from experiments with humans, and the selection of experimental decisions (for, say, the examination of choice potential) that give the greatest compatibility with studies focusing on revealed choice patterns.

The problems identified above are serious ones, yet geographers have done little toward their solution. This is due in no small part to the recency of their explication. There is little doubt in our minds that their solution will dramatically change our level of understanding of spatial phenomena. The purpose of this book is to illustrate a variety of current attempts to achieve solutions, and to highlight not only the results that have so far been achieved but to show some pitfalls and problems that await the unwary researcher.

It should be obvious to the reader that few if any of the problems previously mentioned are *solved* in the essays presented here. To date too little work has been done by too few people in the discipline to accomplish such a goal. However, each essay clearly illustrates a concern for achieving solutions; even those critical of the philosophies and approaches currently in use emphasize the *need* to look more closely at the problems identified in this paper.

The authors represented in the volume belong to no single school of thought, and indeed, implicit in some papers are criticisms of the others.

In most of the essays, there is some borrowing of ideas from other disciplines; this borrowing is at once eclectic and necessary, for geographers appear to be conceptually and methodologically naïve as far as many problems of preference and perception are concerned. A second purpose of this book, therefore, is to provide general information about the degrees of success of the borrowings made by each author.

Human geographers today are less strictly tied to the analysis of the spatial properties of man's artifacts than they were a decade ago. There is considerable evidence of widespread concern in geography with things such as the effects of public policy on man and the effects of changing resource sets on man. Our emphasis on problems related to the dimensions of preference and choice, and our interest in achieving a full understanding of man's use of his environment, falls well within the scope of this concern. Our third purpose, therefore, is to present a range of problems that need to be solved before we can provide serious suggestions for eliminating these worries.

The processes discussed in this volume are generally behavioral in nature. Of particular importance are spatial choice processes and processes of extracting information from the objective environment. Many are also concerned with philosophical problems of the behavioral approach and/or with methods of representing cognitive phenomena in traditional geographic formats such as maps.

The bulk of the papers presented in this book were written for a symposium on "The Multidimensional Analysis of Perceptions and Preferences," which was organized by Golledge and Rushton for the national meetings of the Association of American Geographers at Atlanta in April 1973. Unfortunately, there was insufficient time at the meetings to explore the many interesting problems brought out by authors and commentators—hence the idea of publishing the revised papers and comments to cater to the considerable amount of interest in the subject expressed by those attending the symposium. The original symposium consisted of papers by Tobler, Golledge and Rivizzigno, Rushton, Harman, Lieber, Lueck, and Louviere. Comments were prepared on selections of these papers by Curry, Burnett, Lycan, and Menchik. The session was admirably chaired by Joseph Sonnenfeld. Subsequent to the meetings, authors were invited to revise their papers, and commentators were invited to expand their comments to paper length or to formalize them for publication. Invitations were extended to Hanson and Ewing to add new papers for the volume, and Gould, Goodchild, and Clark were invited to prepare formal comments on groups of the revised papers.

The book itself is divided into three sections. The first section includes papers by Harman and Betak, Burnett, Sonnenfeld, and Tobler. Philosophical problems related to behavioral work in general, the complexity of the human mind, and methods of extracting and representing cognitive phenomena are discussed in the first two papers. Relationships between individuals and their environment are discussed by Sonnenfeld through the medium of personality theory. Tobler clearly and concisely discusses the mathematical bases of methods for representing various types of cognitive phenomena, showing that cognitive cartography can be used as confidently as we use cartographic representations of objective phenomena.

The second section presents a variety of approaches to the analysis of spatial behavior. Golledge, Rivizzigno, and Spector present an experimental design for recovering cognitive configurations of places in urban areas and suggest the exploration of the relationships between the degree of learning about places in the city and urban spatial behavior. A multidimensional scaling procedure is used to recover levels of cognitive information about a sample city. Rushton discusses three approaches to the problem of decomposing space preference functions and finds an amazing degree of coincidence among the methods. He likewise analyzes preferences using multidimensional scaling procedures. Knight and Menchik illustrate how the estimation of preferences for residential land can be used in policy evaluation procedures. Thus, they illustrate a potential practical use of analyses of choice and perceptions. Hanson uses unidimensional scaling procedures to discuss variations in the quantity of cognitive information about places in the city held by urban residents and then illustrates how such information is related to consumer behavior. Although scaling procedures are used to determine the levels of information, regression analysis is used to analyze the hypothesized relations with spatial behavior.

The third section illustrates a variety of problems, theoretical and empirical, that are currently being researched by behavioral geographers. Louviere's paper comments on the need for rigorous experimental designs for the study of spatial behavioral phenomena and suggests mathematical methods of information integration as alternatives to the various scaling procedures used in other papers in the book. Lieber discusses some characteristics of metric and nonmetric methods used in research on the spatial aspects of cognitive phenomena. Lueck and Ewing adopt somewhat different approaches to the migration problem, the first examining preference structures for cities as a variable in the migration process, the latter examining perceptions and preferences of migrants for states. Clark's commentary on these largely empirically oriented papers completes the section.

A number of things are common to all the essays in this volume. First is a deep concern for rigor, objectivity, and a scientific approach to the analysis of behavioral problems. Second is a concern for broadening the scope of existing geographical theory by including process variables. Third is an expression of confidence in the value of quantitatively analyzing behavioral data. Fourth is an awareness that we are now dealing with a relative unknown, the human mind, and that we must become fully aware of the philosophical and methodological problems associated with such dealings. Fifth is an expression of cautious optimism in the ability of geographers to expand the set of relevant variables used to analyze spatial phenomena to include behavioral process variables.

The problem of providing meaningful answers to questions related to spatial choice and spatial behavior is by no means solved. However, if one compares the content of this volume with that of a publication derived from a somewhat similar conference held at the AAG meeting in 1969,[1] it is obvious that considerable progress has been made in that relevant philosophies, theories, and methodologies have all been more extensively investigated and used in the discipline than they were at that time. The need (expressed specifically at that time in papers by Harvey and Olsson) for a more process-oriented approach in geography has been taken to heart by many members of the discipline. Although there have been few attempts to rewrite classical geographic theories from a behavioral view, there is an increased awareness of the limitations of these theories. There has also been a widening of the analytical methods used in the discipline by the introduction and use of various scaling techniques and by the adaptation of cartographic procedures for use on behavioral data. Existential and empirical philosophies have complemented the positivistic ideas of the prebehavioral, multivariate analysis era in the discipline.

There is an increasing awareness among geographers that we can learn much from *selective* reading in other social and behaviorial sciences. We feel that the essays in this volume are indicative of the potential value to the discipline of such interdisciplinary excursions. It is noteworthy, though, that many of the contributors advise caution in the acceptance and use of concepts, models, and theories from outside geography. Such caution is essential if we are to maximize the gains from interdisciplinary contact while minimizing the problems that we are confronted with in our search for geographical knowledge. We offer this volume therefore with a belief that it can contribute to the search for geographical knowledge by stressing some gains and some problems faced in continuing our analytical interest in problems of spatial choice and spatial behavior.

1. K. R. Cox and R. G. Golledge, eds., *Behavioral Problems in Geography: A Symposium,* Studies in Geography, no. 17, Department of Geography, Northwestern University, 1969.

PART I
Philosophy and Methods

CHAPTER 1

ELIZABETH J. HARMAN, JOHN F. BETAK

Behavioral Geography
Multidimensional Scaling, and the Mind

The purpose of the paper is to examine the value of multidimensional scaling[1] as a tool for research into mental structure and process in behavioral geography. The first section outlines why there is a need to evaluate the usefulness of MDS. The second section initiates an evaluation by examining both shortcomings and potential uses of scaling. The discussion does not consider technical aspects of the algorithms. It concentrates on substantive questions of the use of interpretation and scaling within the context of three questions about the psychological structure and operation of the mind that recur in behavioral geographic literature.

An evaluation of scaling in these terms is important for three reasons. First, with the adoption of a cognitive philosophy, the mind is now seen as a crucial variable in the explanation of spatial behavior in geography.[2] Second, scaling is a primary technique employed in geographic research into mental structure and process, notably in respect to the cognition and evaluation of environmental stimuli such as shops, residences, and cities.[3] Yet, and this is the third reason, geographers have made no serious attempt to examine the interface between scaling procedures and the mind. Hence, there has been no obvious effort to examine the value of MDS in research relating to mental phenomena.

One point should be noted here. Geographers are not concerned with researching psychology as such. However, having adopted a cognitive philosophy, they do require theories of the mind to guide research on spatial behavior, namely, theories on how the mind selects, codes, and manipulates information about environmental stimuli for the purposes of spatial decision-making. The conceptualizations described by Briggs [8], Brown and Moore [10], Demko and Briggs [25], and Hudson [46] all indicate the need for such theory. Appropriate theories are not immediately available. Work in psychology has largely been done in a laboratory context and is not always easily adapted to explain spatial behavior in the "real world." Behavioral geographers are therefore forced to spend some time acquiring knowledge of theories of the mind in cognitive psychology and philosophy and then modifying and developing concepts suitable for their purposes. This is the thrust of the work by Kaplan [48].

To date, behavioral geographers have not been successful in developing mental models. Little more is known than is implicit in terms like "cognitive maps," "mental maps," "images," "awareness spaces," and the like, or embodied in the brief conceptualizations of Downs [27], Eyles [29], Golledge [35], Hudson [46], Pocock [61], and others. There is little or no knowledge of how the mind selects and structures information relating to environmental stimuli or how it manipulates this information to make different types of decisions. Yet, it is this type of knowledge that is required if cognitive behavioral geography is to provide general statements on the nature of spatial decision-making and perhaps ultimately contribute to the explanation of geographic process and pattern.

An assessment of the value, and potential value, of MDS for behavioral research essentially involves two pairs of questions. First, what are the limitations of the procedures for research on aspects of the mind? Have geographers taken these into account? (We call these "the problems" of scaling.) Second, what potential has MDS for answering questions about the mind that may be important to behavioral geography? Have geographers attempted to use this potential?

The problems largely relate to the assumptions on which scaling is based. Like many psychological measures, MDS is based on certain assumptions about the mind. This has the effect of allowing MDS procedures to be considered as both a *measure* and as a *model* of psychological structure and process [19]. If considered as a measure, MDS is simply a technique and the assumptions are a set of rules or an algorithm for allocating numbers on an n-dimensional scale. They need not be considered to have any psychological meaning. If MDS algorithms are considered to function as models of psychological structure and process, the purpose of scaling is to discover whether the data fit the model and, therefore, whether the assumptions of MDS may correspond to the structure and operation of the mind.

It can be argued that geographers have used MDS as a measurement technique only and that therefore they do not assume a relationship between the assumptions of the algorithms and mental processes. In all studies of cognition and preference, however, behavioral geographers accept and interpret most of their MDS output as valid descriptions of cognitive and evaluative judgments. In fact, we have no way of knowing *how* reasonable a scaled description is without independent verification. Two possible means of doing this are: (1) confirmation by an alternative data source and measurement procedure and (2) accuracy of predictions made on the basis of the descriptions [30].

The third and remaining course is to accept the MDS output on the belief that the underlying assumptions of the MDS algorithm comprise a reasonable model of mental structure and process. Since behavioral geographers have rarely, if ever, used either of the first two approaches, we must assume that they have adopted the third. As such, geographers should be very aware of the psychological bases of MDS and should interpret output in light of the psychological limitations of the models.

Geographers have not paid much attention to the psychological aspects of scaling. Brief statements largely relating to the appropriate psychological metric are given by Demko and Briggs [25], King [50], and Downs [27]. A discussion on the psychological implications of MDS is conspicuously absent from the review by Golledge and Rushton [37], although this matter is considered in the recent monograph by Brummell and Harman [11]. In empirical studies, most assumptions are adopted without comment. Exceptions to this statement are studies by Demko [24] and Demko and Briggs [25].

This, then, is why it is important to examine the interface between the mind and MDS. First, without an explicit understanding of the mind, geographers cannot be fully aware of the psychological implications of scaling. Hence, they cannot evaluate the strength of MDS technique as measures of psychological processes. This leads to the problems of indeterminate measurement that currently plague behavioral geography. Second, without an appreciation of the relationship between MDS and theories of the mind, it is impossible to design research that makes the best use of the scaling programs for exploring the mind.

Three questions about the mind appear in many behavioral statements in geography. The remainder of this paper discusses examples of both problems and potential uses of MDS in reference to each of these questions. They concern (1) the psychological structure or organization of the mind (this covers information selection, coding, and arrangement in the mind); (2) mental operations, specifically environmental cognition (also termed perception) and evaluation (also termed preference); and (3) the problem of idiographic versus nomothetic research. The latter considers the problem of accommodating individual differences in thought and behavior with group communalities.

PSYCHOLOGICAL STRUCTURE OF THE MIND

MDS is based on a number of assumptions and makes certain inferences about mental structure. It is assumed that stimuli are judged by individuals according to differences between the stimuli on the set of cognitive attributes by which they are characterized. When more than one attribute is involved in making an overall judgment of similarity or preference, the differences on attributes are mentally combined in some way. In all the scaling models it is assumed information about cognitive attributes is organized as a set of continuous dimensions. It is also assumed that these can be identified in the MDS configuration if the axes are rotated to the correct position.

A primary aim of much geographic behavioral research is to identify the information (concepts, cues, constructs, factors, or dimensions) the individual uses in making judgments. The exact nature of this information is not made explicit in scaling but is often inferred from the relative positions of stimuli on dimensions rotated to cover maximum variance. The psychology of cognition provides at least two warnings relevant to the interpretation of dimensions. Neither is well recognized—at least in practice—in geography. First, under the cognitive approach, environmental stimuli are judged on the basis of the *cognitive* meaning of the stimuli and not on the basis of their objective physical attributes. It should therefore *not* be assumed that the dimensions can be meaningfully interpreted directly in terms of the objective nature of the stimuli. Cognitive meaning should be considered first. This can be elicited from alternative sources, for example, from free descriptions of stimuli, elicited constructs, or adjectival checklists. Cognitive meaning will obviously relate to the physical nature of the stimuli in some as yet unknown way, but it is misleading to interpret dimensions directly in terms of their physical makeup. There is no assurance that the physical attributes used to interpret dimensions are either correct or complete. They may, for example, only correlate with the correct dimensions across the sample set of stimuli.

The continuous nature of MDS axes provides a second set of difficulties in the use of the procedure for psychological research. The axes predispose the researcher to believe that the mind differentiates between stimuli on the basis of *continuous* referents, when in fact discrete manifolds may be more appropriate. This point is discussed by Stefflre [68] and Boyd [7]. Evidence also suggests that cognitive information generally relates to a limited range, context, or domain of stimuli.[4] Stimuli belonging to different conceptual domains are not comparable. This idea is recognized only in a broad sense in geography. We do not group shops and residences in the same MDS analysis and expect meaningful output. However, it may be possible that our classification of shopping centers or cities is also inappropriate. Evidence for this conclusion has been found [26, 13, 55].

The problems of continuous or discrete referents and limited domain may provide difficulties in interpretation of MDS outputs if the researcher is not aware of their existence [68, 59]. On the other hand, MDS may be very useful in isolating clusters of stimuli in the configuration. (Such an output is, however, only *suggestive* of separate domains since some deviant solutions produce a similar configuration.) Stefflre [68] advocates MDS be limited to this type of heuristic analysis. The domains isolated by the application of MDS should then be subject to subsequent research and model-building using alternative approaches.

Another main assumption underlying MDS is the belief that the differences an individual sees between stimuli are represented as distances between pairs of stimuli, or a stimulus and an "ideal," in some mental space whose axes are defined by the attributes of the stimuli.

Stimuli separated by small distances are similar, and stimuli closer to the ideal are more preferred. On the assumption of a psychological space, stimuli are located as points by an MDS algorithm in a geometric space. The immediate inference is that the MDS configuration is in some way isomorphic with the individual's cognitive spatial image of the stimuli. If this is not an explicit assumption, it is at least a reasonable inference.

In terms of cognitive psychology, these aspects of MDS are not unacceptable, but they are limiting. A belief in the importance of spatial imagery in thought has been revived in philosophy and psychology after a fifty-year lapse [44, 40, 45]. There is some evidence that even stimuli with no apparent spatial referents are mentally organized on distance-type dimensions [39]. Nonetheless, applications of scaling should be tempered by the recognition that modes other than spatial imagery are important in thought processes—notably a verbal or lexical manifold and some unknown form or forms used in preverbal and unconscious thought [49, 58, 45]. The choice of a particular mode is not always obvious [9], and geographers have no assurance that geographic problems are treated in spatial terms as manifest in MDS configurations simply because it seems logical to geographers.[5]

Again, in this respect MDS may play a schizophrenic role depending on the sensitivity of the user. Although it undoubtedly predisposes the researcher to interpret thought in terms of spatial images, it can be used to search for the use of alternate modes of thought. The simultaneous use of personal-construct elicitation [49] and MDS can explore the extent to which judgments about stimuli are determined by preverbal or unconscious modes. (Such work is currently underway by the authors.) This has serious implications for the large amount of research based on verbal explanations of behavior, as in questionnaires. If preverbal or unconscious modes are important, a discrepancy will occur between the construct and MDS analysis, since the former is dependent on verbal thinking and the latter is not. If, for example, stimuli cluster into three groups in the MDS configuration but only two distinct sets of constructs are elicited, differentiation of a third group in scaling must be based on something more than the constructs verbalized. Results of research by Downs and Horsfall in Baltimore on the cognition of upper- , middle-, and lower-class neighborhoods seem to demonstrate this (Downs, personal communication).

To locate stimuli as points in a geometric space, MDS requires yet another assumption about the nature of the mind, namely, that the psychological space satisfies the requirements of a metric space. This is one point that geographers have paid some attention to. Demko and Briggs [25] and Stefflre [68] discuss how reasonable the three axioms of a metric space are as psychological relations, and conclude the correspondence is more convenient than actual. The psychological distance between stimuli s and r may be different from that between r and s. In a metric space they are assumed to be the same. In the same space, two stimuli located at the same point are assumed to be identical. This does not necessarily hold in the mental image used for preference judgments. Two stimuli at the same point may be ranked equally but need not be identical stimuli. Stefflre [68] believes psychological intransitivities may violate the metric assumption of triangular inequality.

The final assumptions of MDS to be considered in this section relate to the specific metric chosen to derive the n-dimensional space. The metric is crucial since it determines how the distances between stimuli (or points) are calculated and, therefore, how the attributes of stimuli (or dimensions) are combined in judgments of overall similarity or preference. The problem of choosing a Minkowskian metric that corresponds to a psychological metric has been discussed at the theoretical level [23, 4, 19]. There is little evidence concerning the appropriate metric. Most MDS solutions are based on Euclidean geometry. This assumes in the two-dimensional solution, for example, that attributes are combined according to the Pythagorean theorem and the space is easily visualized as a plane. Shepard [66, p. 54] makes a pertinent comment on this: "Despite the highly specific character of these assumptions, their adoption has largely followed the dictates of mathematical convenience— not those of any conclusive empirical evidence." Rushton's [63] work on the nature of trade-offs between size and distance underlying the choice of towns for rural consumers is the closest geographers have come to an actual attempt to examine how dimensions are psychologically combined.

Suggestions as to the appropriate metric remain tentative. King [50], supporting his ideas with reference to psychological research on visual perception, has considered the feasibility of hyperbolic metric. In doing so, he ignores two important points. First, evidence that visual space perception in the real world is hyperbolic is not strong [33, 5]. The Luneberg Theory is based on experiments that are limited to two-dimensional space perception using binocular cues only. Many other cues are utilized in actual fact, including familiarity, perspective, brightness, and the like. Moreover, two of the three binocular cues are effective only within distances of about fifty feet [33, p. 20]. Ironically, recent research using MDS has demonstrated that binocular visual space perception in a nonlaboratory context may be Euclidean, not hyperbolic [60, 57]. The second point King ignores is that geographers are *not* concerned with *visual perception,* that is, immediate perception involving actual uses of the senses in the presence of stimuli. Geographers are concerned with *cognition,* that is, how information about stimuli is selected and coded for use in decision-making in the absence of all relevant opportunities [25]. There is no reason to believe that the geometry of visual perception is also the geometry of the cognitive image. Nor is there reason to believe there is any one appropriate psychological metric. Work by Shepard [66] indicates that the cognitive metric shifts depending on which stimulus attributes subjects pay attention to.

OPERATIONS OF THE MIND: COGNITION AND EVALUATION

Behavioral geographers concerned with the operations underlying spatial choice have generally concentrated on three mental processes: cognition, evaluation of spatial opportunities, and learning. It is postulated that choice among stimuli is a function of the evaluation of stimuli, which is in turn a function of their cognition [8, 10, 25, 45, 35, 31]. Learning affects changes in cognition and evaluation over time [34, 36]. MDS has been used extensively for research on cognition and evaluation, although research efforts in the two areas have generally been separate. Cognition is measured using some form of (dis)similarities data and analyzed using factor analytic or MDS procedures. Evaluation is measured using dominance data for preferences, rankings, or ratings and is largely subjected to unfolding techniques.

The primary aim of both areas is to identify the cognitive information (attributes or dimensions) individuals use to differentiate or choose among alternatives. The secondary aim is to identify the relative importance (weighting or salience) of the various dimensions in a given judgment. Implicit in this work is the belief that the results will eventually assist in explaining and predicting spatial choice behavior.

Two aspects of geographic research put this belief on shaky ground: little attention has been paid to the relevant psychological assumptions of the scaling or unfolding models, on which results of much of the research depend, and no thought has been given to the relationship linking cognition to evaluation, and hence to choice.

One important and relevant assumption, which has not already been considered in the previous section on psychological structure, is that in unfolding models an individual's utility function is single peaked at an ideal point and declines monotonically and symmetrically from there. Carroll [15, 16] has demonstrated that scaling programs are not equipped to handle more complex functions,[6] and a configuration is difficult to interpret if a complex function is implicit in the data. Yet, examples of bimodal functions at least are not difficult to find in geography. In current research on intraurban residential choice, the authors have found that some individuals declare a preference for locations *either* very close to the workplace(s) or in the rural-urban fringe. In the alternative to the unfolding model, the vector model (MDPREF) [16], the usual assumption about the utility function is modified slightly. Preferences are represented as projections on a subject's vector directed toward an ideal point located at infinity. The assumption in this case is that utility increases monotonically away from the origin. In many cases, this is also unlikely in reality.

The relationship between cognition and evaluation for specific stimulus domains has been neglected in behavioral geography. It is important for three reasons. First, the relationship must be specified if the results of the separate studies of cognition and evaluation are to be combined in an explanation of spatial choice decision-making. Second, knowledge of the relationship would eliminate the need for extensive future research on the cognition of stimuli in a given domain, since this could be inferred from the analysis of preferences. Finally, it provides a means of evaluating the limitations of scaling programs based on "internal analyses" of preferences. Internal analysis designates a method whereby stimuli and ideal points are located as points on the basis of preference data only. Coombs's unfolding model is a case in point. By comparison, "external analysis" of preferences occurs when ideal points are mapped into an independently derived cognitive space [16, 22]. Effectively, internal analysis assumes that cognitive and evaluative judgments are alike, whereas external analysis allows them to vary.

Research on the relationship between cognition and evaluation has been given new impetus by recent work of Carroll [15], who sharply distinguishes between the two mental operations. Carroll and Chang have developed a means for the external analysis of preferences— PREFMAP. The algorithm is in fact a set of four models ordered as a hierarchy of increasing flexibility (i.e., fewer binding assumptions). The usual input to PREFMAP is the configuration produced by scaling similarities data. PREFMAP uses preference data to locate ideal points in three cases and an individual vector in the remaining phase in the input cognitive space. PREFMAP provides a unique opportunity for exploring the relationship between evaluation and cognition.

Research to date in other disciplines has been sparse and inconclusive. A number of empirical studies report a similarity between cognitive and evaluative configurations [51, 69, 15]. These give some credence to the assumption on which the Coombs unfolding model is based. Nonetheless, it is still misleading to assume a close relationship holds in all cases. Carroll [15] has demonstrated that internal analysis of preference data produces a configuration radically different in both dimensionality and point location from a configuration derived from similarities data for the same stimuli.

The most suggestive research to date is that of Greene and Carmone [38], who compared configurations produced by four different methods of scaling similarities and preference data for the same stimuli. They concluded that the attributes (dimensions) involved in both types of judgments were similar but that their saliences or relative importance differed.

> In effect, what the unfolding approaches appear to provide is *not* the standard configuration (obtained from similarities data), but a transformed configuration in which the interpoint distances between stimulus pairs are weighted by the importance attached to each dimension in the preference context. (p. 338)

Carroll [15] also describes the difference between cognition and evaluation, as a variation in the importance given certain attributes. This result has not emerged in geographic research—despite efforts to identify the importance of given attributes in studies of both cognition and evaluation of spatial opportunities.

Attention might usefully be paid to PREFMAP—to provide information on how the cognitive image is transformed into a preference space and to provide insight into the type of model most appropriate in representing the data.

IDIOGRAPHIC VERSUS NOMOTHETIC RESEARCH

Is the mind and behavior of an individual unique, *or* are there communalities between groups of individuals? If communalities exist, how can they be estimated and described? Psychologists, anthropologists, and political scientists all recognize the existence of both individual differences and communalities in thought and behavior.[7] Moreover, some have made a conscious effort to estimate and model the various levels within one design.[8]

Behavioral geographers have, in practice at least, never quite decided how they stand on the question. On the one hand, most reviews list research at the level of the individual as one of the definitive characteristics of the field [20, 27]. On the other hand, almost all empirical research reports results generalized for a group. The groups are often defined along socioeconomic or ethnic lines, or in terms of a surrogate representing familiarity with a specific environment. The evidence that such groups have homogeneous cognitive structures is limited and circumstantial. Cognition and evaluation may also depend on personality, sex, and cultural variables [65] as well as the context of data collection [32]. The use of scaling models in geography has generally enforced the practice of assuming group consensus. All scaling algorithms produce output that present an "average configuration." All are, therefore, based on some assumptions of group consensus—for example, homogeneity of cognition and similar utility functions for all individuals.

In addition to assuming consensus for groups that may not be meaningful, geographers do not stipulate the way different individuals relate to the average or group picture. This is true for most MDS analyses based on the scaling of similarities data. It is less true of those involving unfolding models but only because individuals are represented as ideal points by the algorithm, and not because researchers deliberately set out to examine individual differences and how they relate to the group.

There is a very real need to reexamine the definition of groups and the extent to which it is meaningful to aggregate across individual differences. Such questions feed directly into the problems of cross-level inference and aggregation, which have been a constant headache to behavioral geographers. King [50], Harvey [42], and Winkel [74] all discuss these problems from a theoretical point of view. Little attempt has been made to treat them at an empirical level. Again, an exception is provided by Demko [24], who factored similarities arrays in an attempt to find groups with homogeneous cognition on which to perform further analysis. Also, work currently in progress by Harman is concerned with this problem in residential evaluation and choice.

Another of Carroll and Chang's new programs (INDSCAL or INdividual Differences SCALing) is a promising candidate for research on the specification of groups and individual variation. INDSCAL scales (dis)similarities data matrices for each subject. It produces output-defining configurations for both the group and the individuals within it. Although attributes or dimensions of the group space are assumed to be common to all individuals, the salience they are given may vary. INDSCAL also produces a subject or source space, in which individual sources of data are located relative to the origin, axes, and to each other. Normalization of the INDSCAL solution means that the position of an individual relative to the origin can be interpreted as the amount of variance in her/his judgments that has been accounted for. Position relative to the axes represents the salience given to different dimensions. It is therefore possible to identify groups comprised of individuals who think about stimuli in a similar way. In addition, the internal variance of such groups can be estimated, and the manner in which individuals outside the groups deviate can be identified.

In the future, it may be more worthwhile for geographers to search for homogeneous groupings inductively via the subject of INDSCAL. Once groups are defined, questions regarding their internal structure, relationship to specific individuals, or conversely to larger groups will be more readily answered.

CONCLUSIONS

The discussion in the preceding sections leads to one very obvious conclusion. As a tool for geographic behavioral research, multidimensional scaling has both problems and potential. Scaling can only be used to its best advantage if both aspects are recognized. To date, geographers have not fully appreciated either the problems implicit in the procedures or their considerable potential for useful research into the structure and operation of the mind. This may partially account for the lack of substantive progress in work on the nature of the mind in geography despite the proliferation of relevant empirical studies.

Two suggestions are pertinent here. First, geographers need to consider theories of the mind more carefully and how MDS techniques correspond to these. If behavioral research was better grounded in cognitive psychology and philosophy, the problems and potentialities of MDS would be more effectively dealt with. Second, the use of MDS should be more obviously integrated into well-constructed research designs; that is, an explicit conceptualization, preferably derived from an accepted theory of the mind, should be used to define the research problem, to select variables and measures — including MDS — and to guide interpretation [19, 27]. The need to relate MDS as the measure to the conceptualization and problem specification would force recognition of the psychological assumptions on which scaling is based. Burnett [12] and Demko and Briggs [25] report research designed along these lines.

The specification of MDS as a measure is deliberate. The discussion of MDS in this paper highlights the limitations of the psychological assumptions on which the procedures are based. As such, it is easy to concur with those who question the plausibility of MDS as *models* of human behavior, as have Boyd [7], Stefflre [68], and Greene and Carmone [38]. The latter state, "As data reduction and summation techniques, nonmetric scaling methods seem to have much to offer. . . . As useful models of psychological processes, the question is still moot" (p. 338).

To conclude, geographers need to pay more attention to the psychological implications of MDS. The results will be evident in more efficient use of MDS, which may assure that the techniques survive in the field. In addition, behavioral geographers will gain new insight into the nature of the mind— something that is fundamental to an area that has adopted a cognitive approach to behavior.

1. "Multidimensional scaling" is used here as a generic term to cover all the techniques designed to locate n points and/or m individuals in an r dimensional space, where the dimensions represent attributes used by the individuals to differentiate between stimuli. Multidimensional scaling is also used as a specific term to distinguish the subset of models locating stimuli according to (dis)similarities data from the unfolding models that locate individuals as ideal points and stimuli on the basis of preference data. Throughout the paper multidimensional scaling is abbreviated to MDS.

2. The cognitive, or organismic (O), philosophy is the antonym of the stimulus-response (SR), or behavioristic, approach to behavior. The latter postulates that behavior is a deterministic function of the stimulus, whereas the former postulates that the mind mediates between the environment and behavior. In an O approach, there are a number of probable behaviors in response to a given stimulus depending on the mediating effects of psychological processes [17]. Evidence of the adoption of a cognitive approach in behavioral geography is quite strong. It clearly underlies the conceptualizations of Downs [27], Golledge [35], and others. Psychological sources quoted in geographic literature and derived concepts are frequently more cognitive than behavioristic; for example, the "life space" notions of Lewin [53] influenced Wolpert [75]. Hudson [46] reviews cognitive influences in learning in geography. Kelly's [49] personal-construct theory is diffusing through the field [46, 28, 24, 67, 56, 41, 72, 71]. The proliferation of terms like "cognitive maps," "awareness spaces," and so forth, is symptomatic of the same trend. So is the use and definition of the term "perception" to cover cognitive elements as defined, for instance, by Gibson [33] and Arnheim [2]. The cognitive stance in geography is explicitly recognized by Gale [31] and by those who use the term "cognitive behavioral geography" [43].

3. Many of the relevant studies are reviewed in the final section of the paper by Golledge and Rushton [37].

4. This is discussed very specifically by Kelly [49] as Corollary 6, "The Range Corollary," of personal-construct theory. It is also considered in studies concerned with cognitive structures in general—as reviewed by Neisser [58] and Kaplan [48].

5. Beck [6]provides limited evidence that geographers tend to think in spatial terms. If they incorrectly impute this tendency to other individuals, there is a clear risk of the problems of value transference discussed by Downs [27] and Downs and Horsfall [28].

6. Greene and Carmone [38, p.335] note that the later Kruskal procedures and Carroll and Chang's parametric mapping programs allow considerably more flexibility than most scaling procedures in the need for interperson comparability and in the form of the utility functions respectively.

7. The relationship between individual and group is a main component of social psychology [52] and in social welfare [3]. The contextual effects of a group on the behavior of an individual are considered in psychology (for example [65, 73]), in political science [47, 70, 64], and in sociology [21].

8. The problems of estimating behavior across levels have been pointed out by Robinson [62] and Alker [1]. These have been investigated under the label of "cross-level inference" [47, 70]. Lorrain and White [54] have attempted to model across levels by incorporating points of view in a formal representation of the sociometric relations of a group.

LITERATURE CITED

1. Alker, H. R. "A Typology of Ecological Fallacies." In *Quantitative Ecological Analysis in the Social Sciences,* ed. M. Dogan and S. Rokkan, pp. 69–86. Cambridge: M.I.T. Press, 1969.

2. Arnheim, R. *Visual Thinking.* Berkeley: University of California Press, 1969.

3. Arrow, K. J. *Social Choice and Individual Values.* New Haven: Yale University Press, 1963.

4. Beals, R., D. H. Krantz, and A. Tversky. "Foundations of Multidimensional Scaling." *Psychological Review,* 75 (1968), 127–42.

5. Beardslee, D., and M. Wertheimer. *Readings in Perception.* Princeton, N. J.: D. Van Nostrand Co., 1958.

6. Beck, R. "Spatial Meaning and the Properties of the Environment." In *Environmental Perception and Behavior,* ed. D. Lowenthal, pp. 18–29. Research Paper No. 109, Department of Geography, University of Chicago, 1967.

7. Boyd, J. P. "Information Distance for Discrete Structures." In *Multidimensional Scaling: Theory,* vol. 1, ed. R. N. Shepard et al., pp. 213–23. New York: Seminar Press, 1972.

8. Briggs, R. "The Scaling of Preferences for Spatial Locations: An Example Using Shopping Centers." M.A. thesis, Department of Geography, Ohio State University, 1969.

9. Brooks, L. E. "Spatial and Verbal Components of the Act of Recall." In *Readings in Cognitive Psychology,* ed. M. Colheart. Toronto: Holt, Rinehart and Winston, 1972.

10. Brown, L. A., and E. G. Moore. "The Intra-Urban Migration Process: A Perspective." *Geografiska Annaler,* 52B (1970), 1–13.

11. Brummell, A. C., and E. J. Harman. "Behavioural Geography and Multidimensional Scaling." Discussion Paper No. 1, Department of Geography, McMaster University, Hamilton, Ontario, 1974.

12. Burnett, K. P. "The Dimensions of Alternatives in Spatial Choice Processes." *Geographical Analysis,* 5 (1973), 181–204.

13. Burrill, M. F. "The Language of Geography." *Annals of the Association of American Geographers,* 58 (1968), 1–11.

14. Carroll, J. D. "An Overview of Multidimensional Scaling Methods Emphasizing Recently Developed Models for Handling Individual Differences." In *Attitude Research Reaches New Heights,* ed. C. W. King and D. J. Tigert, pp. 235–62. Bibliography Series No. 14, Attitude Research Committee, Marketing Research Techniques, 1971.

15. ———. "Individual Differences and Multidimensional Scaling." In *Multidimensional Scaling: Theory and Applications in the Behavioral Sciences,* vol. 1, ed. R. N. Shepard et al. New York: Seminar Press, 1972.

16. ———. "Models and Methods for Multidimensional Preference Analysis." Mimeo. Murray Hill: Bell Laboratories, 1972.

17. Chaplin, J. P., and T. S. Krawiec. *Systems and Theories of Psychology.* 2nd ed. Toronto: Holt, Rinehart and Winston, 1968.

18. Coombs, C. H. *A Theory of Data.* New York: John Wiley and Sons, 1964.

19. Coombs, C. H., R. M. Dawes, and A. Tversky. *Mathematical Psychology: An Elementary Introduction.* Englewood Cliffs: Prentice-Hall, 1970.

20. Cox, K. R., and R. G. Golledge. "Editorial Introduction: Behavioral Models in Geography." In *Behavioral Problems in Geography: A Symposium,* ed. K. R. Cox and R. G. Golledge, pp. 1–13. Northwestern University, Evanston, Illinois, 1969.

21. Coxon, A. P. M. "Differential Cognition and Evaluation: An Introduction to Carroll and Chang's Multidimensional Scaling Models." Research Memorandum No. 1, Project on Occupational Cognition, Department of Sociology, University of Edinburgh, 1972.

22. Coxon, A. P. M., and C. L. Jones. "Occupational Cognition: Representational Aspects of Occupational Titles." Working Paper No. 1, Project on Occupational Cognition, Department of Sociology, University of Edinburgh, 1972.

23. Cross, D. V. Metric Properties of Multidimensional Stimulus Control. Ph.D. dissertation, University of Michigan, cited in Demko and Briggs (1971).

24. Demko, D. Perception and Preference Structures for Urban Areas in Southern Ontario. Paper prepared for Canadian Council on Urban and Regional Research, 1971.

25. Demko, D., and Briggs, R. "An Initial Conceptualisation and Operationalisation of Spatial Choice Behaviour: A Migration Example Using Multidimensional Unfolding." Proceedings of the Canadian Association of Geographers (1970), 79–86.

26. Downs, R. M. "The Cognitive Structure of an Urban Shopping Centre." Environment and Behavior, 2 (1969), 13–19.

27. ———. "Geographic Space Perception: Past Approaches and Future Prospects." Progress in Geography, 2 (1969), 65–108.

28. Downs, R. M., and Horsfall, R. "Methodological Approaches to Urban Cognition." Paper presented at the 67th meeting of the Association of American Geographers, Boston, Mass., April, 1971.

29. Eyles, J. "Pouring New Sentiments into Old Theories: How Else Can We Look at Behavioural Patterns?" Area, 3 (1971), 242–51.

30. Friedman, M. Essays in Positive Economics. Chicago: University of Chicago Press, 1953.

31. Gale, S. "Inexactness, Fuzzy Sets, and The Foundations of Behavioral Geography." Geographical Analysis, 4 (1972), 337–49.

32. Garner, W. R., H. Hake, and C. W. Eriksen. "Operationism and the Concept of Perception." Psychological Review, 63 (1956), 149–59.

33. Gibson, J. The Perception of the Visual World. Cambridge, Mass.: Riverside Press, 1950.

34. Golledge, R. G. "A Conceptual Framework of a Market Decision Process." Discussion Paper Series, no. 4, Department of Geography, University of Iowa, 1967.

35. ———. "Process Approaches to the Analyses of Human Spatial Behavior." Discussion Paper Series, No. 16, Department of Geography, Ohio State University, 1970.

36. Golledge, R. G., and L. A. Brown. "Search, Learning, and the Market Decision Process." Geografiska Annaler, 49B, (1967).

37. Golledge, R. G., and G. Rushton. Multidimensional Scaling: Review and Geographical Applications. Technical Paper No. 10, Commission on College Geography, Association of American Geographers, Washington, D. C., 1972.

38. Greene, P. E., and F. J. Carmone. "Multidimensional Scaling: An Introduction and Comparison of Nonmetric Unfolding Techniques." Journal of Marketing Research, 6 (1969), 530–41.

39. Handel, S., C. B. DeSoto, and M. London. "Reasoning and Spatial Representations." Journal of Verbal Learning and Verbal Behavior, 7 (1968), 351–57.

40. Hannay, A. Mental Images: A Defence. London: George Allen and Unwin; New York: Humanities Press, 1971.

41. Harman, E. J., and J. F. Betak. "Some Preliminary Findings on the Cognitive Meaning of External Privacy in Housing." Proceedings of Edra 5, forthcoming.

42. Harvey, D. W. "Pattern Process and the Scale Problem in Geographical Research." Transactions of the Institute of British Geographers, 45 (1968), 71–78.

43. ———. "Conceptual and Measurement Problems in the Cognitive-Behavioral Approach to Location Theory." In Behavioral Problems in Geography: A Symposium, ed. K. R. Cox and R. G. Golledge, pp. 35–68. Studies in Geography, no. 17, Northwestern University, 1969.

44. Hold R. R. "Imagery: The Return of the Ostracized." *American Psychologist,* 19 (1964), 254–64.

45. Horowitz, M. J. *Image Formation and Cognition.* New York: Appleton-Century-Crofts, 1970.

46. Hudson, R. "Personal Construct Theory, Learning Theories and Consumer Behaviour." Seminar Paper Series, no. 21, Department of Geography, University of Bristol, 1970.

47. Iverson, G. R. "Contingency Tables without Cell Entries." Unpublished paper, University of Michigan.

48. Kaplan, S. "Cognitive Maps in Perception and Thought." In *Image and Environment: Cognitive Mapping and Spatial Behavior,* ed. R. Downs and D. Stea, pp. 63–78. Chicago: Aldine, 1973.

49. Kelly, G. A. *The Psychology of Personal Constructs.* New York: Norton, 1955.

50. King, L. J. "The Analysis of Spatial Form and Its Relations to Geographic Theory." *Annals of the Association of American Geographers,* 59 (1969), 573–95.

51. Klahr, D. "Decision-Making in a Complex Environment: The Use of Similarity Judgements to Predict Preferences." *Management Science,* 15 (1969), 595–618.

52. Krech, D., R. S. Crutchfield, and E. L. Ballachey. *Individual in Society.* New York: McGraw-Hill, 1962.

53. Lewin, K. *Principles of Topological Psychology.* New York: McGraw-Hill, 1936.

54. Lorrain, F., and H. D. White. "Structural Equivalence of Individuals in Social Networks." *Journal of Experimental Psychology,* 86 (1970), 325–27.

55. Lucas, R. C. "Wilderness Perception and Use: The Example of the Boundary Waters Canoe Area." *Natural Resources Journal,* 3 (1964), 394–411.

56. Lundeen, R. "The Semantic Differential Technique and Personal Construct Theory in Image Measurement." Discussion Paper No. 5, Department of Geography, York University, Toronto, 1972.

57. Matsushima, K., and N. Noguchi. "Multidimensional Representation of Binocular Visual Space." *Japanese Psychological Research,* 9 (1967), 85–94.

58. Neisser, U. *Cognitive Psychology.* New York: Appleton-Century-Crofts, 1966.

59. Nerlove, S. B., and A. K. Romney. "Introduction to Volume II." In *Multidimensional Scaling, Theory and Applications in Behavioral Sciences,* vol. 2, ed. A. K. Romney, R. N. Shepard, and S. B. Nerlove, pp. 1–10. New York and London: Seminar Press, 1972.

60. Nishikawa, Y. "Euclidean Representation of Binocular Visual Space." *Japanese Psychological Research,* 9 (1967), 191–98.

61. Pocock, D. C. D. "Environmental Perception: Process and Product." *Tijdschrift voor Economische en Sociologie Geografie,* 64 (1973), 251–57.

62. Robinson, W. S. "Ecological Correlations and the Behavior of Individuals." *American Sociological Review,* 15 (1950), 351–57.

63. Rushton, G. "The Scaling of Location Preferences." In *Behavioral Problems in Geography: A Symposium,* ed K. R. Cox and R. G. Golledge, pp. 197–227. Studies in Geography, no. 17, Department of Geography, Northwestern University 1969.

64. Scheuch, E. K. "Social Context and Individual Behavior." In *Quantitative Ecological Analysis in the Social Sciences,* ed. M. Dogan and S. Rokkan, pp. 133–56. Cambridge: M.I.T. Press, 1969.

65. Segall, M. H., D. T. Campbell, and M. J. Herskovits. *The Influence of Culture on Visual Perception.* Indianapolis: Bobbs-Merrill, 1966.

66. Shepard, R. N. "Attention and the Metric Structure of the Stimulus Space." *Journal of Mathematical Psychology,* 1 (1964), 54–87.

67. Silzer, V. "Personal Construct Elicitation in Space Preference Research." Discussion Paper no. 1, Department of Geography, York University, Toronto, 1972.

68. Stefflre, V. J. "Some Applications of Multidimensional Scaling to Social Science Problems."
    In *Multidimensional Scaling: Theory and Applications in the Behavioral Sciences,* vol. 2, ed.
    A. K. Romney, R. N. Shepard, and S. B. Nerlove, pp. 211–48. New York and London:
    Seminar Press, 1972.
69. Steinheiser, F. H. "Individual Preference Scales within a Multidimensional 'Similarity'
    Space." *Journal of Experimental Psychology,* 86 (1970), 325–27.
70. Stokes, P. E. "Cross-Level Inference As a Game against Nature." In *Mathematical Applica-
    tions in Political Science IV,* ed J. L. Bernd, pp. 62–83. Charlottesville: University Press of
    Virginia, 1971.
71. Tuite, C. J. "Personal Construct Theory and Neighborhood Cognition." M.A. thesis, De-
    partment of Geography, McMaster University, Hamilton, Ontario, 1974.
72. Tuite, C. J., and J. F. Betak. "The Use of the Repertory Grid Test to Elicit Aspects of
    Neighborhood Cognition." Submitted to *Environment and Behavior,* 1974.
73. Tyler, L. E. *The Psychology of Human Differences.* New York: Appleton-Century-Crofts,
    1965.
74. Winkel, G. H. "Theory and Method in Behavioural Geography." Paper presented at the
    Meeting of the Canadian Association of Geographers, Waterloo, 1971.
75. Wolpert, J. "Behavioral Aspects of the Decision to Migrate." *Papers and Proceedings of the
    Regional Science Association,* 15 (1965), 159–69.

CHAPTER 2

PAT BURNETT

Behavioral Geography and the
Philosophy of Mind

I. INTRODUCTION AND AIMS

A recent and timely feature of behavioral geography is a serious concern about the methodological problems of relating, first, models of the mind, second, procedures for recovering and measuring perceptions and preferences, and, third, overt spatial choice behavior. This concern evinces a much-needed departure from the well-worn and prejudiced debate—given the absence of much evidence one way or another—as to whether behavioral explanations of spatial phenomena will ever in some sense be better than traditional ones.

The new methodological concern is reflected in papers, for example, by Brown and Longbrake [7], Burnett [9, 10], Gale [20], Harman and Betak [34], Louviere [53], and Rushton [76]. Most of these writers attempt to develop operational mathematical models, which connect testable algebraic or geometric statements about mental states or processes with quantifiable statements about observable spatial choices. Burnett [9], for example, uses a multidimensional unfolding formulation [78, p. 25] of shopping place perceptions to predict the allocation of trips to centers by two samples of shoppers. Rushton [76] explains observed route choices from calibratable models of the ways in which subjects mentally combine several different distance stimuli (e.g., cost, effort). Louviere [53] outlines a way in which mathematical behavior theory and analysis of variance may be used to predict mode choice and choice of recreational destinations. In addition, Brown and Longbrake [7] and Harman and Betak [34] examine some of the technical difficulties of measuring facets of minds and resultant spatial behavior. The latter, especially, provide an exhaustive discussion of the potential of multidimensional scaling procedures for the mathematical definition of mental states ("psychological structure of the mind," "perceptions," "imagery," pp. 6–11), and mental events and processes ("operations of the mind—cognition and evaluation," pp. 11–15).

However, underlying this recent work, and also previous work in behavioral geography, is a highly controversial set of beliefs that amount to a crude and unspecified philosophy of mind. These beliefs have apparently been absorbed in part with other borrowings from cognitive psychology. They arise from presently divergent answers to such basic questions as: Is the mind tautologous (logically identical with) observable behaviors [77]? If yes, then what *is* short- or long- term memory, consciousness, the unconscious, perception, and evaluation? If no, then is the mind material or immaterial, that is, is it part of, or to some degree not part of, the physical matter of the body [73]? Further, if the mind does not exist partly or wholly in material form, can it logically be said to have contents (like mental maps), to be an activated brain (as in spatial decision-making), or to cause, and hence explain, behavior (like residential migration)?

All these questions are philosophical in nature, comprising part of the so-called mind-body problem dating from Plato and Aristotle [73]. Different answers to these questions give rise to different definitions and hence models of the mind and of people and human nature. These models in turn afford different explanations of human behavior, including spatial behavior (see for example [15, pp. 3–5]).

Because certain answers to these deep philosophical questions appear to have simply been assumed in behavioral geography and have not been spelt out and examined, this paper has the following aims: (1) to isolate the beliefs about mental states, events, and processes that constitute both the philosophy of mind and the origins of a model of explanation in behavioral geography; (2) to demonstrate the questionable nature of both the philosophy and the explanatory model by appeal to well-developed and conflicting alternative philosophies of mind (behaviorist, materialist, and neodualist); and (3) to suggest alternative ways of viewing mental states and processes and of relating them to individual and aggregate spatial behavior.

II: BELIEFS ABOUT THE MIND IN BEHAVIORAL GEOGRAPHY

The Mind and Its Place in a Model of Geographic Explanation

It is held that human beings employ mental models of the world to organize their spatial behavior, that is, "the mind mediates between the environment and behavior in it" [34, fn. 2].[1] Specifically, the following beliefs seem pervasive and are rarely seriously questioned in behavioral geography (though see [69, 28, 21] for possibly divergent views).[2]

*B*1. Minds exist and can constitute valid objects of scientific enquiry; that is, they do not have peculiarly mental, nonmaterial, or "ghostly" properties, which would place them outside the realm of acceptable scientific discourse.

*B*2. Minds are generally described in psychological and not neurophysiological language. For example, we write articles devoted to the description of preferences and perceptions but not to the description of conditions of neurons and nerve fibres.

*B*3. There is an external world of spatial stimuli with objective properties (industrial agglomerations, central places, residential sites), "outside" the mind.

*B*4. Minds observe, select, and structure information (sense data) about the external world [33, 84]. They thus have processes corresponding to spatial learning and remembering [15, pp. 51–62, 221–88; 22; 23; 26; 28]. They also have states somehow corresponding to mental maps [15, pp. 1–7; 27; 30; 44; 83], perceived distances [6, 25], awareness spaces [8, 13; 15, pp. 162–78; 85] environmental cues [88], multidimensional images of shopping, residential and other locations [9; 15, pp. 148–61; 35], and more or less imperfect spatial knowledge [63, 84, 85].

*B*5. Mental events or processes occur that correspond to thinking about or evaluating spatial information, so that the mind has states describing action spaces [42, 72, 83, 85] and space preference and utility functions [7; 15, pp. 182–220; 45; 57; 65; 74; 75; 76].

B6. Minds are the seat of emotions and sensations, such as environmental stress [8, 86] and satisfactions and dissatisfactions [8, 22]. They are also the seat of attitudes, needs, desires, and motives [45, 59], particularly motives (aspirations) to optimize or satisfice in making locational choices [63, 84].

B7. Spatial choices (such as where to shop or where to market a new product) are made by thinking according to "decision rules" [20, 24, 40, 56, 63]. These rules may be viewed as methods of relating collected and evaluated information about alternatives on the one hand and motives on the other. Spatial choices are hence themselves made in the mind and result from prior mental states, events, and processes [66].

B8. A spatial choice decision is held to be the cause of an overt act, such as search for a new residence, the purchase of a new industrial site, or a shopping trip. Sequences of choices over time by individuals and groups cause overt behavioral processes, like intra- and interurban migration [7, 8, 85]. In turn, these behavioral processes cause changes in spatial structures in the external world, like transitions in urban land use (simulated in [16]). Thus, the normal view of behavioral geography is that ultimately location processes are explained (caused) by mental states, events, and processes (see Golledge and Briggs [24] for a recent exposition of this standard view).

B9. The mental states, events, and processes of different persons, such as preferences and perceptions, are comparable, recoverable, and verifiable [54, 57, 78, 81].

Figure 1 summarizes the philosophy of mind of cognitive behavioral geography and the model of explanation it affords for overt spatial behavior and observable locational processes.

It is somewhat surprising that the belief set {B1, . . ., B9} has not been isolated and queried thus far. Since the beginning of the fifties, and especially in the sixties, there has been a vigorous philosophical debate as to the ontological status of the mind as an object of scientific enquiry.

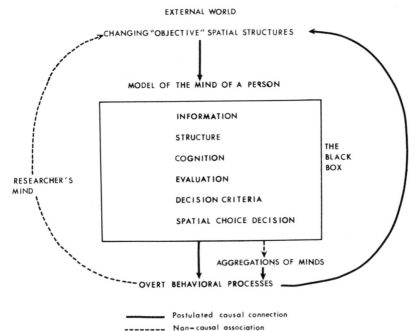

FIG. 1. Relations between mind and behavior in behavioral geography

(The nature of this debate is elaborated below.) Accordingly, a central question has become whether mental events, states, or processes can logically be held to cause, explain, or predict any kind of observable behavior (for example [41, 73, 77, 80, 87]).

The philosophical debate is sometimes explicitly recognized in cognitive psychology, the avowed foundation of behavioral geography [e.g. 34, fn. 2]. Often, however, the debate is recognized only implicitly in the psychological area: first, by an unwillingness to designate whether statements like B1–B9 are true, untrue, or ''as if'' assumptions; and second, by focusing attention on the development of mathematical models that will forecast observable behavior accurately, even if the predictions are derived in a logically debatable manner from dubious postulates about the mind. These two positions are made particularly clear by Harrison and Sarre:

Today, almost all psychologists admit both verbal and physical behavior as valid objects of study. . . . They all accept that at some level, the mind becomes unknowable, so that they are restricted to observing its inputs and outputs. An element of dispute which still pervades concerns the way in which the inaccessible black box should be treated. Most workers are prepared to make inferences about mental behavior which allow explanation of observable behavior in more or less common sense terms, though with the possibility of evaluating the success of predictions based upon the mental model. [35, p. 352]

Stances of these kinds are also particularly evident in work by mathematical psychologists in learning, judgment, choice, memory, and other kinds of mental states or processes of most relevance to geographers (see, for example [2, 31]).

Even without exposure to the controversies of the philosophers and the stances of the psychologists, geographers could have been expected to treat very seriously such questions as "where and what are the mental maps?" Mental spatial phenomena clearly do not belong to the usual category of traditional geographic observables, like plant locations, the sizes and functions of central places, the characteristics of migration streams, and agricultural land uses. It is not common for geographers to treat mental spatial phenomena (assuming they exist) as directly observable. Inferences are usually made about them from other kinds of observable behavior, such as verbal responses to questions permitting the "recovery" of images of places (e.g. [9; 15, pp. 182–230]). Thus, geographers could have noted that it is doubtful whether mental states, events and processes can ever be shown by direct observation to have connections either with real-world spatial objects or with psychological brainstates.[3] Accordingly, the nature and role of minds in deductive, relational, or any other type of model of "scientific" geographic explanation [39, pp. 13–15] should have called forth some serious inquiry.

It seems appropriate, therefore, to digress briefly to examine why behavioral geographers generally appear to have accepted the belief set $\{B1, \ldots, B9\}$, insofar as any belief set is accepted in a science. We will then return to a discussion of the arguments for incorporating a less naïve and more explicit philosophy of mind in future research.

Origins of the Belief Set

Most pertinently, why do the essays in this volume focus attention on investigating the mind as a valid object of scientific enquiry ($B1$); on comparing, recovering, or verifying the "contents" of minds using highly sophisticated multidimensional analysis ($B9$); and on explaining observable spatial behavior from mental events, states, or processes ($B8$)?

Superficially, at least, it seems that behavioral geographers must be committed to this position by the initial and continuing raison d'être for their subject area: "to provide the real reasons why people behave as they do" [38, p. 37] in order to modify traditional location theory. By the end of the sixties, there was some consensus that classical spatial theories were unable to describe, explain, or predict the phenomena of most concern to geographers with a satisfactory degree of accuracy.[4] The phenomena included agricultural land use patterns (e.g. [84]); consumer travel behavior (e.g. [12; 56, pp. 33–35]); the size, spacing, functions, and shapes of market areas of central places (summarized in [28, p. 91]); travel flows in cities and the location and design of transportation nets (e.g. Marble [56]); intraurban and interurban migration streams and the growth of cities (e.g. [8, 85]). Moreover, these "failures" to explain interesting spatial phenomena were clearly ascribed to "unrealistic" assumptions about the mind in classical spatial models (e.g. [63]). Particularly debatable assumptions were:

$A1$. That all persons have minds with perfect information (knowledge) about stated conditions in the external world (for example, about transport costs to or from all possible raw material, production sites and markets in Weberian location theory).

$A2$. That all persons have minds that permit them to think about and evaluate their knowledge correctly and in identical ways (for example, there is a mental process corresponding to a correct evaluation by the household of the utilities of residential space in Alonso-Muth residential location theory).

$A3$. That all persons are governed by identical motives, namely, to optimize utilities or money profits (as in Thünen-like agricultural land use analysis).

$A4$. That locational choices are determined by mental events or processes relating perfect knowledge, its evaluation, and optimizing motives (for example, decision-makers use their minds to trade off accessibility costs and site space utilities, and thus choose an optimal dwelling place in intraurban residential location theory).

The belief set of the behavioral geographer certainly appears more plausible than that of the traditionalist. Accordingly, substituting $B4-B8$ for $A1-A4$ became, and remains, a goal of the behavioral geographer (see the clearest statement of this substitution in the pioneering papers by Olsson and Gale [63]. One of the most recent statements is in Golledge and Briggs [24, p. 1]). Given this substitution of beliefs about the mind as a major goal for behavioral research, a logical focus of attention now necessarily seems to be on the theoretical and empirical problems of mathematically defining the mental states and processes of $B4-B7$ and of mathematically relating them to each other and to overt spatial behavior ($B8$).

The remainder of this paper will use philosophical arguments about the mind to show that the plausibility of the belief set $\{B1, \ldots, B9\}$ is questionable. Accordingly, it is dubious to place such a high priority on developing multidimensional scaling or other models and measurement procedures to define mental states, processes, or events. However, it is not implied that behavioral geographers have been, are, or will be, on a wild goose chase. Rather, much more attention should be given in each piece of research to working out a tenable philosophy of mind—then to defining mental models (or models of man/humans [15, p. 2]) and behavioral predictions to accord with it. Examples of this approach will be given in the conclusion to the paper.

III. THE BEHAVIORIST PHILOSOPHY OF MIND

The Tautology of Mind and Behavior

The philosophical debate about minds, that is, about the "mind-body" problem, is conducted by linguistic rather than empirical analysis. Thus, we ask what statements about minds or what psychological terms must mean and how we can make sense of them, rather than what empirical evidence exists to support beliefs like the behavioral geographers'. Linguistic analysis has been adopted for two reasons.

First, as Brain [80, pp. 60–80] shows, neurophysical evidence about the nature of the human brain is still scant (assuming for the moment that evidence about the brain comprises evidence about the mind). Second, the findings of science do not constitute immutable truths, so that conclusions about mental phenomena based on theories of the moment quickly lose their currency. For example, Hobbes attempted to support definitions of mental states as motions of material particles, using the outdated views of seventeenth-century mechanics [73, pp. 8, 43–52] (for other examples, see the writings of Descartes and Spinoza [73, pp. 19–42]). Consequently, modern linguistic analysis is an attempt to investigate minds in ways that are as independent as possible of the current state of scientific knowledge about human beings.

Behaviorists since Ryle [77] have posited that most mental phenomena can logically be defined only in terms of observable actions, activities, or behavioral propensities. The mind simply does not exist either as a nonmaterial entity or as the inaccessible black box of Figure 1. "The core of the argument is that to talk of a person's mind is 'to talk of the person's abilities, liabilities, and inclinations to do or undergo certain sorts of things, and of the doing and undergoing of these things in the ordinary world.' . . . So putative statements about immaterial or imperceptible occurrences [are] . . . exhibited as disguised hypothetical statements about perceptible behavior" (Hampshire on Ryle [87, p. 27]). Accordingly, behaviorists have shown with some success how key mental constructs—now absorbed by geography in B4–B7—are tautologous with observable behaviors. Mental phenomena are therefore not altogether independent and explanatory of actions, as we would both wish and believe (B8 and Figure 1). The tautologous constructs include: observation, learning, perception and knowing (in B4); thinking, that is, evaluation and decision-making about spatial alternatives (in B5 and B7); and motivations and emotions like satisficing and environmental stress (in B6). (See [77] for behaviorist definitions.)

It is obviously not possible to do justice to the subtlety and multiplicity of the behaviorists' arguments in this limited space (see Wood and Pitcher's anthology [87]). The chief contention is that "independent entity," "inaccessible black box," or "ghostly" views on the mind are "category mistakes" (Ryle [77, p. 16]). The notion of a "category mistake" is hence first simply illustrated with a famous analogy using nonmental phenomena. It is then applied to develop alternatives to behavioral geographers' prevailing beliefs about the mind and to suggest a related, different model of spatial explanation.

The Analogy and Its Spatial Applications

Consider "'a foreigner visiting Oxford or Cambridge for the first time [who] is shown a number of colleges, libraries, playing fields, museums, scientific departments and administrative offices. He then asks 'But where is the university? I have seen where the members of the Colleges live, where the Registrar works, and where the scientists experiment and the rest. But I have not yet seen the University in which reside the members of your University'? It has then to be explained to him that the University is not another collateral institution, some ulterior counterpart to the colleges, laboratories and offices which he has seen. The University is just the way in which all that he has already seen is organized. When they are seen and when their co-ordination is understood, the University has been seen" (Ryle [77, p. 16]). Hence the university exists not as an extra member of the category to which other units belong (e.g., lecture theatres, laboratories); it is not an extra unit that explains the operations of the others. The university is *defined* by the observations of the other units themselves.

Similarly, mental constructs are not "things" which explain many kinds of observable spatial behaviors; they *are* observable behaviors. We cannot say what we mean by mental events, states, or processes *without* talking about the observable spatial actions, activities, or behavioral propensities that commonly describe them.

For example, when we say a person is observing, perceiving, or obtaining information about spatial stimuli in the external world (as in $B4$), we can only denote by this that he/she is performing certain publicly recognized acts or achievements, such as selectively "looking, listening, savoring, smelling or feeling" (Ryle [77, pp. 222–23]). Moreover, we can only state that an individual is learning or has spatial knowledge (as in $B4$ too) if that individual is displaying or can display overtly the ability to do certain things (e.g., locate shopping places on a map with some degree of accuracy). Similarly, characteristic observable kinds of behavior must stand for thinking and evaluating spatial alternatives ($B5$), having optimizing or satisficing motives ($B6$), and making spatial choice decisions (*B*7). "The criteria of motives," for instance, can only be those observable "propensities or trends . . . which show that a person is acting more or less carefully, critically, competently, or purposefully" (Ryle [77, p. 110]).[5]

Impacts on Behavioral Geography

The behaviorist stance clearly has some drastic impacts on the belief set of behavioral geographers. Firstly, if the inaccessible black box and its contents do not exist, and if minds *are* behaviors, what becomes of the existence, recoverability, and verifiability of such favorite things as cognitive images, awareness and action spaces, and space-preference functions? These must all somehow be redefined in terms of the necessary and sufficient overt behaviors for which the mental constructs stand. For example, a mental map would not be an image "in the mind," but solely the ability of a person to reproduce a selected portion of the geography of the external world. Secondly, considerable care would be necessary in establishing causal connections between spatial behaviors and mental events, states, or processes. For example, learning could not be referred to as a *cause* of the more and more frequent use of an effort-minimizing set of shopping centers (as in [27] for example). Learning would be *defined* or *denoted* by that pattern of activity.

It cannot be concluded, however, that a behaviorist stance precludes either explanations of human spatial behaviors or explanations of the impacts of such behaviors on changing spatial structures. Theoretically, at least, mental constructs (e.g., cue perception or learning) can be defined in terms of observable activities (e.g., the verbal importance rating or active avoidance of traffic lights). These activities can then be associated with other overt responses (e.g., route selections) and with spatial structures (e.g., the zonal, concentric, or other land use patterns of cities). The strength of such a model of explanation is that it can consist almost wholly of directly verifiable statements about observables. Some recent work using stimulus-response models of spatial learning seems headed in this direction (e.g. [28, 88]).

However, there are formidable difficulties against the widespread use in geography of a behaviorist philosophy of mind and a behaviorist model of explanation. There are, naturally, logical counterarguments to the approach. These include (1) demonstrations of the behaviorists' failure to account for why humans have always used and correctly applied psychological terms (e.g., Hampshire on language development [87, pp. 27–34] and Shorter's "it is very natural to talk of visual images, and we can make ourselves understood when we do" [87, p. 155]), and (2) arguments that not all mental constructs can be said simply to denote behavior—for example, Quinton's that "perception itself is a causal (and not a behavior-achievement) notion, in that for someone to have perceived something it is necessary that the impact of his environment on his senses is a causally necessary condition of his forming the belief about his environment that he does" [87, pp. 129–34].

The worst problems arise, though, from the mental gymnastics involved in attempting to define those necessary and sufficient activities that can be held to describe pertinent mental phenomena (see, for example, Sibley on "thinking," Brown on "knowing," and Matthews on "mental copies" [87, pp. 75–104, 162–67, 213–48]). Indeed, it seems logically impossible to cover some hypothetical cases behavioristically, such as the paralytic who cannot manifest any experience he has, and who, by behaviorist notions, has no mind! This leads to the conclusion that behaviorist models in geography will often not prove satisfactory. They will either be extremely difficult to specify and test or they will reduce to simple, scientifically barren statements of observable associations between properties of spatial behaviors (e.g., distances traveled on shopping trips) and properties of spatial stimuli (e.g., the sizes of central places). The latter is a route to explanation that geographers have traveled and rejected before.

Consequently, the behaviorist philosophy of mind simply seems to undermine any belief in mental states, events, and processes as real, independent, recoverable, and verifiable entities. In practice, this supports the conclusion that less emphasis should be placed on developing sophisticated models and methods for the explicit purpose of defining such "things" as spatial preferences and perceptions. It also cautions us to be much more critical and careful in forming statements that claim to explain spatial phenomena by "realistic" models of the mind. Similar conclusions are also indicated by both the existence and the substance of a conflict between two further philosophies of mind, namely, materialism and neodualism [73, 80].

IV. MATERIALIST VERSUS NEODUALIST PHILOSOPHIES OF MIND

Materialist and Neodualist Stances and Their
Manifestations in Behavioral Geography

Materialists hold that "thoughts and other mental events or states [e.g., spatial learning, choice, perceptions, and preferences] are simply events and states of the brain . . . not just that the psychological events and states are causally correlated with physical events or states, but that they are the same" [73, p. 4]. Materialists therefore find ways of arguing that:

1. There is no logical reason why psychological descriptions of mental phenomena do not apply to the same material objects (brain states or processes) as neurophysiological descriptions [48, 49, 61, 70];

2. That there are good reasons for thinking that the materialist hypothesis will eventually be confirmed by scientific research [4, 19, 70, 71];

3. That it makes sense to speak of mental events as publicly observable, and not solely as privately accessible, phenomena [32].

Neodualists, on the other hand, posit that the existence of two languages to describe mental phenomena (psychological and physical) denotes an awareness of at least some peculiarly mental, privately accessible, nonphysical, and not-directly-verifiable properties of minds, such as nonlocatable visual images of spatial stimuli (see [14; 17; 51; 52; 80, pp. 134–61; 68; 73, pp. 67–72]). Neodualism constitutes a swing of the pendulum away from the predominantly materialist stances of philosophers and psychologists in the sixties—the decade of rapid advance in cybernetics, neurophysiology, and computer "brains." The present version of dualism differs from the classical one, which Ryle describes and traces from Plato through Descartes to current lay concepts of the mind as the private "ghost in the machine" [77, pp. 11–16]. Neodualists do not argue that human beings have a material body whose behaviors are somehow caused by the activities of immaterial minds, which contain thoughts, emotions, sensations, perceptions, etc. What neodualists claim is that there are ways of speaking about minds that are sensible and that materialist arguments cannot account for.

While it is evident that behavioral geographers do not as a rule operate with a behaviorist philosophy of mind, it is not at all clear what position their beliefs indicate with respect to materialism and neodualism. A materialist stance seems to be suggested by both $B1$ and $B9$ of the belief set in section 2. These assert, respectively, the mind as a valid, material object of scientific enquiry and the comparability, recoverability, and verifiability of the mental states, events, or processes of different persons (e.g., their spatial preferences and perceptions). However, few geographers attempt to use neurophysiological terms, like nerve impulses or information coding in brain cells, to describe the mental phenomena that interest them. Nor do they appear to recognize possible connections between physiological and psychological descriptions of the mind (though see [34] for an exception).[6]

Moreover, other members of the behavioral geographers' belief set appear to endorse old-fashioned Cartesian dualism. Firstly, no specific material location is ascribed to the particular mental events, states, or processes of concern. These include: the mental maps, images, perceived distances, cues, and awareness spaces of $B4$; the subjective space preferences/utility functions and action spaces of $B5$; the emotions and motives of $B6$; and the spatial perceiving, learning, evaluating, and decision-making of $B4$ to $B7$. Secondly, these unlocated mental phenomena are somehow mysteriously conceived as causing observable bodily behavior, in true Cartesian style ($B8$). Lastly, although different persons' mental states and processes (e.g., perceptions, preferences, learning) are held to be recoverable, comparable, and verifiable ($B9$), in practice experimental designs often assume that subjects introspect to provide verbal or other reports on the contents of their private and not publicly accessible consciousnesses. This is especially the case with experimental designs for multidimensional or attitude scaling analyses (as in [9, 25, 26, 35, 42, 44, 45, 50, 57, 59, 65, 81]).

Consequently, behavioral geographers appear at the moment to include both materialist and dualist notions in their belief set and model of explanation—probably simply by default of any discussion of a philosophy of mind as other more important matters claimed attention in initial theory construction. However, materialist and dualist notions *are* mutually contradictory and not complementary. Given a confused belief set and explanatory model, it seems worthwhile, in conclusion to this section of the paper, to summarize some of the principal materialist and dualist arguments about mental phenomena. This should emphasize the point that, ideally in future research, behavioral geographers might first explicitly recognize the controversial nature of any set of beliefs about the mind, second, arbitrarily select one philosophy of mind or other as a basis for their enquiry, third, specifically state their beliefs about pertinent mental constructs in ways that are compatible with their philosophical position, and lastly, frame statements about how mental phenomena could "cause" or "explain" observable spatial phenomena in ways that are consistent with their philosophy of mind.

Arguments for Materialism

Materialists concede that "psychological descriptions differ from physical [physiological] ones . . . in what they mean" [73, p. 3]. The concession is made because it is clear that psychological statements about, for example, spatial learning, preference, and choice, say things about individuals that cannot be said using physical descriptions. Moreover, it is not clear how this can occur unless the differences between the two kinds of language are reflected in differences in meaning. However, materialists argue that "in spite of the difference in meaning between any psychological and physical descriptions, still whatever is described in psychological terms can also be described equally well (though differently) in solely physical terms . . . on this account, the things we describe psychologically are no more than physical things, material objects, or states of affairs and events involving material objects," namely, brain states or events. This view can be held because descriptions having different meanings can nonetheless be about the same things. "We can talk about Alaska by describing it as either the largest or the coldest state in the Union" [73, p. 3].

This position underlies the four major materialist views: the strict identity hypothesis, theoretical materialism, functionalistic materialism and eliminative materialism. It seems sufficient to take only two of these views, namely, Smart's identity hypothesis [79] and Lewis's functionalistic materialism [49], to illustrate in detail the implications of this philosophy of mind for the behavioral geographers' belief set and model of explanation.

Smart's identity thesis is that all mental phenomena in general, and hence the behavioral geographers' mental phenomena in particular, are strictly identical with processes taking place in the brain. The force of "strictly identical" is that it is not logically impossible that every property ascribed to a mental construct can be identified with a property of the brain. For example, it is not logically impossible that every property of perceived distance can be identified with a brain state. Smart supports this view by asserting that when constructs are "described as psychological, the properties in terms of which [the descriptions are made] are neither peculiarly physical nor incompatible with being physical, that is, the words used to refer to such properties are 'topic-neutral' " [72, p. 10]. To elaborate, when behavioral geographers talk of persons having perceptions of distance, they mean no more than "something is going on in these subjects that is like what goes on when they observe the distance between spatially located objects" (compare with Smart's classical example of a person's "seeing a yellowish-orange after-image" [79, p. 61]). By the identity thesis, either psychological descriptions or physical descriptions of mental phenomena may be used to yield "realistic" explanations of observable spatial behaviors. Accordingly, if the thesis is accepted, no modification is necessary to the behavioral geographers' model of explanation of $B8$ and Figure 1.

However, Smart's version of materialism does not account for how psychological descriptions can be, and are, discriminated from physical ones. Lewis's functionalistic materialism tries to allow for this [49]. He gives an account of mental states in terms of "the networks of causal connections which each kind of state has with overt sensory stimulation, behavior and other mental states" (noted in [73, p. 13]). Accordingly, all mental phenomena are defined in terms of their causal roles. For example, a person's satisfactions in choosing a new place of residence will be definable with reference to his/her behavior in making the choice, his/her stated residential needs, and the sensory stimulations the person experiences when he/she is observing alternative housing. Theoretically at least, then, mental states for population groups can be defined by specifying the typical stimuli and the typical sensory, neural, and behavioral responses that are causally associated with each other and with each residential satisfaction state. On this view, though, since mental phenomena must be *defined* by causal connection with behavior as well as with brain states, they cannot afterwards be held to be autonomous entities which themselves explain behavior. In consequence, the adoption of functionalistic materialism by behavioral geographers would demand some modification of their model of explanation of human spatial activities (*B*8 and Figure 1). It seems clear, however, that the specification of the causal connections necessary to define mental states might of itself set up operational "realistic" models of spatial behavior. This obviously could be so in the case of the person's residential choice considered above. A functionalistic materialist philosophy of mind therefore may be an attractive one for the behavioral geographer to consider.

Neodualist Arguments

Neodualist arguments are of two kinds: logical counterarguments *against* materialism and logical arguments *for* dualism. However, both kinds support the contention that mental events have peculiarly mental, nonmaterial properties and, as such, lie outside the accepted domain of the sciences altogether. Neodualist writings, therefore, seriously undermine two key beliefs of behavioral geographers, namely, that mental phenomena constitute valid objects of scientific enquiry (*B*1 in section 2), and that they are identifiable and verifiable by methodologies like multidimensional scaling (*B*9). Neodualist arguments also call into question both the model of explanation of behavioral geography and the subject's whole raison d'être. It is obviously difficult to show how entities that may lie outside the space-time domain of the sciences can explain either spatial behavior or changing spatial structures—let alone permit more realistic explanations than traditional ones!

Only one example of each kind of neodualist argument can be given here; the examples are chosen because of their direct relevance to behavioral geographers' beliefs. First, we may take Shaffer's simple counterarguments to Smart's strict identity hypothesis [73, pp. 67–72]. Shaffer initially remarks that people can and usually do report their mental events, states, and processes without ever being aware of anything about their physiological state. A relevant geographical example is that subjects can obviously report their images of spatial stimuli, such as shopping centers, without noticing any properties of their own neurophysiological conditions (e.g. [9]). Shaffer next remarks that people can only report what kind of mental phenomena they are describing if they have noticed *some* features of them. It follows that, on some occasions at least, when we describe features of mental phenomena in psychological terms, we must be noticing some properties of mental phenomena (e.g., images) that are not neurophysiological.

To illustrate the second kind of neodualist position, we may use Beloff and Kuhlenbeck's arguments [80, pp. 35–53, 137–61]. This is that no *logical* rules can be found to permit an immediately apparent, satisfactory translation of subjects' perceptual spaces into the physical space of their brains. Kuhlenbeck first distinguishes between the "perceptual time-space manifold" of the mind, and the conceptual time-space utilized by the physical sciences (e.g., neurophysiology). He then argues that "consciousness can be intentionally defined, in a satisfactory manner, as any private perceptual time-space system." This system encompasses the visual and spatial imagery familiar to behavioral geography. Kuhlenbeck also provides a wealth of detail as to how subjects do organize and use a perceptual time-space in Euclidean and higher-order dimensions. However, as Beloff then points out (pp. 48–50), to recognize a distinction between the perceptual time-space of people and the conceptual time-space of science is to recognize "one respect in which the reduction of the phenomenal [mental] to the physical poses a problem quite unlike that which occurs in any other field. For, elsewhere in science, however much the properties of the macro-object may differ from those of the micro-object both fit equally well the universal conceptual framework of physical space. Phenomenal objects, on the other hand, cannot be anchored in physical space, nor, it would seem, is there any set of dimensions that would constitute a common phenomenal space for objects belonging to diverse sense modalities. Such an apparent incommensurability between the phenomenal and the physical domains . . . undoubtedly increases one's misgivings" about the strict identity of the two domains, and about the precise nature and meaning of translations or connections between them.

Both these kinds of argument obviously illustrate the principal thesis of this paper: that there are some fundamental, unresolved, and perhaps unresolvable, questions about the behavioral geographers' beliefs about the mind.

V. SUMMARY AND CONCLUSION: DIRECTIONS FOR FUTURE RESEARCH

This paper has attempted to identify the underlying set of beliefs of behavioral geographers about the nature of the mind, together with the model of explanation of spatial behavior which that philosophy affords. The paper has also attempted to show that both the underlying belief set and the model of explanation are dubious because of unresolved controversies about the ontological status of the mind. As a result, it seems that behavioral geographers cannot justify strong claims about providing causal explanations of observable spatial phenomena (e.g., residential migration, consumer travel behavior, the location of economic activities) in terms of "realistic," that is, scientifically specifiable and verifiable, mental states and processes.

However, it does not follow that behavioral models of the mind should be abandoned in favor of traditional ones. Even if it is true that the underlying beliefs of behavioral geographers are questionable, they still appear more plausible than the mental constructs used in classical location theories. The fact remains that behavioral geographers ascribe to individuals such mental events, states, and processes as human beings normally ascribe to each other in ordinary discourse. More importantly, it remains possible that the behavioral geographers' constructs will yield better descriptions and predictions of observable spatial behaviors and processes than classical theories, despite faulty logic or dubious assumptions about mental events, states, or processes. Nonetheless, the direction for future research would seem to be away from trying to reproduce the contents of individuals' black boxes, to (1) providing models of the mind to predict spatial behavior, consistent with an explicitly designated philosophy of mind and (2) determining which of many alternative and possibly fictional models of the mind can describe and predict observable spatial behaviors best. Pocock, in "Environmental Perception: Process and Product" [66], seems to be a harbinger of the first kind of endeavor in geography. He explains spatial behavior using a model of the mind consistent with a strict-identity, materialist philosophy (summarized in Figure 2).

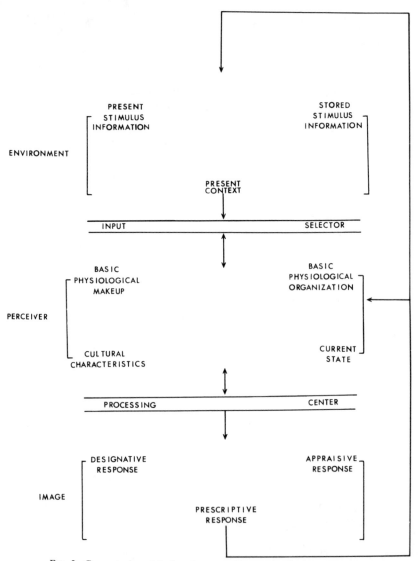

FIG. 2. Conceptual model of environmental perception for image studies

The reorientation provided by the second kind of endeavor would tend to bring geography more into line with the treatment of mental constructs simply as descriptive-predictive devices of overt behavior in psychology, as mentioned above, and in other subject areas. Examples of the latter are afforded by studies of choices of travel mode, brands, and stores in transportation and marketing, using attitude scaling and learning models [1, 29, 36, 60, 62]. Within geography, Hanson [33] appears to stand out with her recent consideration of alternative specifications of models to forecast *observable* destination choice frequencies for recurrent travel, from the subjective familiarity, location, and destination attribute assessments of subjects. She also outlines a research methodology to better specify and test her preferred model:

$$P_{ijb}{}^n = f \left(\sum_{k=1}^{m} I_{kj} L_{ijk} Q_{ijk} \, P_j \, H_j \, T_b{}^n \right), \tag{1}$$

where

$P_{ijb}{}^n$ = probability the ith destination is chosen by the jth individual on the nth trip for trip purpose b

f = approximate functional form

I_{kj} = importance of the kth destination attribute to the jth individual ($k = 1 \ldots m$)

L_{ijk} = level of information jth individual has about kth attribute of the ith destination

Q_{ijk} = amount of attribute k that the jth individual perceives i to have

P_j = personal characteristics of individual j (age, sex, education, occupation)

H_j = household characteristics anotated with individual j (income, car ownership)

$T_b{}^n$ = trip type of the nth trip for purpose b

Clearly, through most of this discussion, my sympathies have been with D'Andrade, who recently declared: "It seems unlikely that people have stored in their memories huge matrices of the sort (our measurement procedures call forth) . . . nor is it apparent that people have an internal representation like the spatial plot produced by MDS procedures'' [in 78, vol. 2, p. 5]. Perhaps it is time to grapple with the philosophical, as well as the modeling and measurement issues that this kind of intuitive unease reveals.

ACKNOWLEDGMENTS

This paper was stimulated by discussions with members of the Philosophy Departments of the three unversities in Sydney, New South Wales, Australia. I am particularly indebted to Alan Olding, my friend and colleague at Macquarie University, who ensured that I took his course on the philosophy of mind, and came to understand at least a little of it. The encouragement of Reginald G. Golledge, of the Department of Geography, Ohio State University, was also greatly appreciated, as were the comments of Gunnar Olsson, Gerard Rushton, and others.

1. This philosophy of mind is prevalent outside behavioral geography in the social science disciplines concerned with the relations between the physical environment and human behavior (see, e.g., the comprehensive annotated bibliography compiled by Bell et al. [3], the standard anthology edited by Proshansky, Ittelson, and Rivlin [67], and the newer work collected by Downs and Stea [15].

2. Relph [69] adopts a phenomenological view that denies the dualism of an external, objective world and an internal, mental perception of it. Golant [21] views humans as biological organisms simply responding to external stimuli. Golledge and Zannaras appear to employ similar stimulus-response models [28, pp. 62–67]. However, the models are combined with learning concepts that seem to imply the orthodox view of the mind mediating between external stimuli and spatial behavior (see especially p. 67).

3. It can be argued, in extension, that experiments with the temporal lobes of the brain, which result in loss of a subject's ability to provide, for example, correct verbal and motor memory behaviors, do not demonstrate necessarily the "observability" of the mind. Such experiments simply demonstrate associations between brain cells and memory behaviors. They reinforce the questions about the mind elaborated below—for example, are the memory behaviors *themselves* the mind (behaviorism); are the brain cells the mind (materialism); or does some nonmaterial entity intervene between cells and behavior to cause presence or absence of memory (neodualism)?

4. Whether or not the traditional theories *are* unsatisfactory is still a matter of debate, with various resolutions depending on the participants' subjective and ultimately arbitrary criteria for assessing theories [39, pp. 15–18].

5. It may be said that this is too strong an interpretation of the Rylean philosophy of mind. It is the one that has certainly been endorsed by behavior psychologists following Skinner [35, p.352]. One of Ryle's most famous critics, Hampshire, on the other hand, argues behaviorists "have not decided whether (a) no mental states 'stand for' imperceptible (=ghostly) processes or states; all 'designate' some imperceptible . . . pattern of behavior: or less drastically (b) that the statements involving mental concepts are in principle testable . . . by observation of the behavior of the person concerned" [87, p. 40].

6. This may be compared with some of the work of environmental psychologists, like Kaplan [46, 47], who attempt to explain behaviors in terms of inherited brain structures for the coding and processing of spatial information.

LITERATURE CITED

1. Aker, D. A., and J. M. Jones. "Modelling Store Choice Behavior" *Journal of Marketing Research*, 8 (1971), 38–42.
2. Atkinson, R. C., G. H. Bower, and E. J. Crothers. *An Introduction to Mathematical Learning Theory.* New York: Wiley and Sons, 1965.
3. Bell, G., et al., eds. *Urban Environments and Human Behavior: An Annotated Bibliography.* Stroudsberg, Pennsylvania: Dowden, Hutchinson and Ross, 1973.
4. Bernstein, R. J. "The Challenge of Scientific Materialism." *International Philosophical Quarterly,* 2 (1968), 252–75.
5. Brand, D. "Separable and Simultaneous Travel Choice Behavior." Resource paper for the Engineering Foundation Conference, "Issues in Behavioral Travel Demand and the Valuation of Travel Time," Berwick Academy, Maine, 8–13, July 1973. Forthcoming in *Issues in Behavioral Travel Demand and the Valuation of Travel Time,* ed. P. Stopher and A. Meyburg. Washington: Transportation Research Board.
6. Briggs, R. "On the Relationships between Cognitive and Objective Distance." Paper read at the Fourth International EDRA Conference, Blacksburg, Virginia, 17 April, 1973.
7. Brown, L. A., and D. B. Longbrake. "Migration Flows in Intra-Urban Space: Place Utility Considerations." *Annals, Association of American Geographers,* 60 (1970), 368–84.
8. Brown, L. A., and E. G. Moore. "The Intra-Urban Migration Process: A Perspective." *Geografiska Annaler,* 52B, (1970), 1–13.
9. Burnett, K. P. "The Dimensions of Alternatives in Spatial Choice Processes." *Geographical Analysis,* 5 (1973), 181–204.
10. ———. "A Three-State Markov Model of Choice Behavior within Spatial Structures." *Geographical Analysis,* 6 (1974), 53–68.
11. ———. "Decision Processes and Innovation: A Transportation Example." Paper submitted to *Economic Geography.*
12. Clark, W. A. V. "Consumer Travel Patterns and the Concept of Range." *Annals of the Association of American Geographers,* 58 (1968), 386–96.
13. ———. "Measurements and Explanation of Intra-Urban Residential Mobility." *Tijdschrift voor Sociale en Economische Geografie,* 61 (1970), 49–57.
14. Cornman, J. W. "The Identity of Mind and Body." *Journal of Philosophy,* 18 (1962), 486—92.
15. Downs, R. M., and D. Stea, eds. *Image and Environment: Cognitive Mapping and Spatial Behavior.* Chicago: Aldine, 1973.
16. Drewett, J. R. "A Stochastic Model of the Land Conversion Process: An Interim Report." *Regional Studies,* 3 (1969), 269–70.
17. Fields, L. "Other Peoples Experiences." *Philosophical Quarterly,* 22 (1972), 19–43.
18. Fodor, J. A. "Functionalist Materialism." In *Psychological Explanation,* J. A. Fodor, pp. 90–120. New York: Random House, 1968.
19. Fyerabend, O. K. "Mental Events and the Brain." *Journal of Philosophy,* 11 (1963), 295–96.
20. Gale, S. "Remarks on the Foundations of Locational Decision-Making." *Antipode,* 4 (1972), 41–79.
21. Golant, S. M. "Adjustment Process in a System: A Behavioral Model of Human Movement." *Geographical Analysis,* 3 (1971), 203–20.
22. Golledge, R. G. "Conceptualizing the Market Decision Process." *Journal of Regional Science,* 7 (Supplement 1967), 239–58.

23. ———. "Process Approaches to the Analysis of Human Spatial Behavior." Research Paper, Department of Geography, Ohio State University, 1969.

24. Golledge, R. G. and R. Briggs. "Decision Processes and Locational Behavior." *High Speed Ground Transportation*, 7 (1973), 81–100.

25. Golledge, R. G., R. Briggs, and D. Demko. "The Configuration of Distance in Intra-Urban Space." *Proceedings of the Association of American Geographers*, 1 (1969), 60–65.

26. Golledge, R. G., and V. L. Rivizzigno. "Learning about a City: Analysis by Multidimensional Scaling." This volume.

27. Golledge, R. G., and G. Rushton. *Multidimensional Scaling: Review and Geographical Applications*. Commission on College Geography Technical Paper No. 10, Washington: Association of American Geographers, 1972.

28. Golledge, R. G., and G. Zannaras. "Cognitive Approaches to the Analysis of Human Spatial Behavior." In *Environment and Cognition*, ed. W. H. Ittelson. New York: Seminar Press, 1973.

29. Golob, T. F. *The Development of Attitudinal Models of Travel Behavior*. Warren, Michigan: Research Laboratories, General Motors Corporation, 1972.

30. Gould, P. "Problems of Space Preference Measures and Relationships." *Geographical Analysis*, 1 (1969), 31–44.

31. Greeno, J. G. *Elementary Theoretical Psychology*. Reading: Addison-Wesley, 1968.

32. Gunderson, K. "Asymmetries and Mind-Body Perplexities." In *Materialism and the Mind-Body Problem*, ed. D. M. Rosenthal, pp. 1–52. New Jersey: Prentice-Hall, 1971.

33. Hanson, S. E. "On Assessing Individuals' Attitudes Towards Potential Travel Destinations." Paper read at the 15th Annual Transportation Forum, San Francisco, 10–12 October, 1974 (*Proceedings* forthcoming).

34. Harman, E. J., and J. F. Betak. "Behavioral Geography, Multidimensional Scaling, and the Mind." This volume.

35. Harrison, J., and P. Sarre. "Personal Construct Theory and the Measurement of Environmental Images: Problems and Methods." *Environment and Behaviour*, 1 (1971), 351–73.

36. Hartgen, D. T. *A Note on the Ability of Socio-Economic Variables to Explain Attitudinal Bias towards Alternative Travel Modes*. Albany, New York: New York State Department of Transportation, 1972.

37. Harvey, D. W. "The Problem of Theory Construction in Geography." *Journal of Regional Science*, 7 (Supplement, 1967), 211–16.

38. ———. "Conceptual and Measurement Problems in Geography." In *Behavioral Problems in Geography*, ed. K. R. Cox and R. G. Golledge, pp. 35–68. Northwestern University Studies in Geography, no. 17, 1969.

39. ———. *Explanation in Geography*. London: Edward Arnold, 1969.

40. Hinman, J. "Controversial Facility-Complex Programs: Coalitions, Side-Payments, and Social Decisions." In *Research on Conflict on Locational Decisions, Discussion Paper 8*. Philadelphia: Regional Science Department, University of Pennsylvania, 1970.

41. Hood, S., ed. *Dimensions of Mind*. London: Collier-Macmillan, 1961.

42. Horton, F. E., and D. R. Reynolds. "Effects of Urban Spatial Structure on Individual Behavior." *Economic Geography*, 47 (1971), 36–49.

43. Huff, D. "A Topographical Model of Consumer Space Preferences." *Papers, Proceedings of the Regional Science Association*, 6 (1962), 157–73.

44. Jackson, L. E., and R. J. Johnston. "Structuring the Image: An Investigation of the Elements of Mental Maps." *Environment and Planning*, 4 (1972), 415–28.

45. Johnston, R. J. "Activity Spaces and Residential Preferences: Some Tests of the Hypothesis of Sectoral Mental Maps." *Economic Geography*, 48 (1972), 199–211.

46. Kaplan, S. "The Role of Location Processing in the Perception of the Environment." Mimeo, Department of Psychology, University of Michigan, 1973.

47. ———. "The Challenge of Environmental Psychology: A Proposal for a New Functionalism." *American Psychologist,* 27 (1972), 140–43.

48. Kim, J. "On the Psycho-Physical Identity Theory." *American Philosophical Quarterly,* 3 (1966), 227–35.

49. Lewis, O. K. "The Argument for the Identity Theory." *Journal of Philosophy,* 1 (1966), 17–25.

50. Lieber, S. R. "A Comparison of Metric and Nonmetric Scaling Models in Perceptual Research." Paper read at the Special Session "Multidimensional Scaling of Preferences and Perception," 69th Annual Meeting, Association of American Geographers, Atlanta, 18 April 1973.

51. Locke, D. *Perception and Our Knowledge of the External World.* London: Allen and Unwin, 1967.

52. ———. "Must a Materialist Pretend He Is Anaesthetized?" *Philosophical Quarterly,* 21 (1971), 217–302.

53. Louviere, J. J. "After MDS, or the Role of Mathematical Behavior Theory in the Analysis of Spatial Behavior" Paper read at the Special Session, "Multidimensional Scaling of Preferences and Perception," 69th Annual Meeting, Association of American Geographers, Atlanta, 18 April 1973.

54. Lowenthal, D. "Geography, Experience, and Imagination: Towards a Geographical Epistemology." *Annals, Association of American Geographers,* 51 (1961), 241–60.

55. Lynch, K. *The Image of the City.* Cambridge: M.I.T. Press, 1960.

56. Marble, D. F. "A Theoretical Exploration of Individual Travel Behavior." In *Quantitative Geography, Part 1: Economic and Cultural Topics,* ed. W. L. Garrison and D. F. Marble, pp. 33–53. Northwestern University Studies in Geography, n. 13, 1967.

57. Menchik, M. "Residential Environmental Preferences and Choice: Empirically Validating Preference Measures." *Environment and Planning,* 4 (1972), 379–500.

58. Morley, C. D., and J. B. Thornes. "A Markov Decision Model for Network Flows." *Geographical Analysis,* 4 (1972), 180–93.

59. Murphy, P. E., and R. G. Golledge. "Comments on the Use of Attitude As a Variable in Urban Geography." Discussion Paper No. 25, Department of Geography, Ohio State University, 1969.

60. Myers, J. G. *Consumer Image and Attitude.* Berkeley: University of California Institute of Business and Economic Research, 1972.

61. Nagel, T. "Physicalism." *Philosophical Review,* 3 (1965), 339–56.

62. Nicholaidis, G. "Quantification of the Comfort Variable for Use in Disaggregate Mode Choice Models" (preliminary draft). Warren, Michigan: Research Laboratories, General Motors Corporation, 1973.

63. Olsson, G., and S. Gale. "Spatial Theory and Human Behavior." *Papers and Proceedings of the Regional Science Association,* 2 (1968), 229–42.

64. Olsson, G. "Inference Problems in Locational Analysis." In *Behavioral Problems in Geography,* ed. K. R. Cox and R. G. Golledge, pp. 14–34. Northwestern University Studies in Geography, no. 17, 1969.

65. Peterson, G. K. "A Model of Preference: Quantitative Analysis of the Visual Appearance of Residential Neighborhoods." *Journal of Regional Science,* 7 (1967), 19–32.

66. Pocock, D. C. D. "Environmental Perception: Process and Product." *Tijdschrift voor Economische en Sociale Geografie,* 64 (1973), 251–57.

67. Proshansky, H. M., W. H. Ittelson, and L. G. Rivlin, eds. *Environmental Psychological: Man and His Physical Setting.* New York Holt, Rinehart and Winston, 1970.

68. Putnam, H. "Psychological Predicates." In *Art, Mind, and Religion,* ed. W. J. Capitan and D. D. Merrill, pp. 37–48. Pittsburgh: University of Pittsburgh Press, 1967.

69. Relph, E. "An Inquiry into the Relations between Phenomenology and Geography." *Canadian Geographer,* 16 (1970), 193–201.

70. Rorty, R. "Mind-Body Identity, Privacy and Categories." *Review of Metaphysics,* 1 (1965), 25–54.

71. ———. "In Defense of Eliminative Materialism." *Review of Metaphysics,* 1 (1970), 112–21.

72. Roseman, C. C. "Migration as a Spatial and Temporal Process." *Annals, Association of American Geographers,* 61 (1971), 589–98.

73. Rosenthal, D. M., ed. *Materialism and the Mind-Body Problem.* New Jersey: Prentice-Hall, 1971.

74. Rushton, G. "The Scaling of Locational Preferences." In *Behavioral Problems in Geography: A Symposium,* ed. K. R. Cox and R. G. Golledge, pp. 197–227. Northwestern University Studies in Geography, no. 17, 1969.

75. ———. "Behavioral Correlates of Urban Spatial Structure." *Economic Geography,* 47 (1971), 49–58.

76. ———. "The Removal of Non-Additivity of Stimuli Effects in a Space Preference Function." Paper read at Special Session, "Multidimensional Scaling of Preferences and Perceptions," 69th Annual Meeting, Association of American Geographers, Atlanta, 18 April 1973.

77. Ryle, G. *The Concept of Mind.* New York: Hutchinson, 1949.

78. Shepard, R. N., A. K. Romney, and S. B. Nerlove, eds. *Multidimensional Scaling: Theory and Applications in the Social Sciences.* 2 vols. New York: Seminar Press, 1972.

79. Smart, J. J. C. "Sensations and Brain Processes." In *The Philosophy of Mind,* ed. V. C. Chappell, pp. 101–9. Englewood Cliffs: Prentice-Hall, 1962.

80. Smythies, J. R., ed. *Brain and Mind: Modern Concepts of the Nature of Mind.* London: Routledge and Keagan Paul, 1965.

81. Sonnenfeld, J. "Equivalence and Distortion of the Perceptual Environment." *Environment and Behavior,* 1 (1969), 83–99.

82. Stegman, M. A. "Accessibility Models and Residential Location." *Journal of the American Institute of Planners,* 35 (1969), 22–29.

83. Tobler, W. R. "The Geometry of Mental Maps." This volume.

84. Wolpert, J. "The Decision Process in a Spatial Context." *Annals, Association of American Geographers,* 54 (1964), 537–58.

85. ———. "Behavioral Aspects of the Decision to Migrate." *Papers and Proceedings of the Regional Science Association,* 15 (1965).

86. Wolpert, J., and D. Zillman. "The Sequential Expansion of a Decision Model in a Spatial Context." *Environment and Planning,* 1 (1969), 91–104.

87. Wood, O. P., and G. Pitcher, eds. *Ryle: A Collection of Critical Essays.* New York: Doubleday, 1970.

88. Zannaras, G. *An Analysis of Cognitive and Objective Characteristics of a City: Their Influence on Movement to the City Center.* Ph.D. dissertation, Department of Geography, Ohio State University, 1973.

CHAPTER 3

JOSEPH SONNENFELD

Multidimensional Measurement
Of Environmental Personality

Geographers and psychologists seemed to exchange roles during the early period of environmental perception studies. Behaviorally oriented geographers were inclined to focus on person variables in perception [4, 5, 7, 9], whereas psychologists working in related areas appeared to be emphasizing stimulus variables [1, 8, 16, 17]. This was not really so odd an arrangement, considering that geographers had long been aware of the significance and complexity of the stimulus environment and thus were more likely to be intrigued by the role of the relatively unknown person variables, while the reverse was probably true for those psychologists probing the stimulus field.

With the spread of behavioral interest, however, concern for the person seems to have declined; many behavioral geographers now appear to be focusing on environmental or stimulus variables.[1] And while the perceptual transformation of these variables is emphasized, a fair amount of stimulus control is still implicit.[2]

Being from the earlier group of behavioral geographers, I have tended to retain a bias favoring person rather than stimulus. I recognize that there is a significant stimulus dimension to sensing and perceiving, but I consider the stimulus to be important only to the extent that it can be associated with some kind of overt behavior, which implies that it need not produce or elicit such behavior. If this is the case, then one may question the utility of emphasizing either environmental (stimulus) or perceptual (sensitivity, attitude) variables rather than more explicit sources of behavioral variability, such as personality and response set, for getting the kind of understanding of environmental behavior that permits prediction.

A second bias that I seem to have retained is a preference for dealing with behavior at the individual rather than the group level. Though information about an individual's group memberships is often needed to explain some of his behaviors, behavior itself occurs because an individual decides to behave. Sensing and perceiving mechanisms function at the level of the individual. It is the individual who values, who relates images to previous experiences; and it is the individual who represents the group, and who brings pressure to bear on those who violate group norms. Although one can calculate group preferences and perceptions, one cannot assume behavioral significance for these, since group behaviors may be a function more of the impact of certain influential individuals than of consistent individual perceptions and preferences.

A third bias, more recent in developing, is against the use of attitude and preference measures for predicting behavior. Attitudes relate to beliefs and values and may influence behaviors; but attitudes also derive from behaviors. And though a type of behavior may have a consistent impact, any given behavior may also have quite different impacts. Because feedback is obviously related to impact, quite different attitudes can result, depending on reasons for the behavior, its social context, and the environment toward which it is directed.

Attitudes toward recreation, for example, are a function of one's past recreational behaviors; these are conditioned by experience in a specific environment, which may have either reinforced given recreational attitudes or tended to extinguish them—and similarly with attitudes toward pollution, the need for population control, and the risk of natural hazards. In other words, attitudes may be a reasonable measure of the impact of past behaviors, but one with no necessary implication of such impact for subsequent behaviors, which can occur for reasons that may relate only minimally to the attitudes in question.

The preference-perception distinction is equivalent to that between attitude and belief [2]. Preferences, like attitudes, are oriented. Perceptions, like beliefs, simply indicate awareness or knowledge of a situation. Though values can and do condition the nature of perceptions and beliefs, neither carries any necessary value connotation to indicate degree of approval or appreciation of that which is perceived or believed.

Expressed preferences and actual behaviors do not necessarily coincide, especially if behavior is defined as real-world action directed to, or having impact on, some element or feature of the environment. I do not characterize responses to test questions meant to elicit an individual's preferences for certain environmental elements or conditions, from which perceptions or cognitive structures subsequently may be inferred, to be behaviors in this sense. Rather, the behavior of choice is here only an artifact of the test situation. As with attitudes, expressed preferences from a limited set of alternatives are not adequate for predicting the behaviors of the individuals being tested, were they to be faced with responding to the real-world equivalent of test stimuli [3, pp. 213 ff.]. Some form of behavior validation in the ''real world'' is necessary before such extrapolation can be made from test results.

Consistent with these biases I have moved from an initial concern with perception, and the attitude and preference equivalents of perception, to an emphasis on behavior and its sources in personality. This shift in focus has been facilitated by the rather clear evidence that patterns of test response that distinguish *between* populations also occur *within* populations [10, 11]. This suggests that there are influences other than culture or subculture or social role that form environmental attitudes and preferences. Thus there can be considerable individual variation within any group in terms of things such as landscape tastes or in the way individuals characterize environment or environmental relationships— for example by indicating a high sensitivity to hazards or risk, or social isolation, or aesthetic quality of setting. These kinds of concerns are a function of person rather than of stimulus or environment, which is the reason why I have begun to probe personality and, more specifically, environmental personality [12]. A personality concept emphasizes the relationship between person and environment as the source of most behavior, but it focuses on the person rather than on the environment and thus permits identification of equivalently behaving individuals, regardless of environmental context; this is especially important for cross-cultural analysis. In addition, personality implies behavior or a predisposition to behave and not simply a predisposition to perceive or to develop attitudes or values that may or may not produce behaviors. This concern for behavioral validation of attitudes and values may seem excessive, but it is through behavior that perceptions, individual attitudes, and values are validated.

TEXAS STUDY

I am currently involved in a study of a diverse set of Texas populations, which focuses on perception and personality variables in a manner more or less consistent with the positions I have stated above. The "more or less" disclaimer refers to the fact that this study is still in its initial stages and has not yet expanded into an examination of the real-world behaviors that are considered essential for validating the personality constructs so far based only on test responses. What follows is a kind of rationale for the tests used, not in terms of specific test results, but rather in terms of what may be inferred from tests that ostensibly focus on the community environment but produce measures of personality rather than of environmental qualities.

This study, in its initial phase, attempts to make an inventory of the environmental attitudes and sensitivities of regional populations in Texas. The following general hypotheses are being tested: (1) that differences will be found in the environmental perceptions of populations in different regions as a function of different environmental exposures and experiences; (2) that differences will be found in the environmental perceptions of population groups within regions as a function of such variables as age, sex, urban-rural residence, socioeconomic status, other-environment experience, and personality; and (3) that similar environmental personality types will be found among all populations though the environmental manifestations of personality traits may vary considerably from area to area as a function of different environmental exposure and experience; the proportion of individuals of a specific type of personality may also vary as a function of cultural and environmental selection for or against certain personality characteristics by the predominant population and environment of a region.

Hypothesis (1) suggests, simply, that people in a state as diverse environmentally as Texas will differ in their environmental attitudes and sensitivities as a result of having adapted to their diverse environments. Thus sensitivity to water deficiency should differ for East Texas and West Texas populations. Sensitivity to pollution should differ for urban and rural populations, as should sensitivity to crowding and noise. Environmental tastes should also vary: preferences for coasts, mountains, forests, and the desert as vacation and home environments should in large part be conditioned by the experience or nonexperience of these. Similarly, the perception of climate in terms of qualities and intensities and risks should be influenced by regional experiences with drought, freeze, flooding, or hurricane.

Hypothesis (2) suggests that in addition to the differences that distinguish different regional populations are those that occur within each of these populations, related to the fact that no population is really homogeneous either in the sensing capacities and experiences or the values of its members. Thus age and health factors may influence sensitivity to pollutants of various kinds. Similarly, living standard differentials between Latins, Blacks, and Anglos will condition sensitivities to quality of the physical environment, given the prior need for improvement of more basic quality dimensions of the social environment, for example, housing, schools, and jobs. Differences in education and other-environment experience will affect environmental values, as will occupation and related activity variables.

In any culturally homogeneous population one may find many subcultures, each consistent with the others in some respects, but also different in other respects. Young and old constitute separate subcultures, and similarly male and female, different religious groups, and different ethnic groups. Different social and activity groups may also be identified, ranging from birdwatchers to mountain climbers, and including members of social organizations concerned with improving the quality of the community environment. These represent associations of compatible personality types, who derive from a variety of more conventional groups; and, depending on level of commitment, these may also constitute subcultures of a kind. In effect, not only will environmental sensitivities and values differ from region to region in Texas, but these may also vary considerably within any given region.

Hypothesis (3) suggests that personality types are transregional as well as transcultural; the aesthetically sensitive and insensitive, risk takers and risk avoiders, those who value the different or exotic and those who instead prefer the traditional and historical may be found among all groups in all regions, though what is valued by each will be affected by that which each has experienced locally, within a context of both social and geographic environment. The aesthetically sensitive among Latin, Black, and Anglo, or among young and old, may differ in what each considers attractive and thus in how each experiences any given aesthetic attraction; similarly, risk takers will vary in their classification of a given environment or activity as risky. Thus, specific behaviors and values in different areas may differ, but their sources in personality may be essentially the same; and conversely, similar behaviors in different areas may derive from different predisposing conditions of personality and environment. This should suggest that observed behaviors, and the manifestations of these on the landscape, are not adequate indicators of a population's sensitivities and values, at least not from the standpoint of prescribing remedial action for environmental deterioration and planning for environmental quality generally.

Procedures

Tests were designed to establish the existence of regional variation in environmental sensitivities and attitudes and to include measures of personality elements as developed recently in a model of environmental personality (see Figure 1) [13]. Students were the subjects for the initial phase of this study. Texas was divided into seven geographically distinct regions, and a sample of junior high and high schools randomly selected from each of these regions. For the first run of the test, school districts

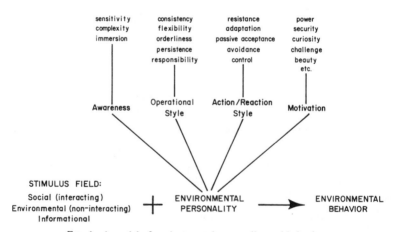

FIG. 1. A model of environmental personality and behavior

were chosen from comparably sized communities. Six of the seven districts selected served communities under 10,000 in population; the remaining district was only slightly larger (10,074).

Students were chosen for this study for a variety of reasons. For one, they constitute a captive audience, which means access to all groups—social, ethnic, and racial—to an extent and under conditions that normally are not possible, given work schedules of adult males, difficulty of contacting members of minority populations, and variability of conditions under which testing would have to take place. In addition, most of the tests were verbal and required fair linguistic competence. In Texas this would tend to exclude many of the Spanish-speaking community as well as marginal literates among non-Latin populations as well. This was the reason for working with students in the upper grades, though it was apparent that we were still dealing with marginal levels of literacy among some eithth graders, at least in terms of what our tests required of them.

Granted that a student sample excludes large segments of a community population, we have assumed that differences in student perceptions and personalities will also represent differences in their community and home environments. However, the students do constitute a more homogeneous group in exposure and experience than their parents, so that within-group variability may not be as apparent; and given the impact of communication media, neither may between-group differences be as apparent. But this also suggests that any within- and between-group differences found may indicate the existence of yet greater differences in the adult community. More critically, as it has turned out, the student group is directly involved in a rather important measure of community viability, specifically, the rate of out-migration.

Students completed six tasks over a two-day period of testing. They prepared a residential history as part of a personal data inventory; they evaluated their home community, using an adjective checklist; they completed a semantic differential test designed to permit definition of a wide variety of familiar and unfamiliar environments; they viewed and indicated preferences for contrasting landscapes as depicted by a set of colorphoto slides; they constructed what each considered an ideal community; and they thought and wrote about postgraduation plans.

Since my main concern during the initial phase of this study was to verify between- and within-region differences in environmental perception, personality, and behavior, the personal data form was restricted to soliciting little more than identifying information on age, sex, and residential history. This last was for indications of the effect of gross environmental experiences (exposures) and the diversity of these on environmental perceptions and personality, to which the remaining tasks contributed more explicitly.

Community Perceptions

The community evaluation is based on a checklist of terms for describing the home community. The list includes ninety-nine terms, any of which can be checked by the student as descriptive of his "home territory." Previous use of this type of test indicated that the number of items checked could not be attributed to size of the area included as home territory, but rather seemed to be a function of the complexity of respondent perceptions. Thus the fact that the size of a community differs, or by some "objective" standard is a more heterogeneous community than another, should not influence the number of items checked. Objective dimensions of a community may influence choice of certain items when the respondent has a basis for comparing his home community with others he has experienced; but this still requires a sensitivity to such difference on the part of the respondent, and this sensitivity is basically what I wanted to measure.

The checklist provides a number of indices. These include (a) a *complexity index* based on total number of items checked, (b) an *interaction index* based on checked items that suggest internalizations of environmental *qualities* (e.g., "dangerous") by contrast with items that suggest a subjective evaluation of objective home environment characteristics (e.g., "ugly"), (c) *positive* and *negative* indices based on items that indicate a positive or negative evaluation of the home environment, and (d) an *activity index* based on items that depict the community in action terms (e.g., "aggressive," "busy"). Complexity index scores are taken as one of the indications of student's sensitivity to, or awareness of, his own environment, with the specific items checked defining the nature of this sensitivity. Consistency in group definitions of the community environment not only suggests the existence of a group perception but also constitutes a measure of the community as perceived environment, which, in turn, is one basis for understanding the community as behavioral environment [14].

Landscape Preferences

This test requires choices between natural landscapes as depicted by a select set of colorphoto-slides. These slides are projected in pairs, and students are expected to choose one of each of a set of twenty-nine pairs of slides. This is a modified version of a test used many times previously for indications of the landscape preferences of populations differing both in culture and environmental experience. It has the advantage of being nonverbal in nature, and this is especially useful for cross-cultural work or where the question of linguistic equivalence or competence is at issue. Previous studies [10, 11] have shown between-group differences related both to culture and environment, and within-group differences related to sex, age, education, and environmental experience. Comparison of photo-slide tests with other test data has also suggested the role of personality as a source of difference, related to preferences for what is considered exotic or exciting (risky) in environment.

A number of changes were made for the Texas study. The original set of fifty pairs of slides was reorganized and, with some additions, reduced to a new set of twenty-nine pairs. To the original set of four indices, which indicated degree of preference for topography (relief), vegetation, water, and temperature, four new indices were added: (*a*) a *space index*, indicating preference for closed or "filled in" landscapes as opposed to more open spaces (e.g., a narrow canyon versus open plain or a forest versus a grassland); (*b*) an *aridity index*, not necessarily consistent with the original water index, which was based simply on the presence or absence of observed water bodies or flows; (*c*) a *mobility index*, which considers apparent accessibility differences of the landscapes depicted; and (*d*) a *social index*, based on preference for landscapes showing people, or otherwise indicating the close presence of man: houses, roads, bridges, and the like. Most of the slides depicted landscapes that lacked any obvious cultural features.

Two runs of the slides were required, which also represented a change from the original test design. For the first run, students were requested to choose from each pair of slides that place they would most like to spend a vacation—money or time being no object. Having completed the first run, they were then asked to rate the slides once more, but now to choose places they would prefer for long-term residence, at least for a year or more. In addition to the eight indices for each of the two runs, the differences in slides chosen for first and second runs provide the basis for an additional index, a *consistency index*. And since there is no way of knowing from any of these indices whether choices represent preference for the more or less exotic environments, specific slides were also compared with the surrounding community environment; differences between these and student choices for short-term residence provided an *exotic index*. Combined with the consistency index, this also indicates preference for the conventional community environment and thus constitutes an additional measure of adaptation.

In an earlier study, a list of places—more and less exotic—provided the basis for a similar type of comparison between preferences for short- and long-term visiting [12], but this presented the problem of choosing places (e.g., Greenwich Village) that might be relatively unknown to large segments of a given population (e.g., Mexican-Americans in Texas). This was much less of a problem with the photo-slides, since the locations of places were not identified for the students.

In addition to providing a measure of adaptation, test results also suggest differences in level of curiosity and, combined with data from other tests, the level of student contentment with community, such as is capable of being translated into environmental mobility, albeit only a potential mobility at this point. Within-group analysis of the consistency and exotic index scores also provides a basis for distinguishing equivalent environmental personalities across groups, since these are free of the regional bias associated with the environmental (topography, vegetation, etc.) indices, which should vary as a function of adaptation to the regional environment [10].

Environmental Meaning

The third test makes use of the semantic differential technique and is designed to get measures of the range of meaning of a variety of more and less common environments and environmental elements (e.g., the seasons, storms, the ocean, wilderness). Earlier research with the semantic differential [11] suggested its utility as a measure of between- and within-group similarities and differences in level of environmental adaptation, at both a cross-environmental and cross-cultural level. And combined with results of the photo-slide tests, the semantic differential also permitted probing into certain personality dimensions (involving, e.g., attribution of danger and excitement to environmental elements) not otherwise interpretable from photo-slide choices, with correlations also between positive and negative environmental orientations and preferences for certain types of landscapes.

The test used in this study involved two sets of concepts, one of climatic elements (e.g., spring, summer, storms, night, etc.) and the other of environmental types (the ocean, wilderness, home town, etc.). The same bipolar scales (seventeen) were used for both sets of concepts.

Group scores are derived from individual scale responses for each concept, and these provide the basis for between-group comparisons; both direction of difference between groups and within-group consistency of scale scoring are important. At the individual level, mean scale responses across all concepts may be suggestive of critical environmental personality traits and provide the basis, through fractionating of populations (establishing quintiles), for combining like personalities into groups that are not biased by regional differences in adaptation level. In addition to mean scale responses, a set of *difference* (*D*) scores is obtained that allows for a measure of perceived differentness of the test concepts, one from the other (e.g., winter versus summer, ocean versus mountain, wilderness versus big city). A set of objective scales (e.g., hot-cold, wet-dry) provides a measure of sensory sensitivity or adaptation, while a set of subjective scales (e.g., beautiful-ugly, exciting-dull) constitutes an equivalent measure of environmental "bias."

These *D*-scores are analyzed at both individual and group levels to provide not only indications of group differences in sensitivity and adaptation but also within-population variation, which can be related to landscape choices and other test results. It provides, in effect, cross-test verification for environmental personality typing.

Symbolic Community

As a fourth task, students were asked to "design" their own community. The stimulus for this was the "self-social symbols task" developed by Ziller[3] [18], who asked respondents to locate important social-others in some relation to self, using a variety of both structured and unstructured spatial formats. Social personality is shown to have rather interesting spatial and locational dimensions, within the context of an abstract social space. Because community patterns involve social as well as environmental associations, which also have spatial and locational dimension, a test was devised that allowed students to construct maps of ideal communities. The test requires that a set of twelve "place types" be located within the confines of a bounded (4 × 5 inch), though unscaled, space. In addition to locating place types individually or in groups, students are asked to encircle those elements that are to be included as part of their own group (neighborhood).

Two kinds of map measurements are obtained: (a) the position of each community element on a Cartesian coordinate system overlay and (b) the location of individual place types relative to student's home.

Position measurements provide the basis for judging the significance of upper/lower, left/right, and central/peripheral locations. Centering student's home at zero permits easy computer calculation of the distance from student's home to place locations, as well as the absolute dispersion of community elements, based on the sum of the distances from each point to every other point. Since no scale appears on maps, distances have no real meaning for cross-map analysis. In order to allow within- and between-group comparison of distances from student's home to various place locations, the distance vectors for each individual are standardized by converting these to z-scores [6], which normalize individual map distributions. Mean X and Y values are also calculated to provide a measure of skewedness of locations in respect to home residence.

The ratios of distances between student's home and place locations provide the basis for a set of scale-free indices, which also permit comparison across maps. These include a *rivalry index* (distance to sibling's home compared with distance to parent's home), an *alienation index* (parent's home: friend's home), a *nature index* (recreation: park), an *authoritarian index* (closest social other: police), a *tradition index* (school: church), a *pragmatic index* (job or shopping: park), and a *fear index* (hospital: police).

Students were requested to take home a copy of this task to be completed by a parent. The difference between parent and student responses yields a *consistency index*.

This test, treating symbolically ideal community associations, yields responses conditioned by current community experiences as well as by contentment with existing social relationships. It also suggests reasons for student responses to other tests and thus provides a basis for analyzing within-group differences in both community evaluation and environmental preference in more explicit social and activity terms. And because this task does not involve reference to any specific kind of environment, it is also possible to identify like individuals across groups, in terms of the social, activity, and environmental associations they prefer. This permits clearer distinction between the role of adaptation level and personality in accounting for differences in environmental preferences.

Postgraduation plans

In this final task, students were asked to indicate whether they planned to remain in their home community after completing their schooling or whether, instead, they intended to move elsewhere, for a better job and/or for raising a family. Each was asked to state his reasons for wanting to stay or to leave.

Students were then asked to consider an alternative: under what conditions might they consider changing their minds about staying or leaving? If they initially indicated that they expected to be leaving the community, under what conditions might they instead decide to stay; and, similarly, if they initially indicated a preference for their home community, what would make them consider leaving for a new location?

Written responses undergo a content analysis. Critical environmental and social elements are identified as well as student value orientations: e.g., primary concern for job (for security or opportunity reasons), for more leisure time activities (active or passive), and for an improved family environment or quality of environment generally. The specifics of these orientations are also noted, i.e., the kinds of social and environmental elements at issue and the stimulus role of these in residential expectations or projections.

A more direct measure of mobility and mobility potential was obtained by asking students to indicate how often they took trips to (*a*) a close town or city larger than their own (within approximately a 25-mile radius) and (*b*) a larger city or metropolitan area (within approximately a 100-mile radius). Some data on extended summer or recreational travel were also obtained. With the exception of this last, data on incidence and range of year-round travel are considered to constitute behavioral measures of perceived home community deficiency, and are being related to statements on residential or migration plans in order to indicate the extent to which such plans are based on personal knowledge of what exists elsewhere, thus providing one means for distinguishing the positive from the negative pressures for change in residence.

CONCLUSIONS

It is clear that the individual student's attitudes toward community and relationships with community elements are relevant in all of the tests given.[4] Together these provide a basis for probing both the environmental and personality dimensions of migration. In the case of the school districts involved in this study, the rural-urban exodus is at issue, a continuing phenomenon of the Texas and national scene. Problems of population expansion (urban congestion and suburbanization) and of population decline (community deterioration and abandonment) exist not only because of simple numerical changes in residence but also because of the select nature of that population which remains and that which leaves. The behaviors of those who opt for residential stability will no doubt differ from the behaviors of those who opt for change— these latter based on values colored both by an earlier other-environment experience and by the motivations that produced a demand for change. The concept of the nonnative as a distinctive environmental personality [9] becomes especially relevant for understanding behavior and conflict in urban settings.

In effect, through a kind of multidimensional analysis of community attitudes and environmental preferences, we get information that enlightens us about more than stimulus attributes, even though it was a specific stimulus or stimulus complex that elicited the student's response. We see responses as characterizing the person—as sensor, evaluator, and potential behaver—rather than as characterizing environment. We look at behaviors such as migration as the product of environmental personality rather than as the result of any given environmental condition or situation. Such manipulation of test data implies that the stimulus field is nondefinitive; the same community can be either repulsive or attractive apart from specific environmental characteristics. It is obviously not any objective set of community elements that is varying, but rather the perception of these.

To conclude, the sensing and perceptual transformation of environmental stimuli are not random group processes. There are reasons in other than stimulus why the individual perceives and behaves as he does, reasons that are specific to him, and, to varying degrees, to the different groups of which he is a member. One of these groups is made up of like personalities who, by definition, have equivalent behavioral disposition. Such disposition is complexly determined and liable to change; but once established, it can be used as a guide to prediction of behavior under any of a variety of stimulus situations. All one needs to know is how the specific stimulus is perceived. Perception does not automatically produce behavior, nor do test-elicited attitudes or preference measures necessarily predict behavior. Yet such measures, adequately validated for meaning, may indicate the direction that behavior will take once the behavioral threshold is reached. Whether such threshold *is* reached is at least part of what the study of environmental personality is all about.

1. See, for example, the papers by R. G. Golledge, S. R. Lieber, J. J. Louviere, V. M. Lueck, and G. Rushton in this volume. Golledge has stated that the current emphasis in his work "serves only as a staging point: once we've determined how to represent cognitions of environments, we can go back to the important task of determining individual differences and similarities in how environments are represented and used." Another indication that behavioral geographers are becoming more concerned about person variables, according to Golledge, is "the intense interest in personal construct theory by a sizeable group of U.S. and British geographers. . . ." (personal communication, 1974).

2. This is especially apparent in efforts to predict group behavior. Groups are presumed to behave consistently if they perceive environmental elements consistently. Whether distorted or not by perceptual transformation, if consistency exists, then the stimulus provides the key to prediction.

3. My original source for information about the "self-social symbols task" was a series of six papers by Ziller and his associates reporting on research supported by the National Science Foundation, 1960–68, mimeo.

4. For some preliminary analyses of data from this study see [15].

LITERATURE CITED

1. Beck, R. "Spatial Meaning and the Properties of the Environment." In *Environmental Perception and Behavior*, ed. D. Lowenthal, pp. 18–41. Research Paper No. 109, Department of Geography, University of Chicago, 1966.
2. Bem, D. J. *Beliefs, Attitudes, and Human Affairs.* Belmont, California: Brooks/Cole, 1970.
3. Jahoda, M., and N. Warren, eds. *Attitudes.* Baltimore: Penguin, 1966.
4. Lowenthal, D. "Geography, Experience, and Imagination: Towards a Geographical Epistemology." *Annals, Association of American Geographers,* 51 (1961), 241–60.
5. Lucas, R. C. "Wilderness Perception and Use: The Example of the Boundary Water Canoe Area." *Natural Resources Journal,* 3 (1964), 394–411.
6. McNemar, Q. *Psychological Statistics.* New York: John Wiley and Sons, 1949.
7. Saarinen, T. F. "Perception of the Drought Hazard on the Great Plains." Research Paper No. 106, Department of Geography, University of Chicago, 1966.
8. Sommer, R. "The Ecology of Privacy." *Library Quarterly,* 36 (1966), 234–48.
9. Sonnenfeld, J. "Variable Values in Space and Landscape: An Enquiry into the Nature of Environmental Necessity." *Journal of Social Issues,* 22 (1966), 71–82.
10. ———. "Environmental Perception and Adaptation Level in the Arctic." In *Environmental Perception and Behavior*, ed. D. Lowenthal, pp. 42–59. Research Paper No. 109, Department of Geography, University of Chicago, 1967.
11. ———. "Equivalence and Distortion of the Perceptual Environment." *Environment and Behavior,* 1 (1969), 83–99.
12. ———. "Personality and Behavior in Environment." *Proceedings, Association of American Geographers,* 1 (1969), 136–40.
13. ———. "Behavioral Dimensions of Cultural Geography." *Environment and Behavior,* 4 (1972), 268.
14. ———. "Geography, Perception, and the Behavioral Environment." In *Man, Environment, and Space,* ed. P. English and R. C. Mayfield, pp. 244–51. New York: Oxford University Press, 1972.
15. ———. "Environmental Perception, Personality, and Behavior: The Texas System." *Man-Environment Systems,* 4 (1974), 119–25.
16. Stea, D. "Space, Territory, and Human Movements." *Landscape,* 15 (1965), 13–16.
17. Wohlwill, J. F. "Amount of Stimulus Exploration and Preference As Differential Functions of Stimulus Complexity." *Perception and Psychophysics,* 4 (1968), 307–12.
18. Ziller, R. C. *The Social Self.* New York: Pergamon, 1973.

CHAPTER 4

WALDO R. TOBLER

The Geometry of Mental Maps

In modern cartography, one distinguishes between two classes of theory. The first covers the geometrical content of a map and the second treats the substantive content of a map. The geometrical content is extremely well understood. Here the concern is with the *configuration* of control points and the *scale, orientation,* and *location* of this configuration relative to one of the celestial bodies. The theory of the substantive content of geographical maps, on the other hand, is quite unsatisfactory, incomplete, and disjointed—an assertion which I think will be proved by the history of the next several decades. Given this state of the cartographic art, it seems prudent to begin an investigation of mental maps by concentrating on those parts of cartography wherein the achievement of definite results can be anticipated with some certainty, and this is the strategy adopted here. The entire focus is thus on the geometric content of mental maps. It is probably possible to obtain some results via the bivariate modulation transfer function for geographical maps considered as two-dimensional scalar fields, since some theory is beginning to emerge for this restricted class of geographical maps, but this is ignored in the present discussion.

In the classical cartographic paradigm, one knows that the position of any point on the two-dimensional surface of the earth can be established by two independent measurements. In a triangulation one observes angles; in a trilateration one measures distances; and in a traverse one employs a combination of distance and direction measurements. These empirical data are obtained using a variety of instruments, the precise nature of which seems strongly dependent on the available technology. If we wish to estimate a mental configuration that relates terrestrial points to each other, we need to obtain comparable empirical data. But the measuring devices will differ. There are some fairly obvious ways of obtaining data on mental configurations and a few that are more subtle. One can ask people to draw maps, which I would not consider a very good procedure since it confounds drawing ability with geographical knowledge. One can devise questionnaires to elicit estimates of distances or directions, or a combination of the two, between places. One can use a method of paired comparisons, obtaining a rank ordering of distances or directions. One can investigate associations between places (e.g.: given the name of a place, cite another place whose name comes to mind most readily; or, cite a place adjacent to the named place; and so on). Alternately one can infer a configuration from a behavioral pattern. Clearly we are still at the stage where our instruments can be improved. In all of this we assume that the subjects being studied have a representation of their environment and that this is somehow maplike and can be observed by some type of measurement procedure. I am not convinced that the basic assumption is meaningful, but I have been unable to devise an experiment that would force me to give it up. Clearly, some representation of the environment is required, but whether this is hierarchical or maplike is not known. Experiments with computer robots able to move within a complex environment, such as are now under way, may be more illuminating than inferences from biological subjects [2].

    Let us take a cartographic posture and assume that we have obtained, by some empirical procedure, a set of estimated relations between places. If it is reasonable to consider these relations to be distances, then we can use the formula known to every high school student. The map-maker's problem is to find the coordinates, given the distances, and not, as is the usual case in high school, the other way around. In two dimensions N points give rise to $2N$ coordinates, the unknowns, and to $N(N-1)/2$ symmetric distances, the data, not all of which may have been observed. In general there will be more equations (one for each distance) than unknowns. Each equation can be approximated by a linearization, and the entire problem can then be written as a matrix equation. Starting from an estimated initial configuration, one iterates on the least-squares solution; and in the cartographic case where the initial guess is a good one, that solution converges rapidly (see [25]). An exactly analogous demonstration is available for relations that can be considered angles. N points taken three at a time yield $N(N-1)(N-2)/2$ possible measures, assuming symmetry. High school trigonometry again yields directions as a function of the coordinates. This is linearized using Taylor series and an initial guess for x and y, and the usual solution is again given by iterative least-squares methods.

A variation or combination of the foregoing methods can easily be devised if a combination of distances and angles has been observed. More importantly, in a two-dimensional space of constant curvature three coordinate locations (determining scale, orientation, and position of the configuration) are arbitrary so that if the number of observations, appropriately distributed, exceeds $2N - 3$, then one apparently has excessive information. An axiom of all of the empirical sciences is that every measurement is to some extent wrong. The redundancy of information is thus not only most desirable, it is really necessary. Unquestionably, one of the most important innovations in cartography during the last two centuries has been the development of methods of taking into account the empirical error axiom. We now know that redundant measurements provide a method of evaluating the internal consistency of empirical data. In the cartographic field, the inverse covariance matrix defines the error at each point of the configuration, and this is usually illustrated graphically by the drawing of small error ellipses at each point. It is easy to see how this might be applied to mental maps. Suppose, for example, that a large number of people have estimated the distance (or direction) between points, e.g., between cities in the United States. We can use the mean of the individual distance (or direction) estimates, weighted by the inverses of their standard deviations, to obtain the configuration as a set of points and can also obtain the standard error of the estimate at each point. These standard errors may be more important than the average estimates since they tell us something about the variance of the process. It seems to be a common fault of beginners to present an average mental map without indicating the degree of fuzziness of this map, as measured by the standard error.

The error, it must be stressed strongly, is always relative to some ideal. In the present context the model will always be a geometry. There are of course innumerably many different geometries so that one has no assurance that one's data will not fit some different geometry better than the one currently used as the model. The previous examples solved the triangulation and trilateration problems assuming a plane. Suppose for example, that it is assumed that the mental map or configuration will fit best on the surface of a sphere, of unknown radius. Then the triangulation or trilateration procedure must be modified. On a sphere one only need solve the problem a number of times using a different radius each time. Suppose, to illustrate this, that the maximum observed distance is $\hat{D}$. This distance is an upper bound on the length of the arc of some great circle on a sphere of (unknown) radius R. Thus $0 \leqslant \hat{D} \leqslant k\pi R$, with $0 < k \leqslant 1$. Solve the problem for a sequence of k's, say, from 0.1 to 1.0 in steps of 0.1. At each stage the radius is given by $R = \hat{D}/\pi k$. A simple solution procedure is to work in a three-dimensional Euclidean space after reducing every distance to a chord distance by a transformation. The least-error solution yields an estimate for k, and thus R. The configuration of points is then placed on the sphere by well-known equations, choosing one point and one direction arbitrarily. Alternately the solution can be computed directly on a sphere by using spherical trigonometry. Thus, by assuming that the number of dimensions is two and that the metric is given by the spherical distance formula, we find both the configuration and the curvature of the spherical space. It is a natural generalization for a cartographer to consider spaces that are not flat since solutions to geodetic triangulations on an ellipsoid have been available for more than one hundred years [8]. It is easiest on surfaces of constant curvature because it then does not matter where one is on the surface. This can obviously be generalized to higher-dimensional spaces of constant curvature. For Riemann spaces of variable curvature or for more general Finsler spaces, the problem seems much more difficult [19, 6]. In principle a torus, a piece of Swiss cheese, a potato, or the geometry induced by modern transportation systems, and so on, could be chosen as the geometric ideal to which the adjustment procedure should be modeled. In psychology the multidimensional scaling procedures have been extended to include the Minkowski metric, with the "city-block distance," or Manhattan geometry, as a special case [20]. It also comes as something of a shock to the metrically minded cartographer to learn that one can also determine a set of rectangular coordinates for points, say A through E, when given only the relations of the sort $AE < BC$; the distance from A to E is less than the distance from B to C. Although no numbers are specified in this exercise, the geometry is quite rigidly determined. Kendall has shown that one only needs to know adjacencies to obtain metrical solutions [12]. The reason is that the redundancies in the geometrical conditions override the lack of quantitative observations. One does not need to have numbers to determine the geometrical configuration of points on a map, and the more observations one has, the less the dependency on numerical values; $N(N-1)/2$ increases much faster than $2N-3$ [21].

It is possible to be somewhat more specific. The Luneberg model, for example, asserts that visual space is three-dimensional Lobachevskian, that is, the model is a pseudosphere [14]. Certain in variances are required of visual objects, and these are said to require the hypothesis of a space of constant curvature. It has similarly been proposed that modern transportation systems induce a two-dimensional metric of constant negative curvature of the surface of the earth. An experiment to test this model for mental maps would require estimates of distances between pairs of places located at varying distances and directions from the observer. The hypothesis is then fairly clear; the estimated distances are a predictable function of the true distances and the distance from the observer. But I would suggest that this hypothesis could also be rejected and that one might find that the experiment would simply show that the errors of distance estimation increase with increasing distance from the observer. That is, the space might become more fuzzy the farther away one goes, and there is not a consistent bias in the distance estimation. The true situation must be more complicated than this because each point in the estimated configuration has about it an uncertainty that is a tensor function of location, not just one number. This uncertainty is generally approximated by the simpler error ellipse. Any satisfactory model would have to describe the spatial pattern of the variation in the size, eccentricity, and orientation of these error ellipses. As a reasonable first approximation, the standard error at each point of the configuration defines a scalar function of position (i.e., a single number), and this is somewhat easier to evaluate than the tensor function.

The result of many of the foregoing estimates and manipulations is a configuration, that is, a set of coordinates for the N points. One may now wish to compare this configuration with some other configuration, a "true" configuration or a configuration obtained for some different group or at a different time period or under alternate experimental conditions, and so on. The similarity between two mental maps, or between a mental map and some standard, is to be measured. To keep the exposition simple, it is convenient to consider only the two-dimensional Euclidean case, but this does not detract from the generality of the argument. Comparable methods are easily available for any model one chooses to specify.

If we can identify corresponding entities in the two images, we can construct a table of correspondences. One set represents coordinates of the jth point in one image, and the other set represents the coordinates of the associated point in the other image. We now assume that there exists a mapping between the sets, and we wish to investigate the properties of this transformation. We can estimate the relation by noting that there is in this a formal similarity to the problem of producing two superimposed contour maps from observational data on scattered locations. We can thus use standard contour-drawing computer programs to create empiri-cally a picture of the functions as a transformation of a coordinate grid. Two recent dissertations at the University of Michigan use this technique with empirical data from Toledo (United States) and from Cologne (Germany). The method has long been used in cartography to study ancient maps [24]. To obtain the distorted grid, we must use an interpolation procedure to go from the isolated observations to a field of data, in effect invoking two assumptions. The first assumption is that the functions are effectively, at least piecewise, continuous and everywhere defined. It is also convenient to assume that they are one-to-one and single valued. The conventional wisdom seems to admit to these types of assumptions. Lynch [15], for example, reports that informants draw rubber-sheet maps of cities. He does not actually provide the evidence but comments on informant drawn maps as follows:

> There was a strong element of topological invariance with respect to reality. It was as if the map were drawn on an infinitely flexible rubber sheet; directions were twisted, distances stretched or compressed, large forms so changed from their accurate scale projection as to be at first unrecognizable. But the sequence was usually correct, the map was rarely torn and sewn back together in another order. This continuity is necessary if the image is to be of any value. (p. 87)

The second assumption required for the interpolation procedure is that one can predict the values of the function at unobserved locations from the values at observed locations. As has been outlined most clearly by Heiskanen and Moritz [9, chap. 7], based on Wiener's theory, the statistical validity of such interpolation (really a prediction procedure) depends on a knowledge of the two-dimensional autocovariance function of the data, and this is equivalent to theoretical knowledge of the process that produced the observations. The apparent efficacy of the double-contour interpolation procedure is therefore somewhat misleading and spurious, or contains implications concerning the process governing the generation of the observations. This circularity should not be given too much weight; illustration of the transformation using the deformed grids appears useful. Naturally, since all objects, for example in a city, can be located with respect to latitude and longitude coordinates, the interpolation procedure can very easily be extended to draw complete deformed street maps, not only the distorted grid and not only those items cited by informants. Finite-difference methods can also be used to obtain the partial derivatives of the functions from the deformed grid, and these can be used to investigate the type and amount of distortion, as described below.

An alternate to the foregoing empirical-graphical contouring procedure is to postulate an explicit form for the relation between the sets. It is too much to expect that the empirical data will give an exact fit to the postulated function so that it is appropriate to use least-squares methods. Thus, it is desired to find the numerical values of the parameters such that the appropriate residual is minimized. We still need to choose a specific model. The simplest postulate is the two-dimensional equivalent to a linear regression line, namely, a Euclidean transformation [23]. This transformation is insensitive to rotations, translations, and changes of scale, but calculates how large these are. It measures only the association between the two configurations. Using this model it is easy to compute a quantity exactly equivalent to the usual Pearsonian correlation coefficient, as the ratio of the regression variance to the total variance. One such computation, using data from Toledo, yielded a fit of circa 80 percent between a configuration calculated from questionnaires and the usual city map [7].

To a cartographer, a natural, literal interpretation of the statement "everyone has his own point of view" would be to assume a viewing point in space, which might thus result in a representation similar to a low oblique aerial photograph with the area near the viewer enlarged relative to distant locations. Mathematically this is the statement

$$u = \frac{a_{11}x + a_{12}y + a_{13}}{a_{31}x + a_{32}y + a_{23}}$$

$$v = \frac{a_{21}x + a_{22}y + a_{22}}{a_{31}x + a_{32}y + a_{23}}$$

as is well known. The solution requires that the coordinates of the viewing point in space be found when given the coordinates of corresponding points in the original and the image. This is the space resection problem of the photogrammetrist, and solution algorithms are readily available [4, pp. 36–44]. Thus, although the hypothesis is a bit implausible, it is easy to test and provides an alternate to the interesting joint-space solution illustrated by Lieber [13]. The projective hypothesis also has other interesting implications. Under a projective transformation all straight lines remain straight, and the cross-ratio is an invariant. One might design an investigation specifically focused on these invariants, and this strategy can be carried over to other postulated transformations. This would be F. Klein's suggestion, investigating invariants along a hierarchy of geometries. It would be, for example, very interesting to have a measure of the magnitude of a departure from one-to-oneness or of the magnitude of departures from differentiability or from continuity, thus explicitly measuring the amount of agreement with Lynch's statement. I am not aware of proposals for any such measures.

Other possible specific transformation rules come to mind rather readily, of course. One such is the general least-squares complex polynomial, which is mathematically very simple. Requiring this solution to be analytic, of course, specifies that the transformation be conformal. From a substantive point of view, a conformal transformation might be justified on the grounds that it requires that the transformation, in the immediate vicinity of any point, be a simple change of scale. This property of conformal transformations can be visualized by imagining that one is looking at the original surface through a microscope mounted on wheels and constructed in such a way that any movement over the viewing surface changes the amount of magnification. At any one time it is possible to see only a small portion of the transformed original through the eyepiece of the microscope, and each small portion will be seen at a different magnification but is otherwise identical to the original. In the present context the surface under scrutiny might be the area of a city, seen in larger magnification in familiar parts. Kabrisky [11], going beyond the evidence, puts forth the related suggestion that the visual field is conformally represented on the mammalian cortex of the brain. I am not aware of any physiological evidence for a comparable representation or localization of geographical information in the brain. And there are arguments against conformality, in spite of its apparent plausibility. The very mathematical simplicity that renders conformality an appealing hypothesis also severely circumscribes the possible transformations. The more conservative scientific approach would be to let the data speak for themselves, that is, design the experiment to explicitly test the hypothesis of conformality. The cartographic point of view also suggests that consideration be given to equal area mappings and to quasi-conformal cartograms. For this we need Tissot's results on the distortion of two-dimensional transformations, assuming a two space with a Riemann metric [22].

Given a differentiable transformation, the ratio of the distance dS at a location in the u,v image to the corresponding distance ds in the x,y original is given by

$$\frac{dS}{ds} = \left[g_x{}^2 \cos^2 \alpha + 2g_{xy} \sin \alpha \cos \alpha + g_y{}^2 \sin^2 \alpha \right]^{1/2}$$

where the g's are particular combinations of the partial derivatives U_x, U_y, V_x, V_y. These quantities may be obtained by formal differentiation of the functional equations or from finite-difference graphical methods from the empirical contour nets, perhaps after smoothing. The distance ratio defines the scale at any particular position on a map. The thing to notice is that the distance ratio depends on an angle α. There is no such thing as the scale at a particular position on a map, but rather at each location there are an infinite number of scales, one in each direction. The scale equation, of course, represents an ellipse, Tissot's indicatrix, and has a major and minor axis, as do all ellipses. These represent the major and minor scale axes. If they are of the same magnitude, the ellipse becomes a circle, and the transformation is conformal. The areal exaggeration is defined as the product of these axes. The maximum angular distortion at the location in question is given by a trigonometric function of the scale axes. There are thus several well-defined quantities that can be used for the evaluation of mental maps. In order to obtain these quantities, it is necessary to compute the partial derivatives, and we can establish hypotheses based on these derived quantities. For example, it is now possible to postulate that the areal exaggeration of a mental map is proportional to knowledge that one has of the location in question. One might ask informants to estimate distances (or to draw a map, etc.) between places (e.g., stores) with which they are familiar in a city. Then one would expect each person's actual knowledge of an area to be proportional to the product of the travel propensity and the distribution of activities, and the total knowledge of all persons to be the sum over the entire area of all of these products. The result of course is a convolution integral in two variables. This then is the expected distribution of places cited for a large random sample of informants. Models similar to this have been proposed for specific urban population distributions by Moore [17], Moore and Brown [18], and Dacey [5], and they have also included estimates of the expected spatial arrangement of the variances. For the usual models of city population densities and of spatial interaction fields, the maximum of $k(x,y)$ is expected to lie between the residential location of the individual and the center of the city. A specific hypothesis now might be that the standard error of the positioning of any place (as computed from many observations pertaining to the relative location of that place) should be related to the lack of knowledge concerning that place. That is, the standard error of the estimate should be inversely proportional to how well the area is known. This seems a rather trite statement, but certainly testable. The alternate hypothesis, that the mental image is proportional to the amount of knowledge, either for an individual or for a number of individuals, is now also stated in a testable manner. And this might equally apply to cities, to an entire county, or to the entire world. The convolution integral and the areal exaggeration of the mental image are definite—

albeit unknown—numbers and are directly comparable. In principle they are capable of being measured independently of each other. Given an expectation (the convolution integral) one may be able to calculate an expected mental map based on such hypotheses.

One can also work with the distances. Suppose one has, for N places on the earth, an estimate of their separation as judged by people. This will yield $N(N-1)/2$ distance estimates. Each place will be connected to $N-1$ places, and one can form the ratio dS/ds for each pair. Assuming that the locations are known, it is also possible to compute the directions relative to some arbitrary initial reference. We can then write the $N-1$ equations and, as long as $N-1$ exceeds three, can form the least-squares estimate of the coefficients. The distance ratios, however, refer to finite and not infinitesimal values so that it may be more appropriate to weight them by a function, normalized so that the smallest distance in the set has largest weight. The least-squares solution is then the usual weighted case. The g's here can be related to Gauss's first fundamental form, from which the curvature, and thus the implicit geometry, might be calculated. This process can then be repeated for each of the N locations. When the curvature is known at every point, the geometry is known. Of course, we have only a finite set and not a continuum, which must be postulated.

Other measures of the distortion at a single location have been used in the theory of map projections. Generally they describe a combination of angular, areal, and distance distortion. Included here would be Jordan's [10] measure, the Jordan-Kavraisky measure, the mean scale ratio, or the several measures proposed by Airy [10, 1]. A detailed discussion of these various quantities has been given by Biernacki [3] and by Meshcheryakov [16].

Global measures are then obtained by taking either the supremum of one of the foregoing or by the average value taken over all locations. One can thus obtain several overall measures of the degree of correspondence of spatial configurations. Each measure is slightly different, but they all tend to be monotonically related so that it usually does not matter which measure is employed, unless of course there are compelling reasons for a particular choice. As an example, the total error might be defined for a mental map of the world by

$$\frac{\displaystyle\int_{-\pi}^{\pi}\int_{0}^{2\pi}\int_{0}^{2\pi}\left(\frac{dS}{ds}-1\right)^{2}\cos\varphi\,d\alpha\,d\lambda\,d\varphi}{\displaystyle 2\pi\int_{-\pi}^{+\pi^2}\int_{0}^{\pi}\cos\varphi\,d\lambda\,d\varphi},$$

but there are several other possibilities.

In summary it is postulated that one can elicit information concerning locational configurations from people and that these configurations can be embedded in a two-dimensional continuum which is sufficiently like conventional maps that they can be compared. Approached conservatively as a classical cartographic problem, the hypotheses are sufficient to allow the derivation of a number of potentially useful measures. The theory of the adjustment of observations leads to the use of the inverse covariance matrix for the weighting of data from several measurements and for the specification of the error variances. This theory also provides adjustment procedures that vary depending on whether the data are collected in a graphical mode or as a traverse, a trilateration, or a triangulation. Furthermore, departures of any configuration from a specified continuous model can be measured using Tissot's theorem. Global measures such as those suggested by Airy, Jordan, and others may also be valuable for measuring overall changes in the preception of configurations over time. Different individuals can be expected to have different perceptions, and this may be interpreted as different viewing points, in the sense of photogrammetry. One is thus led to inquiries concerning projective invariants, affine invariants, or other metrical and nonmetrical properties of the geometry of mental maps.

ACKNOWLEDGEMENT

Partial support for this study was received under NSF Grant GS 34070X.

LITERATURE CITED

1. Airy, G. "Explanation of a Projection by Balance of Errors." *Philosophical Magazine*, 22 (1861), 409–21.

2. Arbib, A. *The Metaphorical Brain*. New York: John Wiley and Sons, 1972.

3. Biernacki, F. *Theory of Representation of Surfaces for Surveyors and Cartographers*. Trans. from Polish, Washington, D.C.: U.S. Department of Commerce, 1965, pp. 53–147.

4. Church, E. *Analytical Computations in Aerial Photogrammetry*. Ann Arbor: Edwards, 1936.

5. Dacey, M. F. "Two-Dimensional Urban Contact Fields." *Geographical Analysis*, 3 (1971), 109–20.

6. Finsler, P. *Uber Kurven und Flachen in Allgemeinen Raumen*. Basel: Birkhauser, 1951.

7. Franckowiak, E. "Location Perception and the Hierarchical Structure of Retail Centers." Ph.D. dissertation, University of Michigan, Ann Arbor, 1973.

8. Gauss, C. F. "Untersuchungen über Gegenstande der Höheren Geodasie, 1844." In *Ostawald's Klassiker der exaten Wissenschaften*, Nr. 177. Leipzig, 1910.

9. Heiskanen, W., and H. Moritz. *Physical Geodesy*. San Francisco: Freeman, 1967.

10. Jordan, W. "Zur Vergleichung der Soldnerschen Koordinaten." *Zeitschrift für Vermessungswesen*, 4 (1875), 175–90.

11. Kabrisky, M. *A Proposed Model for Visual Information Processing in the Brain*. University of Illinois, Urbana, 1966.

12. Kendall, D. G. "Construction of Maps from Odd Bits of Information." *Nature*, 231 (1971), 158–59.

13. Lieber, S. R. "A Joint-Space Analysis of Preferences and Their Underlying Traits." Discussion Paper No. 19, Department of Geography, University of Iowa, Iowa City, 1971.

14. Luneburg, R. K. "The Metric of Binocular Visual Space." *Journal of the Optical Society of America*, 40 (1950), 627–42.

15. Lynch, K. *The Image of the City*. Cambridge, Mass.: M.I.T. Press, 1960.

16. Meshcheryakov, G. "The Problem of Choosing the Most Advantageous Projections." *Geodesy and Aerophotography*, 4 (1965), 263–68.

17. Moore, E. G. "Some Spatial Properties of Urban Contact Fields." *Geographical Analysis*, 2 (1970), 376–86.

18. Moore, E. G. and L. A. Brown. "Urban Acquaintance Fields: An Evaluation of a Spatial Model." *Environment and Planning*, 2 (1972), 443–54.

19. Riemann, B. "Uber die Hypothesen welche der Geometrie zu Grunde liegen." In *Collected works of B. Riemann*, ed. H. Weber, pp. 272–86. New York: Dover, 1953.

20. Shepard, R. "The Analysis of Proximities." *Psychometrika*, 27 (1962), 125–40, 219–46.

21. ———. "Metric Structures in Ordinal Data." *Journal of Mathematical Psychology*, 3 (1966), 287–315.

22. Tissot, M. A. *Mémoire sur la représentation des surfaces et les projections des cartes géographiques*. Paris, 1881.

23. Tobler, W. R. "Computation of the Correspondence of Geographical Patterns." *1964 Papers, Regional Science Association*, 15 (1965), 131–39.

24. ———. "Medieval Distortions: The Projection of Ancient Maps." *Annals, Association of American Geographers*, 56 (1966) 351–61.

25. Wolf, P. R. "Horizontal Position Adjustment." *Surveying and Mapping*, 29 (1969), 635–44.

CHAPTER 5

PETER GOULD

Cultivating the Garden: A Commentary and Critique
On Some Multidimensional Speculations

"Cela est bien dit," répondit *Candide, "mais il faut cultiver notre jardin."* —Voltaire, *Candide*

I feel a lot of sympathy for Candide, for I know exactly how he felt after the last, but inevitably long-winded, theoretical exposition of Dr. Panglos. Theoretical and philosophical speculations are fine, of course, and there is no plausible reason why works of a speculative and empirical nature should be undertaken by one and the same person. And yet . . .

And yet it would be much more intellectually convincing and satisfying to see some data tucked away in a corner of just one of these papers. Like the anticipation of death, facts can have a wonderfully concentrating effect on the *mind* [1]—a word much in evidence in two of the papers, but a word whose meaning has consistently eluded me through both the philosophical and the technical discussions. Indeed, I strongly suspect that none of us knows what a "mind" is when it really comes down to it. We know what *people* are; we know they think, learn, and evaluate; and we know they do these things with their brains rather than their big toes. But *mind,* so far as I can tell, is simply a word denoting a convenient concept that includes all intellectual processes together with concomitant personality traits. For example, we say: "She has an absolutely first-rate mind," meaning she thinks, learns, and evaluates rapidly and accurately; "She has an inquiring mind," meaning she has an inquisitive nature or personality; "Why is he so bloody-minded?" meaning why has he such an aggressive and truculent personality; "I've a good mind to wallop you," meaning I have thought hard about the merits of bringing my hand into sharp contact with a portion of your anatomy; "Mind the bus," meaning cognize with rapidity the oncoming public conveyance before it squashes you on the pavement, and so on. In common, accepted, everyday speech, we use the word and its derived forms to mean thinking, learning, and evaluating, together with characteristics of personality that may often be linked to the former abilities. We seem to need such a concept for common discourse, but do we need a philosophy of it? I get increasingly impatient with philosophers of science who never undertake an actual investigation of anything. I am even more impatient with Burnett, who has demonstrated in the past that she has a fine mind, for taking them seriously—even in Sydney pubs.

What do we have here? Poor old economic man is stuffed with straw once again and knocked down, an easy task that seems to convey a total misunderstanding of the utility of normative models. Sets of exaggerated assumptions, supposedly underpinning behavioral geography, are laid out inaccurately. Ideas from cognitive psychology, an area notorious for its lack of accepted positions, are stated to be the avowed foundation of behavioral geography (with one footnote to one unpublished paper in support). An irrelevant and meaningless analogy is given, presumably for its tone of authority. Alternative "stances" of the materialists and the neodualists are put forward, but then, after the exposition is all over, we are told to choose one, any one, and work from there. It is rather like a conjurer saying, "Pick a card, any card." After eighty-one pages, what, *exactly,* has been clarified?

The normative model of economic man has the considerable merit of clarifying infinitely complex reality. It provides a set of *usable* assumptions as firm criteria to set up an ideal against which actual behavior may be gauged. When actual behavior falls short of the normative, we are in a position to ask sensible questions about information, motivation and evaluation, and the varying degrees to which these may be important in a particular case or study. No one has ever put forward such an explicit simplification as reality. Rather, like any model, it is a simplifying, contingent structure that helps us order, and make some degree of sense out of, extreme complexity. By definition, models make varying demands of abstraction and simplification. Goodness of fit will depend both upon the complexity of what we are trying to understand and the severity of the underlying mapping—the contingent, homomorphic transformation—that we put forward as a model.

Most fruitful sets of assumptions in science tend to be simple and *usable*. But what can we derive from those that are purportedly the foundations of behavioral geography? What can we deduce from a statement that says minds exist and are not ghostly? What is a "state" corresponding to a "mental map"? And who believes we hold multidimensional (and presumably orthogonal?) images of shopping locations in our heads? Surely we have, in Downs's words, the *capacity to generate* information, preferences, and opinions that sometimes can be structured collectively to account for much of the variation in them. That is all—but that is really quite a lot, because it means we can impose useful, clarifying, contingent structures upon a mass of initially disparate data or observations. Such activity seems to be only a formalization of a very basic, human ability to seek and impose patterns, presumably because there are strong evolutionary principles of survival underlying such skills [8]. This is a very different thing from supposing we are inching along a continuum toward some ultimate truth. Such a notion has the archaic smack of religion to it, but should we have patience with such mystical nonsense?

As for the analogy with the university in Burnett's paper, what does it mean? In the first place, *the university* is itself a mental construct whose content would include many nonmaterial, nonobservable things. In neither specialized nor common usage is it defined by a set of observations about offices and laboratories. But quite apart from the total inadequacy of such a description, how can the notion of *mental constructs* be analogically equated with *the university?* Who has ever said the university explains or accounts for anything? In brief, what is the point?

There are a number of other matters with which I could take issue. For example, the mysticism of neodualist writings only undermines other assumptions if you make an act of faith in some nonmaterial world where rational intellectual inquiry is impossible (so where do we go from here?). The notion of a "projection of the visual scene on the irregularly convoluted surface of the observer's brain" appears meaningless; the idea that observable associations are scientifically barren seems odd; and if you really think that the approaches of multidimensional scaling are dubious, then why put forward the bet-hedging contradiction that geographers are *not* on a wild goose chase? We all equivocate, but such timidity seems out of place given the generally assured tone of other statements. But I do not want to be accused of taking passages out of context, and there is not room here to pursue all my questions, many of which, I am sure, other readers will share.

I have somewhat the same difficulties with Harman and Betak, especially their constantly reiterated idea that the multidimensional scaling algorithms have something to do with "the structure and operation of the mind," that they are based upon "certain assumptions about the mind," or that they "comprise a reasonable model of mental structure and process." So far as I can determine, the algorithms of MDS are just that—algorithms, that is, step-by-step, iterative procedures that generate graphical representations of similarities between things. Sometimes these pictures are usefully interpretable, sometimes they are not. Their interpretability depends upon the scientific imagination and creativity of the person doing the research, the quality of the data employed, and the prototheories, educated guesses, and intuitive hunches generated by the observer. But surely nothing is claimed for the algorithm and procedures themselves other than the fact that they may generate useful, but temporary, patterns, those contingent structures we use to order reality. Nor can such inanimate procedures "make certain inferences about mental structure." It is people who make inferences: for example, inferences that objects (stimuli) close together in a space are more alike than those far apart [4]. Such an inference reflects our common concept and usage of distance in everyday language, and what other interpretation could possibly be considered as tenable? But to infer further, that people carry multidimensional spaces in their heads, and use them for making decisions, is unwarranted—at least as fas as my own personal experience is concerned, together with that of others I have consulted. In any event, decision-making is a process, while the configurations of MDS, with *very* rare exceptions [6] are static, structural expressions.

When people write papers, they should endeavor to convey information as clearly as possible. If "internal" and "external" analyses,

PREFMAP algorithms, and INDSCAL techniques are seen as promising methods for geographic research, it is the duty of those bringing them to the attention of others to state clearly why busy people should take time off and learn them. The best way to illustrate the utility of a new approach is by example, to demonstrate that by using new ways of approaching problems we can achieve insights difficult to obtain in other ways. Otherwise writing deteriorates into a simple listing of techniques, and readers start suspecting that *one-up-man-*, rather than *scholar-*, ship is the major concern. For example, it would be useful to know exactly how INDSCAL might illuminate something—and I am tempted to say *anything*. If the data generated by a group of n people can be structured to yield, for example, two dimensions, what do we gain by going back and producing n individual diagrams with the two axes stretched by varying amounts? Are we not simply generating n idiosyncratic representations? And why? For what purpose? Why, as geographers, are we interested in such individualistic details? And how much further do we push back— to psychoanalytic studies that tell us that some Lolits (Little Old Ladies in Tennis Shoes) avoid certain stores because they have red shutters and that as children they had a traumatic experience in a house with red windows? It is quite possibly true, but do we really want to go this way? I suppose one could always argue that even intensely individual psychoanalytic studies have led to considerable insights about much deeper, underlying themes and structures (the Oedipus complex, for example), but I do not see the geographic equivalent emerging from such inquiries.

Again, I have a number of smaller points to argue with: axes in MDS spaces are defined by the investigator, not the attributes of the stimuli, and their location is *totally* arbitrary—even to their origin, let alone their orientation. Why people still insist upon placing such right-angled axes into a cluster of points is quite beyond my comprehension—a legacy from the old factor analytic days, I suppose. As for what metric is employed, I have seen this question discussed *ad nauseam* ever since geographers learned about the generalized Minkowskian form; but if people are really interested, why do they keep talking instead of actually going out and investigating the question—by doing some research, instead of reviewing and repeating what everyone else has said? Furthermore, are we prepared to construct hyperbolic spaces, and publish them in our articles and reports? If we are not, or if such spaces are beyond the skill of present publishing methods, then what is the point of pursuing *essentially* graphical methods when we cannot represent on a flat piece of paper the configuration?

The paper by Sonnenfeld raises other problems, mainly because its publication may be premature. We have here a description of a research design that probes down to the level of individual personality. I confess to being uncomfortable with the notion of "environmental personality," in which "the relationship between person and environment [is] the source of most behavior." The evidence seems quite strong that most intellectual abilities, many personality traits, and much behavior are all strongly governed by heredity [3], but I am totally unqualified to comment here. Perhaps a psychiatrist, or even a psychologist, will find the concept of environmental personality fruitful.

I must also confess, however, to a feeling of bemusement at certain phrases employed in the proposal. That a "relationship between preferences and behavior may be less than perfect" seems too obvious to comment upon, if for no other reason than that perfect relationships are *never* discovered. That "individuals can be found . . . who differ from the norm in landscape tastes" also seems obvious, since the norm is defined by the individuals. If they are not identical, then some will deviate from the mean. Or have I missed something vital? Finally, are all birdwatchers compatible personality types? We await, with great anticipation, the results of such a research design.

Tobler's paper is of a different order. Although data are once again completely absent, which is a pity because a number of his suggestions cry out for pedagogic examples, we do have a number of imaginative ideas for quite concrete research. What is worth pointing out, in a wholly positive sense, is that there is little here that is substantively new. Rather, we have an example of applying, of thinking through, well-known concepts in cartography to a new area. Such applications of old concepts to a new field raise a number of tantalizing possibilities, because they are openly founded upon the tenuous assumption that the representation people have of their environment is maplike. With all due respect to some of the other contributors to this volume, perhaps whether this is the case or not does not really matter. What is of importance at the moment is that the information people generate can sometimes be structured as a map, and I suspect that Tobler's distinction between such maplike representations and hierarchies may not be very useful. Could we not have both, in the sense that we have overwhelming evidence of spatial clumping [9] and any map might be thought of as a set of nested regions?

Perhaps one of the most provocative ideas to emerge from Tobler's transference of cartographic concepts is the idea that the error in a mental configuration may vary considerably over the space. We could, quite literally, construct an error map, whose analysis might be highly indicative of variations in spatial information, for it is redundancy of information that allows us to reduce error, whether upon a map or in a more conventional transmitting channel.

Further provocative ideas emerge as the question of knowledge (information) is faced directly. If total knowledge is proportional to the distribution of population and travel propensities, and travel propensities are in some way a function of distance overcome or effort expended, then the old gravity model appears once again, and information may be predictable to a fairly high degree. Certainly, at scales larger than the city proposed by Tobler, there is considerable evidence that spatial information *is* highly predictable [5]. Further, the degree to which a generated configuration matches an actual one can also be estimated, and after scale and rotational differences have been "partialed out," the residuals can be mapped as vectors showing the spatial variation in the distortion. Thus we have two sources of discordance: the discordance of error, measured by the error ellipses, and the discordance due to systematic distortion. Both may be related to information, which will depend in turn upon relative location and the pattern of the information-generating population. But any gravity calibration will itself be distorted by the pattern (autocorrelative) effects of the map [2]. It would seem that a number of research threads are coming quite close together here and may be shown ultimately to be part of the same strand at a much deeper, more fundamental level [10].

Add to these possibilities, all seemingly well within the reach of experiment, the possibilities for examining appropriate geometrics and investigating the degrees to which conformal mappings are actually characteristic of such configurations, and we have a provocative statement to guide the direction of future inquiry in this area.

The papers in this section are radically different, but I think four remarks are worth making—just as simple reminders, for they really contain nothing new. First, *all* our structures, patterns, and maps that we seek or impose upon the world are *contingent* and temporary. It does not matter what hat we wear, in what seemingly limited and constrained capacity we inquire, we seek to know as human beings; and in these basic, truly fundamental terms, we have the capacity—almost the necessity—to impose ordering structures upon the chaos around us. *All* such structures are contingent, though some may last for millennia as religious dogmas, while other last for days or weeks, as Bohr and his brilliant young co-workers in Copenhagen well knew during the twenties [7]. The inquiries going on in behavioral geography today are not marching, or even tiptoeing, along a continuum to ultimate truth. We are imposing simplifying, hopefully more understandable, structures upon sets of data gathered in areas that interest us. Twenty years from now, with hard work, creative thinking, and some luck, they will be seen as very temporary structures indeed.

Secondly, if we are going to drive our inquiries in human geography back to the individual level, and perhaps deeper into the human psyche, we have an obligation to state our reasons and expectations. Such extreme microstudies are far from traditional scales of geographic research and appear to center more and more in areas of inquiry cultivated by others in the human sciences. Do not mistake me; I am *not* drawing boundary lines, and I am *not* denying the necessity of following problems wherever they may lead. But I am voicing what I think is a valid, if somewhat traditional, concern when I note that when the geographer moves ever further from the traditional areas of interest, into and through the often fascinating border zones lying between the traditional disciplines, he should bring some of the things we know with reasonable certainty to bear in areas where spatial insights and perspectives are presently lacking. It strikes me that this is exactly what Tobler has done, but I see little evidence of such transference of insight in the others. What, with some reasonable exactness, do we hope to find by going back to individual behavior? Are we making unspoken commitments of faith, by drawing analogies with microbiology, that by going down in scale to the individual components of society we can build truly well-founded theory up from the ground level? If so, the recent history of microbiology should give us pause: understanding at the molecular level does not necessarily help at all in understanding how billions of molecules in living systems function as larger systems. And what about the problem of aggregation, so well posed by Wilson [11]? Ten Lolits shopping at four stores produce one trillion possible spatial configurations. What price the geography of individual behavior now?

Thirdly, we must stop messing about with the latest algorithms just because they are there. Coming from one who has butterflied his way around technique-space for the past decade, such a statement may seem inappropriate, if not downright hypocritical. But perhaps there is some difference between exploring the geographical utility of approaches in the sort of period of technical poverty that characterized geography in the fifties and sixties, and running around with the latest MDS algorithm, trying to find something, anything, that will fit it now.

Finally, we might pay more attention to the concept of information, the raw fuel of so much individual behavior. Little mention is made of it, except in the paper by Tobler, despite its crucial, deeper importance for understanding the configurations, structures, and flows characterizing human society in geographic space. We *must* try to handle this slippery substance and begin, even falteringly and crudely, to measure it. People, after all, think with, learn about, and evaluate . . . *what*? Information, of course. Perhaps, if behavioral geographers turn their thoughts to information, they may be able to justify by eventual insight, rather than hope, the individual approach to geographic understanding.

LITERATURE CITED

1. Boswell, J. *Life of Johnson.* London: Oxford University Press, 1961.
2. Curry, L. "A Spatial Analysis of Gravity Flows." *Regional Studies,* 6 (1972), 131–47.
3. Eysenck, H. *The Inequality of Man.* London: Temple Smith, 1973.
4. Foucault, M. *Les mots et les choses.* Paris: Gallimard, 1966.
5. Gould, P. *People in Information Space.* Lund: Gleerups, 1975.
6. Guttman, L. "The Non-Metric Breakthrough for the Behavorial Sciences." In *Automatic Data Processing Conference of the Information Processing Association of Israel,* 1966.
7. Hoffman, B. *The Strange Story of the Quantum.* Harmondsworth: Penquin, 1959.
8. Polanyi, M. "Experience and the Perception of Pattern." In *Modelling of Mind,* ed. K. Sayre. Notre Dame: University of Notre Dame Press, 1963.
9. Simon, H. *The Sciences of the Artificial.* Cambridge, Mass.: M.I.T. Press, 1969.
10. Smith, T. "Set Determined Processes and the Growth of Spatial Structure." Seminar Presentation, The Department of Geography, Pennsylvania State University, December, 1974.
11. Wilson, A. *Entropy in Urban and Regional Modelling.* London: Pion, 1970.

PART II
Perspectives on Analyzing
Preferences and Choices

CHAPTER 6

REGINALD G. GOLLEDGE, VICTORIA L. RIVIZZIGNO, ARON
SPECTOR

Learning about a City
Analysis by Multidimensional Scaling

The purposes of this paper are to illustrate a research design for uncovering the cognitive spatial structure of a city held by a sample of its residents and to illustrate a method for representing cognized environments so that differences between cognized and objective environments can be measured and examined.

The long-run purposes of such an investigation are to assist in *understanding* relations between human spatial behavior and the environments in which behavior takes place, to *explain* the patterns of human activity that take place in such environments, and to allow more successful *predictions* of human behavior in different objective environments.

DEFINITIONS

A number of concepts and terms used in this paper are not as yet widely used in geography. Before presenting the design format and discussing analytical results, we offer definitions of the most critical of these concepts and terms.

Spatial cognition is defined by Hart and Moore [22] as "the knowing and internal or cognitive representation of the structure, entities, and relations of space; in other words, the internalized reflection and reconstruction of space in thought." Since cognitive representations are internal, their configuration must be inferred; these inferences are usually made from verbal reports, drawings, or relational judgments. The cognitive representations sought in this paper consist of locational arrangements of places in the city as recovered from subjective judgments made about the position of each place relative to the others. Each *place* exists at a specified *location* in space, and can be described in a number of different ways. Each descriptor of a location is called an *environmental cue,* and any given location may be described by a number of different cues (e.g., the name of a road intersection or a major building or sign at the road intersection). For an environmental cue to be useful at more than an individual level, it must be commonly identified, recognized, and used to describe a location. While *specific* cues vary from city to city, and from area to area, some *classes* of cues (such as signs, landmarks, buildings, parks, and so on) are found frequently throughout developed countries. Classes of cues found in lesser-developed areas tend to differ somewhat from the ones used in this study, but even in such areas the *use* of environmental cues by residents appears to be somewhat similar to that of residents of more-developed areas [1]. The cognitive representations recovered from the experimental phase will be checked against a two-dimensional Euclidean map of the actual locations; this map is termed the *objective reality* of the locations.

BACKGROUND

Until recently the bulk of geographic research related to urban environments was concerned with the physical and socioeconomic structures of the city. This bias is clearly evident in the emphasis given to such topics in urban texts (such as [2, 24, 31, 43]) and in terms of the quantity of articles published in major geographic journals. Complementing this long-held interest, there is now in existence a strong concern for examining the city as a behavioral unit or a system of behavioral units. Studies examining the images of places held by resident and nonresident populations (e.g., [9, 13]), preferences for places as migration opportunities [12, 20, 28, 34], perceptions of places in the city [35, 44], and so on, are emphasizing the fact that cities are not just physical entities, but are places in which people operate, make decisions, and exist. Thus it has been suggested [1, 10, 16, 19, 29] that the *cognitive representations* of cities held by people may substantially influence their commerce with such environments. Such representations should be of critical importance in activities such as selecting routes for travel in the city, deciding on which shopping facilities or recreational opportunities to use, choosing a destination for a move of residence, selecting a mode of transportation to use, and so on.

An increased quantity of information has been collected about the *general cognitive* structure of cities. Lynch, in an imaginative pioneer work [29], identified nodes, districts, paths, edges, and landmarks as the structural components of urban images, and was able to compile composite "maps" of Boston, Los Angeles, and Jersey City from information obtained by sampling residents of those cities. Appleyard [1] recognized both linear and areal components of urban images, providing evidence from Venezuela to show that many of the fundamental spatial components observed in North American cities were also observable in other areas of the world. Gulick [21], Lee [26], and de Jonge [11] have also corroborated the idea that a city's spatial image could be compiled. At a different scale, Winkel et al. [40], Carr and Schissler [6], Carr [5], and others, demonstrated that some elements of the urban environment were more readily impressed on the minds of residents than others, thus suggesting that a city consisted in part of a series of places described by environmental cues linked in some way to provide a cohesive cognitive structure. In other research, Golledge, Briggs, and Demko [14] showed that by concentrating on a variety of place-specific cues and recovering spatial information about their interpoint distances through multidimensional scaling procedures, a basic "map" of the cue locations could be constructed. Zannaras [45] also researched the problem of an individual's ability to recognize and use cues in differently structured cities, while Briggs [4] investigated the relationship between perceived and "real" interpoint distances in the city. More recently Mackay [30] and Zeller and Rivizzigno [47] have used multidimensional scaling to recover and analyze cognitive configurations of places in urban areas.

Empirical investigations of cognitive aspects of cities have thus pointed to the existence of areal, linear, and point-locational components of representations of places such as cities [6, 14, 23, 29]. Some difficulty has arisen, however, in trying to incorporate all these elements into a single cognitive map or model. There appear to be several plausible explanations for this. First, each component may be most applicable at a certain scale and be less relevant at others. Second, each component may vary in its importance and/or accuracy depending on, say, the occupational relationship between a subject and the city. Third, difficulties may arise in compiling a cognitive map because of distance or directional biases induced by the location of subjects in the city (e.g., a subject living and working in the south of the city may have informational biases about the city different from one living in the center, the north, the east, and so on).

What appears to have come out of all this research is convincing evidence that cognitive representations of urban areas can be recovered both from individuals and from groups of individuals. Comparatively little is known however about (a) how cognitive images of urban areas change over time, (b) how much similarity there is between representations of cognitively stored information and "real world" physical structures, (c) the nature of biases and distortions as revealed in representations of cognitive structures, and (d) how representations vary from group to group and from place to place. It is to these and other questions that the current research is directed.

CONCEPTUAL FRAMEWORK

Tolman [39] has suggested that learning about an environment essentially consists of learning the location of places and the paths that connect them. Developmental theorists such as Piaget [32, 33] and Werner [42] suggest that an adult's understanding and representation of space results from his interactions with elements in the physical environment rather than from perceptual copying of that environment. Our hypotheses overlap both these conceptualizations. Fundamentally we accept the ideas that learning about an environment results primarily from interacting with it and that cognitive representations of physical environments are built up with increasing accuracy and complexity over time. Like Tolman, we argue that individuals learn where certain places are in the environment and develop a variety of ways to get to and from and between the places. As more ways are explored, more places become known; as more places become known, some hierarchical ordering of places develops based on the place's significance to an individual. Significance can accrue from continued interaction (as with a place of work), or because of social, historical, or other criteria of importance.

As information is absorbed about specific places, there is a spillover effect on surrounding areas and locations in those areas. Carr and Schissler [6] have shown that regular travelers over a given route tend to recognize and remember more details along the route than do intermittent or new users of a route. This suggests that as places become "well known" their environs become better known also. Thus we can hypothesize that an individual's cognitive representation of a large-scale environment is a constantly evolving one, with the most significant places acting as "primary nodes" and anchoring the representation at specific points. Briggs [4] has suggested that systems of primary, secondary, tertiary, and minor-order nodes will be found in cognitive representations and that these nodes will be linked by paths to form a cohesive "map" of the environment.

At this stage we must impress on the reader that we do not suggest that individuals carry nodal information in their minds in the form of Cartesian coordinates or any similar type of recording mechanism. Following Piaget, we do suggest that adult individuals have an understanding of concepts such as proximity or closeness, dispersion, clustering, separatedness, and orientation. In other words, *spatial relations* are understood (if only implicitly) and cognitive representations are based on each individual's interpretation of the elements of spatial relations. Of course the precise interpretation that is given to elements (such as closeness or separatedness) varies among individuals; these interpretations are probably also influenced by whether they are used to judge relations between primary nodes, secondary nodes, or between primary and minor nodes. It is possible that two primary nodes may be judged as being "close" in space and that two minor nodes exactly the same physical distance apart may be judged to be quite "far apart." The essence of our hypothesis here however is that as places become better known to individuals, their spatial relations become better known. We further hypothesize that frequency of spatial interaction with a place will influence the ability of an individual to successfully integrate a given place into an accurate representation of an environment.

The preceding conceptualization has little scope unless it can be generalized to groups of individuals. Therefore, we suggest that any given macroenvironment has within it a selection of places that have a high probability of being defined as primary nodes by large subsets of the population of the area (and perhaps also by populations outside the area). It should be possible to define a widely accepted primary node set for any environment. Such a node set should provide the anchors for cognitive representations of the environment; as population members become more aware of the spatial relations among members of this node set, they should be able to make judgments about them that reflect their knowledge of these relations. Individuals who are very well acquainted with a given primary node set should have little difficulty in reproducing their spatial relations; others less well acquainted with them should distort such relations (in a variety of ways), but these distortions should become less evident as the degree of knowing increases. We might further hypothesize that accuracy of information about any given area is a function of the node and path set of that area (i.e., whether it contains primary or other nodes and if so how many and how they are connected). Thus the relations between a given area and the rest of the environment should depend on its node/path structure, and the accuracy of knowledge of the elements of an area will depend on the level of knowledge of its major nodes. For example in an area which has a single primary node, other places may be referred to that node when being cognitively assimilated. If the dominant node is "misplaced" in some way, the likelihood of misplacement of subordinate places and the distortion of the spatial relations among such places should be increased. As the degree of "misplacement" of the primary node changes, so too should the degree of misplacement of other elements of the area change.

The first problem facing us at this stage is to determine if a set of primary nodes exists in a sample area. Given that such a set does exist, we face the problem of discovering the nature of the cognitive configuration of such nodes (i.e., whether their spatial relations can be interpreted in Euclidean terms or whether other geometries must be used to explain these relations).

EXPERIMENTAL DESIGN

A pilot project was undertaken at Ohio State University in 1972 to develop viable methods of data collection, to estimate the probabilities of sample cooperation in data collection phases, and to obtain experience with sample outputs obtained from experiments with a variety of scaling programs. The experimental design illustrated in this paper evolved out of this pilot project.

DATA COLLECTION METHODS

Data from the pilot study consisted of scale values derived from paired comparison, stimulus comparison, and triadic comparison experiments (see [18, 41]). Results from the pilot study indicated that subjects hadconsiderable difficulty making triadic comparisons and became bored quickly with stimulus comparisons but were able to handle paired comparisons quickly and efficiently. The major study therefore used only paired comparison proximity judgments.

Drawing on a variety of published works and extensive prior investigation in Columbus, a number of types of environmental cues were selected. A list of eighty-four locations was then compiled; one or more of the environmental cues existed at each location. Subsets of this list were then given to approximately 230 summer-school students at Ohio State University. Each subset had twenty locations; a variety of cue types were presented in each subset; consecutive subsets had 75 percent overlap with previous subsets (Fig. 1). Subjects were first instructed to pick the place(s) they "knew best" and give these a maximum scale score of nine (on a nine-point scale); they then chose the location(s) they "knew least" and gave them a score of one. All other locations were to be given scores between one and nine, indicative of the *relative* amounts of knowledge/familiarity subjects had of places. This normalized the scaling procedure of each individual. Next, subjects recorded the frequencies with which they visited each place and the sources of their information about each place. The list was then reexamined, and if any subject was more familiar with a given location by a cue name other than that provided, the alternate cue name was recorded. Each subject was then requested to provide a number of locations (and their cue names) other than those on the list. These places were then added to the original list of eighty-four places to make a composite list of locations and cues for the city. This list was then reduced to those location/cue name combinations that were given high scores (eight or nine). A simple ratio was then developed between the number of persons who gave scores of

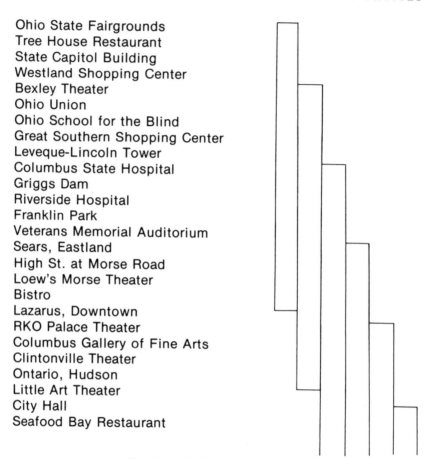

Ohio State Fairgrounds
Tree House Restaurant
State Capitol Building
Westland Shopping Center
Bexley Theater
Ohio Union
Ohio School for the Blind
Great Southern Shopping Center
Leveque-Lincoln Tower
Columbus State Hospital
Griggs Dam
Riverside Hospital
Franklin Park
Veterans Memorial Auditorium
Sears, Eastland
High St. at Morse Road
Loew's Morse Theater
Bistro
Lazarus, Downtown
RKO Palace Theater
Columbus Gallery of Fine Arts
Clintonville Theater
Ontario, Hudson
Little Art Theater
City Hall
Seafood Bay Restaurant

FIG. 1. Overlapping subsets of cue types

eight or nine on the location and the number of people exposed to the location (Table 1). High ratios indicated that most of the people exposed to the location/cue name were "very familiar" with it. The twenty-four places with the highest ratios were then chosen as the subset of places most likely to be best known in Columbus—these constituted the location/cue set for the major study.

Once locations were decided, each site was examined to see if it could be described by multiple cues. Since a dominant purpose of the study was to collect time-oriented data concerning knowledge of proximities of places, it was considered essential to minimize *learning effects* and *pair-order effects*. Learning effects were mitigated by presenting the

TABLE 1

PRELIMINARY TEST: LOCATIONS IN RANK ORDER

Location	Familiarity Ratio
1. Ohio Union	.866
2. Long's Bookstore	.810
3. Lane Ave. at Olentangy River Rd.	.795
4. Morse Rd. at I-71	.785
5. OSU Football Stadium	.754
6. Gold Circle Store, Olentangy	.741
7. Ohio State Fairgrounds	.733
8. Northland Shopping Center	.732
9. Morse Rd. at Karl Rd.	.730
10. Broad St. at High St.	.674
. . . .	.
82. Thurber Towers	.050
83. Great Southern Shopping Center	.033
84. Bexley Theater	.033

same location on consecutive *trials*, subdividing the cue set into three locational subsets, and offering a different locational subset on each trial. Because the pilot experiment had forcibly brought home to us the fact that individuals had varying degrees of familiarity with cue names and that this noticeably affected their judgmental process, some locations were used consistently on all trials to provide anchors for comparison procedures and to allow aggregation over the entire cue set. Initially, pair-order effects were to be minimized by randomly arranging the order of stimulus pairs on each trial. However, since we were uncertain about the transitivity of cognitive distance judgments (i.e., distance *AB* might not be cognized the same as *BA*), it was decided to maintain a uniform bias in pair presentation on successive trials by ignoring pair-order effects.

LATIN SQUARE DESIGN FOR CUE PRESENTATION

Since the dominant aims of this research task involved determining if MDS could provide interpretable representations of cognitive information obtained from both individuals and groups, some control was exercised over subject selection for the experimental phase. In particular, locational and occupational biases were held constant by limiting the study to students and faculty members at Ohio State University. (Once the methodology and experimental design have been verified, expanded subjective groups can of course be used.)

It takes time to build a cognitive representation of a city—how *much* time we do not know. Since it is rather impractical to track the life history of an individual or a group to uncover the development of their information processing and recording mechanisms, we have assumed that, in order to cope with the exigencies of everyday living, a skeletal node/path framework is built up by every urban individual, and that spatial modifications are made to this cognitive node/path set as information is continuously received about the external environment [16]. We also assume that the preliminary node/path set is initially tied to the activities of living, working, and recreating and that there are major places in each city that will form part of the skeletal cognitive image of a city for the majority of individuals. The learning process then becomes one of continuously adding bits of information to the prime or skeletal node/path set and modifying locations and spatial relations among the cognitively stored bits of information until some relatively accurate cognitive transformation of objective reality is obtained. The nature of this transformation is of course not clear yet—some urban subgroups may adopt a time transformation of objective reality, some a cost transformation, some a simple distance transformation, and so on. (The type of transformation is probably a function of the type of society— i.e., whether it is mechanized, capitalistic, geographically educated, and so on.)

Given these assumptions, it is reasonable to infer that long-time residents of an area, and/or populations acutely aware of the city as a whole, constitute a group who would know very well (within the limits of their own cognitive transformation) the relative position of well-known places. Such individuals can form a "control group" that provides an asymptotic representation of the selected locations. It may further be assumed that others in the city constantly move towards such asymptotic representations. Once control group asymptotes have been established, one can then measure the rate of learning about an environment; it should also be possible to categorize environments as cognitively easy or difficult to learn about and to operate in (see [46]).

Our subject population therefore has a control group, an experimental group of absolute newcomers to the city, and another experimental group of individuals who have some knowledge of the city but may not have obtained the locational precision of the control group. Sixty subjects were used in the data collection phase, broken down into three subgroups: (1) city newcomers—twenty-five, (2) intermediate length

TABLE 2

SAMPLE STRUCTURE

1. Newcomers	a(8)	b(8)	c(9)
2. Intermediate	a(8)	b(8)	c(9)
3. Control	a(3)	b(3)	c(4)

residents—twenty-five, and (3) control group—ten. Each subgroup is further broken down into three subsets—*a, b, c* (Table 2). Subdivision into smaller groups allows for the use of a modified Latin square design in the presentation of stimuli.

The twenty-four locations were also divided into three groups with a high degree of overlap between groups. Group I contained locations 1–9 and 22–24; group II contained locations 7–18; group III contained locations 16–24 and 1–3. Each location was allocated to one of the three cue sets, some locations being allocated to each cue set (Table 3). Each subject group follows the same experimental design given in nine trials over a six-month time period (Table 4). Here, in trials 1, 4, and 7, subject subset *a* will use cue set 1 and be given location group I; subject subset *b* will use cue set 2 and be given location group II; subject subset *c* will use cue set 3 and location group III. In trials 2, 5, and 8, subject

TABLE 3

LOCATIONS AND CUE SETS

Cue Set 1	Cue Set 2	Cue Set 3
1. Ohio Union	Ohio Union	Ohio Union
2. Westland Shopping Center	Westland Shopping Center	Westland Shopping Center
3. OSU Football Stadium	St. John Arena	OSU Football Stadium
4. Drake Union	Drake Union	Lincoln-Morrill Dormitories
5. Hudson St. at I-71	Hudson St. at I-71	Hudson St. at I-71
6. N. High St. at Morse Rd.	Graceland Shopping Center	Graceland Shopping Center
7. Ohio State Fairgrounds	Ohio State Fairgrounds	Ohio State Fairgrounds
8. Gold Circle, Olentangy	Gold Circle, Olentangy	Gold Circle, Olentangy
9. N. High St. at 15th Ave.	Long's Book Store	Mershon Auditorium
22. Eastland Shopping Center	Sears, Eastland	Eastland Shopping Center
23. Greyhound Bus Station	Greyhound Bus Station	Greyhound Bus Station
24. Port Columbus Airport	Port Columbus Airport	Port Columbus Airport

TABLE 4

CUE-TRIAL ALLOCATIONS

Trial 1, 4, 7	aII	b2II	c3III
Trial 2, 5, 8	b2I	c3II	a1III
Trial 3, 6, 9	c3I	a1II	b2III

S_s=a, b, c; cue sets=1, 2, 3; location groups=I, II, III.

subset a will use cue set 1, location group III; subject subset b will use set 2, location group I; and subject subset c will use cue set 2, location group II. In trials 3, 6, and 9, subject subset a will use cue set 1, location group II; subject subset b will use cue set 2, location group III; subject subset c will use cue set 3, location group I. In this way each group will have confusion minimized by using only one cue set on all nine trials, but, to prevent boredom and to minimize learning of places at each trial, each will be given the mixes of locations in one of three subsets of the twenty-four locations. The overlap of cue-set presentations to groups allows us to aggregate across groups if so desired and to make between-group comparisons with a high degree of confidence in the compatibility of the results.

The essential pieces of data collected from each respondent were scale values of the proximities of pairs of points. For each location group, $n(n-1)$ 2 paired comparisons were made. Subjects responded to the following instructions:

> Presented below are 66 pairs of locations. Read through the entire list and then assign a score of 1 to that pair(s) of locations which are closest together and a score of 9 to that pair(s) of locations which are farthest apart. After having assigned 1's and 9's to those locations which are respectively closest together and farthest apart, go back through the list of location pairs and assign each remaining pair a number between 1 and 9. The number assigned to each pair should correspond to the relative closeness or amount of spatial separation of those locations. Circle the number that best represents your answer.

ANALYTICAL METHODOLOGY

Earlier, we mentioned the problem of combining areal, linear, and point-located information into a single cognitive representation. To avoid this problem we concentrated only on using specific places (points) in the data collection phase. This allowed us to work with the "psychological distances" between places and to compare configurations derived from such distances with a map of "objective reality" of the places.

Data collection methods were designed to have a subject make a subjective judgment concerning the interpoint distances between pairs of points or to judge the degree of proximity between points. The inference made from such judgments was that at least ordinal level data could be generated from the subjects' responses. Following Shepard [36], Coombs [8], Kruskal [25], and others interested in nonmetric scaling, it was presumed that such ordinal level data would contain a *latent spatial structure*. In other words, a set of interpoint distances could be generated such that the order of these distances correspond to the order of the original judgments. Given a set of ordered distances, the task was then to find a space of minimum dimensionality such that, when the points were plotted in that space, the order of their interpoint distances was maintained. A variety of algorithms available for achieving such a configuration [15] were experimented with, and program KYST (a combination of the best parts of TORSCA 9 and KRUSKAL 6M) was chosen as the analytical device.

To ensure that subjects' configurations and the map of "objective reality" had the same potential orientation and the same scale, the matrix of objective distances between the twenty-four sample locations was subjected to the same algorithm. The pilot study [18] showed that the goodness of fit (stress) between such a configuration and the original interpoint distances is excellent with imperceptible distance or directional distortions being evident. Configurations obtained from both the control group and the experimental group can then be compared directly to this map, and "locational errors" for all two-dimensional cases calculated. "Locational errors" are calculated from the Cartesian coordinates of the locations of places on the MDS representations of original interpoint distances and subjects' configurations.

Data from the pilot experiment raised some doubts regarding our ability to interpret the MDS configurations in terms of a geographic coordinate system. To satisfy these doubts we inputted the two-dimensional coordinates of our twenty-four stimulus points together with sets of coordinates determined from an objective map of the same points, into an algorithm (PROFIT) which uses linear and nonlinear correlation procedures for determining optimal fits of properties (independently determined physical measures) to the MDS output. In this case the program determined a direction for our geographic vectors in a two-dimensional space such that the projection of the stimulus points on to these vectors corresponded optimally to the inputted property values [7]. In the linear case, correlations of .97 and .98 were obtained for the N-S and E-W axes respectively; in the nonlinear case, correlations of .91 and .89 were obtained for the two property vectors.

EXPERIMENTAL RESULTS: THE CONTROL GROUP

Since the collection of data for the experimental groups is incomplete at this time, we present here only results for the control group of ten long-term residents of Columbus. This group consisted of six males and four females. Four of the males and one of the females were senior graduate students in geography. The other two males were geography faculty members; the three remaining females were undergraduate students. Nine of the control group were white, one was black. Length of residence in Columbus varied from as little as four years to as long as twenty-five years.

The MDS configuration obtained by simultaneously considering the judgments made by the entire group (i.e., using group mean scaled responses) produced a configuration with stress of .1887—good to fair (Fig. 2). To highlight the type of distortions and exaggerations observed in various configurations, we present a simplified grid of the sample area devoid of the actual points used in the experiment. The grids are generalizations or summaries of the main variations found in each configuration. They are compiled by interpolating grid lines between points on the configuration in the same manner that contour lines are interpolated on a map of discrete elevations. Obviously some of the finer displacements and distortions cannot be shown on the relatively coarse grids we use here for illustrative purposes. More precise "contour" maps will be produced as relevant computer software becomes available.

The group configuration exhibited a number of peculiarities. First, there was an obvious exaggeration of short distances; second, there was

FIG. 2. Control-group grid

a tendency to collapse the N-S extension along the main axis of the configuration, leading us to infer that these N-S distances were generally underestimated. This is in direct contrast to the interstitial areas between NSE and W axes, where distances appear exaggerated. Third, there seemed a tendency to exaggerate E-W distances close to the center of the map and to "pull in" the E-W extremities somewhat. Fourth, there was a noticeable distortion in the N-E where interpoint distances between places were considerably exaggerated. On the whole the group tended to exaggerate shorter distances and distances between well-known points (which included several in the NE) and to compress somewhat longer distances between relatively well known places. Distances between places not so well known, or across segments of the city not well known, appear to be exaggerated and distorted.

Simplified grids for the individual members of the control group are shown in Fig. 3. Although each has its own distinctive pattern of distortion, there are several striking similarities among group members. At this stage we shall report on only these similarities—fuller explanations of the nature of each configuration are not attempted in this paper.

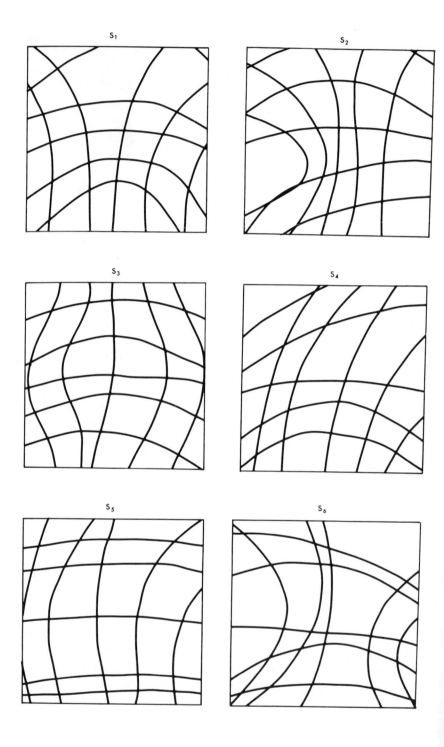

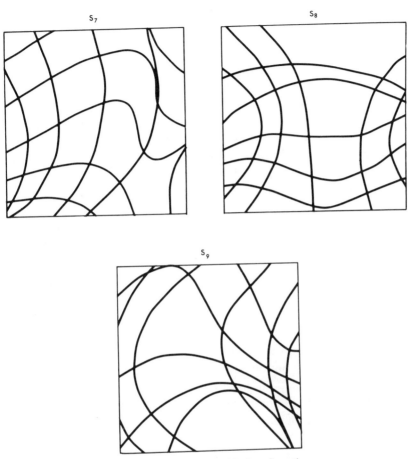

FIG. 3. Grids fitted to individual configurations

Significant similarities include (1) a pronounced exaggeration of shorter distances (for example by subjects S_3, S_4, S_5, S_6, S_7, S_8, S_{10}), (2) a pronounced exaggeration of interpoint distances in the NE (S_1, S_3, S_4, S_5, S_6, S_7, S_8, S_9, S_{10}), (3) a northward "pull" of downtown locations (S_1, S_2, S_4, S_6, S_7, S_9) and, conversely, a southward "push" of the same locations is apparent on S_3, S_5, S_8, and S_{10}, and (4) except for S_9, a noticeable compression of W locations towards the center (S_1, S_2, S_6, S_7, S_8, S_{10}).

As opposed to the general trends outlined above, there are some unique features in each configuration that may be partly explained by location of home site and major interaction patterns. Examples of these unique features include the pronounced W bias of S_9; the southward "push" of E locations by S_7; the compression of the spread of locations in the extreme E and W by S_8; the tendency to "fill in" a relatively blank NW area with "northern" information by S_1 and S_2.

The descriptions presented here bear further and closer examination. The reasons for the similarities and differences have not as yet been fully documented, although numerous possible reasons come to mind and will be investigated as part of our ongoing research. Perhaps the first step is to improve our methods of fitting grids to the MDS configurations, and to develop methods for transforming "real" maps of Columbus to fit the particular map projections obtained from our sample respondents. Since the cartographic procedures to be used are of critical importance to our interpretation of the MDS configurations, we will make some comments on them before concluding the paper.

THE MAPPING PROBLEM

At present we are experimenting with a number of ways of representing the cognitive output obtained from our research. To date we have concentrated only on point locations, which can be quickly and easily superimposed on a simplified base map of Columbus. Alternate ways of illustrating output include:

  a. A series of computer-drawn map transformations of the urban area based on the locational relations found in cognitive output, geographically illustrating the process of convergence from fragmented city information to some form equivalent to objective reality [38]

  b. A computer movie of the learning process based on maps derived from the MDS output

  c. Mathematical models related to the process of learning about the environment with parameters that can be estimated for differently sized and shaped cities

Tobler is currently experimenting with the mathematics of mental maps and has modified basic MDS models to incorporate directional as well as distance relations. Postulating that the areal distortion of a mental map is proportional to knowledge that one has of a set of locations, and describing the areal distortion by a set of partial derivatives related to coordinate locations, he has suggested a method for calculating *expected mental maps* from the expectation of the hypothesized areal distortion [38, pp. 25–26]. Such mapping procedures appear applicable for graphic representations of our cognitive configurations.

SUMMARY

Some of the questions raised by the approach suggested in this paper are:

1. What does one know (or learn) about an urban area?

2. How does one assimilate this information and how does the assimilated information influence decision-making in the urban area?

3. What types of urban places are the easiest (or most difficult) to operate in?

4. How does possession of (or access to) an automobile influence the development of knowledge about an urban area (and of course the ability of people to use those areas)?

Some fruitful lines of continued investigation in the area of cognitive mapping are:

1. Selecting environmental cues that have a high probability of being primary orientation nodes for large segments of an urban population

2. Defining equally identifiable cue names for such places to overcome the learning effects of continually using one cue name for each place

3. Developing methods for using more locations without the tedium of a complete paired comparison or stimulus comparison experiment

Once these problems are solved, it will become more appropriate to examine such things as the distance and directional biases evident in configurations recovered by the MDS method, to inspect locational errors for each cue to find *why* it may be dislocated in a specific way, to see if some places are perennially mislocated by significant segments of urban populations, and to discover if there are pronounced biases in configurations that are primarily due to the location of subjects (either home location or job location).

ACKNOWLEDGEMENT

The research for this paper was supported in part by NSF grant #GS-37969.

LITERATURE CITED

1. Appleyard, D. "Styles and Methods of Structuring a City." *Environment and Behavior, 2* (1970), 100–118.

2. Berry, B. J. L., and F. Horton. *Geographic Perspectives on Urban Systems,* Englewood Cliffs: Prentice-Hall, 1970.

3. Briggs, R. *The Scaling of Preferences for Spatial Locations: An Example Using Shopping Centers.* Master's thesis, Department of Geography, Ohio State University, 1969.

4. ———. "Cognitive Distance in Urban Space." Ph.D. dissertation, Department of Geography, Ohio State University, 1972.

5. Carr, S. "The City of the Mind." In *Environment for Man,* ed. W. R. Ewald, pp. 197–232. Indianapolis: University of Indiana Press, 1965.

6. Carr, S., and D. Schissler. "The City as a Trip: Perceptual Selection and Memory in the View from the Road." *Environment and Behavior,* 1 (1969), 7–35.

7. Chang, J. J., and J. D. Caroll. "How to Use PROFIT, a Computer Program for Property Fitting by Optimizing Nonlinear or Linear Conditions." New Jersey: Bell Laboratories, 1972.

8. Coombs, C. H. A. *A Theory of Data.* New York: John Wiley and Sons, 1964.

9. Cox, K. R., and G. Zannaras. "Designative Perceptions of Macro-Spaces, Concepts, a Methodology, and Applications." Discussion Paper No. 17, Department of Geography, Ohio State University, 1970.

10. Craik, K. H. "Environmental Psychology." In *New Directions in Psychology,* vol. 4, ed. T. M. Newcomb, pp. 1–121. New York: Holt, Rinehart and Winston, 1970. 1–121.

11. DeJonge, D. "Images of Urban Areas: Their Structures and Psychological Foundation." *Journal of the American Institute of Planners,* 28 (1962), 266–76.

12. Demko, D., and R. Briggs. "A Model of Spatial Choice and Related Operational Considerations." *Proceedings, Association of American Geographers,* 3 (1971), 49–52.

13. Doherty, S. M. "Residential Preferences for Urban Environments in the U.S.A." Discussion Paper No. 29, L.S.E. Department of Geography, November, 1968.

14. Golledge, R. G., R. Briggs, and D. Demko. "Configurations of Distance in Intra-Urban Space." *Proceedings, Association of American Geographers,* 1 (1969).

15. Golledge, R. G., and G. Rushton. *Multi-Dimensional Scaling: Review and Geographic Applications.* AAG Technical Paper No. 10, 1972.

16. Golledge, R. G. *Process Approaches to the Analysis of Human Spatial Behavior.* Discussion Paper No. 16, Department of Geography, Ohio State University, November, 1970.

17. Golledge, R. G. "The Geographical Relevance of Some Learning Theories." In *Behavioral Problems in Geography: A Symposium,* ed. K. R. Cox and R. G. Golledge, pp. 101–45. Northwestern University Studies in Geography, no. 17, 1969.

18. Golledge, R. G., and V. Rivizzigno. "Learning about a City: Analysis by MDS" Unpublished manuscript, Department of Geography, Ohio State University, 1973.

19. Golledge, R. G., and G. Zannaras. "Cognitive Approaches to the Analysis of Human Spatial Behavior." In *Environment and Cognition,* ed. W. Ittelson, pp. 59–94. New York: Seminar Press, 1973.

20. Gould, P. "Problems of Space Preference Measures and Relationships." *Geographical Analysis,* 1 (1969), 31–44.

21. Gulick, J. "Images of an Arab City." *Journal of the Institute of American Planners,* 29 (1963), 179–98.

22. Hart, R., and G. T. Moore. "The Development of Spatial Cognition: A Review." Place Perception Report No. 7, Department of Geography, Clark University, 1971.

23. Harrison, J. D., and W. A. Howard. "The Role of Meaning in the Urban Image." *Environment and Behavior,* 4 (1972), 389–412.

24. Johnson, J. *Urban Geography.* Oxford: Pergamon, 1967.

25. Kruskal, J. B. "Multidimensional Scaling by Optimizing Goodness-of-Fit to a Nonmetric Hypothesis." *Psychometrika,* 29 (1964), 1–27.

26. Lee, T. "Psychology and Living Space." *Transactions of the Bartlett Society* (1963–64), 11–36.

27. ————. "The Psychology of Spatial Orientation." *Architectural Association Quarterly,* 1 (1969), 11–15.

28. Lieber, S. "A Joint-Space Analysis of Preferences and Their Underlying Traits." Discussion Paper No. 19, Department of Geography, University of Iowa, July, 1971.

29. Lynch, K. *The Image of the City.* Cambridge, Mass.: M.I.T. Press, 1960.

30. Mackay, D. B. "Spatial Images and Spatial Behavior." Unpublished manuscript, School of Business, University of Indiana, Bloomington, 1973.

31. Murphy, R. *The American City.* New York: McGraw-Hill, 1966.

32. Piaget, J. *The Child's Construction of Reality.* New York: Basic Books, 1954.

33. Piaget, J., and B. Inhelder. *The Child's Conception of Space.* 1948. Rpt. New York: Norton, 1967.

34. Rushton, G. "Preferences and Choice in Different Environments." *Proceedings, Association of American Geographers,* 3 (1971), 146–49.

35. Saarinen, T. F. "Perception of Environment." C.C.G. Resource Paper No. 5, *Association of American Geographers,* Washington, 1969.

36. Shepard, R. N. "Metric Structures in Ordinal Data." *Journal of Mathematical Psychology,* 3 (1966), 287–315.

37. Shepard, R. N., et al. *Multidimensional Scaling: Theory and Applications in the Behavioral Sciences.* 2 vols. New York and London: Seminar Press, 1972.
38. Tobler, W. "The Geometry of Mental Maps." This volume.
39. Tolman, E. C. "Cognitive Maps in Rats and Men." *Psychological Review,* 55 (1948), 189–208.
40. Winkel, G., R. Maleck, and P. Thiel. "The Role of Personality Differences in Judgments of Roadside Quality." *Environment and Behavior,* 1 (1969), 199–224.
41. Wish, M. "Notes on the Variety, Appropriateness, and Choice of Proximity Measures." Mimeo., Bell Laboratories' Workshop on M.D.S., June, 1972.
42. Werner, H. "The Concept of Development from a Comparative and Organismic Point of View." In *The Concept of Development,* ed. D. B. Harris, pp. 125–48. Minneapolis: Minneapolis Press, 1957.
43. Yeates, M., and B. Garner. *The North American City.* New York: Harper and Row, 1971.
44. Zannaras, G. *An Empirical Analysis of Urban Neighborhood Perception.* Master's thesis, Department of Geography, Ohio State University, 1969.
45. ———. *Cognitive Images of Urban Environments and Their Influence on Spatial Behavior.* Ph.D. dissertation, Department of Geography, Ohio State University, 1973.
46. Zannaras, G., and R. G. Golledge. *The Perception of Urban Structures: An Experimental Approach.* Proceedings, EDRA II, Pittsburgh, 1970.
47. Zeller, R., and V. Rivizzigno. "Mapping Cognitive Structures of Urban Areas Using MDS: A Preliminary Report." Discussion Paper No. 42, Department of Geography, Ohio State University, 1974.

CHAPTER 7

GERARD RUSHTON

Decomposition of Space-Preference Functions

INTRODUCTION

For those who conceptualize the spatial choice process as the subjective selection of the most preferred alternative from a subset of alternatives, the methodological task has been seen to be the recovery of a preference function that yields a ranking of all conceivable spatial alternatives on a scale of preferredness. One of the several methods of identifying and calibrating spatial preference functions is based on the scaling of arbitrarily defined combinations of stimuli from a matrix of paired comparisons of relative frequencies of choices. In this paper, extensions of this methodology are proposed to accommodate some of its limitations.

In the application of paired comparisons methodology to spatial choice, confusion between stimuli is assumed to be inversely related to the subjective utility difference between the stimuli. The more two stimuli are confused (i.e., evidently considered interchangeable in the choice process), the closer is their subjective utility. Relative frequency of choice between two alternatives in the restricted choice situation where both are present and one is chosen has often been the operational measure of stimuli confusion, though Tversky has noted the restricted theory of decision-making that such a measure assumes [10]. If, however, these assumptions are accepted, the derivation of a preference scale can be accomplished by nonmetric multidimensional scaling [9; 5, pp. 61–64]. Each paired comparison is an independent estimate of the preferential distance between the stimuli combinations, and the assumption implicit in the adoption of the nonmetric scaling methodology is that there exists a scale consisting of real values for the stimulus combinations such that distances as measured from the scale will increase monotonically as the original preference distances increase. A number of heuristic algorithms and a great deal of computational experience now exist to construct such scales [6, 11, 12].

Two problems limit the usefulness of such scales. One is the problem of decomposing the scale values to identify the quantitative contribution to any given scale value of the individual stimuli. (An individual scale value in a space-preference scale refers to a combination of several stimuli, and the interstimulus distances from which the original scale is constructed are comparisons of the preference distance between any two multistimulus combinations.)

A number of arguments support the desire to partial out the effects of individual stimuli. Since magnitudes of individual stimuli can often be controlled, an issue of some practical importance is the degree to which a given stimulus must be changed in order to achieve a desired spatial response effect. At other times the issue is to predict the spatial response effects of predicted (noncontrolled) changes in the stimulus magnitudes. Control of the distance stimuli is achieved through relocation of the objects from which choice is made, relocation of the person making the choice, or manipulating the variables that affect the value of the operational measure of distance (for example, transport-system improvements). The pursuance of any of these issues is expedited if the relative contributions of individual stimuli to the preference value are known.

Because of the combinatorial nature of paired comparison designs, relatively few stimuli can be examined in a particular experiment. But if the individual contribution of one stimulus to subjective worth in relation to the rest is already known, further experimentation can systematically evaluate other stimuli in turn. Consequently, the problem of dealing with many stimuli is solved when the problem of partialing out individual stimulus effects is solved.

Decomposing the preference function by separately identifying the abstract entities that contribute to subjective worth and developing a function that combines their separate effects by rules of combination to produce the final joint effect can become the basis of a methodology for extrapolating preference rules beyond the immediate domain of experience in which they were measured. One criticism of existing methodology is that the only valid section of the preference function is that which surrounds the normal domain of experience, even though many interesting applications require comparisons of alternatives at the margins of current experience—for example, planning applications in which predictions of the behavioral responses to novel arrangements of spatial alternatives are required or applications to new environments of preference functions calibrated elsewhere. This criticism stems from two considerations, one technical, the other conceptual. Conceptually, the problem is linked to the belief of some behavioral scientists that it is only in the act of choosing that people can reveal their preferences; yet, by definition, actual choices must belong to the domain of experience. This restricted set of spatial alternatives about which preferences are revealed by the choice process is only a subset of the set of alternatives about which one would like to make valid statements. Because the recovered preference functions exposed by this methodology are undefined outside the restricted subset of alternatives, the preferredness of those that are novel combinations of the relevant stimuli can never be known. The technical consideration that restricts the domain of the recovered function is related to the design of the scaling algorithms most frequently used to determine the functions. With the exception of the conjoint measurement models discussed by Lieber in this volume, the multidimensional scaling models used merely assign a scale value to the stimulus combinations for which empirical data exist. There are no readily agreed upon rules for the extrapolation of these preference functions beyond the actual stimulus combinations observed. It follows from the nature of this problem that its solution requires changes in the conceptual as well as the technical basis of the methodology. Such changes can now be proposed.

UTILITY THEORY

A number of propositions and theorems in utility theory provide the basis for an extension of the space-preference methodology [4]. The preference ordering of stimulus alternatives provided by the MDS model can be connected to a real-valued utility function. Some notation must be introduced: let the set X of elements x, y, z be the spatial alternatives between which a decision must be made. Then, $x \leq y$ means that x is not preferred to y, and $x \approx y$ means that x is indifferent to y. Fishburn states the relation between preference orders and utility functions as

A number $u(x)$ can be assigned to each x in X so that if x and y are in X, then $x \leq y$ if and only if $u(x) \leq u(y)$. If this is true, then the utility function u on X preserves the ordering of $\leq$ and [the proposition above] permits us to go back and forth between preferences and utilities. [4, p. 344]

DECOMPOSING THE JOINT SCALE

The problem of decomposing the joint scale is that of finding a function that combines the individual effects of the attributes such that the preference ordering of alternatives on this function maintains the original ordering of alternatives. Three methods of deriving this function will be described and evaluated with empirical data. In all three cases, one starts with a preferential judgment measure that represents the joint effect of several independent stimuli. These are not separably measurable on compatible scales but rather represent units that would generally be regarded as incommensurable.

A Graphical Method from Two Trade-off Curves

The simplest function is one that decomposes the joint effects into the sum of individual effects. This decomposition rule would correspond with the assumption that the utility of the combination of attributes equals the sum of utilities assigned to the individual attributes. Stated generally [3, p. 436],

$$u(x_1, x_2, \ldots, x_n) = u_1(x_1) + u_2(x_2) + \ldots + u_n(x_n)$$

for all x in X where u is a numerical utility function on X (the "joint-effects" function) and u_i is a numerical utility function for the ith factor. Two such individual attribute utility functions are derived below by the graphical method described by Fishburn [3]. Required for the construction of the individual utility functions are any two indifference curves, that is, curves joining combinations of the stimuli (x_1 and x_2) between which the consumer is indifferent. It follows that all utility differences between points on one curve and points on the other curve are equal, and this fact becomes the basis for deriving the utility scales of individual stimuli. If, taking any point on one curve (Fig. 1, A) and holding the value of x_1 constant, one solves for the corresponding value of x_2 on the other curve, then the utility difference between the two values of x_2 ($A - B$) is the same as the utility differences between two other points where the value of x_2 is held constant and the corresponding difference in the x_1 variable between the two curves is computed ($C - B$). By progressing up the curves in a steplike fashion, a continuous function for each stimulus can be graphed connecting measurement units of the stimulus with units of utility (Fig. 1). The achievement effected by this methodology is that of transforming the incommensurable units in which the original stimuli were measured to measures of utility that are standard, and therefore comparable between the two stimuli. If a third stimulus is introduced and two indifference curves are defined between it and one of the original two stimuli (the second, for example), the derived utility scales can be transformed to effect internal consistency between all three by making the scale unit for the third stimulus comparable to that of the first two. (The scale units of the first two are already comparable.) This is achieved by computing a weighting parameter (y_i)

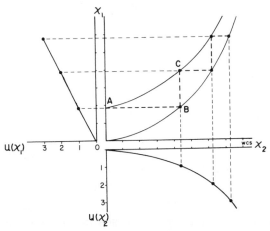

FIG. 1. Deriving individual utility scales from a joint-preference scale

that uniformly stretches (or compresses) the utility scale of the third stimulus by the same proportion that the utility scale of the second stimulus must be stretched or compressed to make it conform to the scale it had when originally calibrated with respect to the first stimulus [3, p. 437]. This parameter is the reciprocal of the slope of the regression line between the utility scale values of the second stimulus as calibrated independently with respect to the first and the third stimuli respectively.

Least Squares Fit to the Scale Values

This method assumes that magnitude estimation of the subjective worth of a stimulus combination has been made. Then a function is fitted by least-squares procedures to the scale values. A variety of functions can be fitted, and the coefficient of determination can be used as criterion for selecting the most appropriate one. The independent variables are the original stimulus values and the dependent variable is the scale values reflecting the joint effects of the stimulus combinations.

Conjoint Measurement

This method operates on the order relationship of the scale values for the stimulus combinations [12]. The individual stimuli are regarded as row and column effects on the joint effect as measured by the scale values for the stimulus combinations. Various rules of combination can be investigated that operate on the individual stimulus values to provide joint-scale values whose order is compared with the corresponding original order. The particular combination rule and associated function parameters that best recreate the original order is accepted as the decomposition function sought.

AN EMPIRICAL EXAMPLE

Fifteen combinations of two stimuli were selected from the thirty combinations for which paired comparison preference similarities had been computed in an earlier work [9]. The particular fifteen were chosen because they occur in the primary domain of choice and were known to follow an area of the preference surface that included approximately similar levels of preference (Table 1). This matrix of similarities was scaled by the nonmetric multidimensional scaling algorithm TORSCA-9 (Table 2) [11].

TABLE 1

PAIRED COMPARISON PREFERENCE DISTANCES BETWEEN THE FIFTEEN
COMBINATIONS OF DISTANCE AND TOWN SIZE CLASSES

16	0														
27	−1.00	0													
11	0.25	0.16	0												
17	0.50	0.50	0.17	0											
22	0.50	0.50	0.25	0.50	0										
28	0.50	0.25	0.03	0.39	0.50	0									
23	0.35	0.50	0.32	0.04	0.30	0.13	0								
6	0.50	0.37	0.26	0.05	0.21	0.08	0.05	0							
29	0.36	0.39	0.12	0.39	0.33	0.44	0.05	0.27	0						
18	0.24	0.50	0.28	0.30	0.50	0.39	0.44	0.23	0.18	0					
12	0.50	0.32	0.50	0.05	0.38	0.30	0.18	0.12	0.02	0.09	0				
24	0.49	0.50	0.44	0.35	0.45	0.48	0.23	0.18	0.50	0.11	0.16	0			
1	0.50	0.40	0.41	0.39	0.42	0.43	0.25	0.37	0.19	0.11	0.28	0.04	0		
7	0.49	0.43	0.49	0.30	0.43	0.39	0.30	0.38	0.15	0.12	0.37	0.11	0.15	0	
13	0.50	0.50	0.44	0.46	0.46	0.46	0.39	0.45	0.50	0.35	0.45	0.19	0.28	0.30	0

TABLE 2

SCALE VALUES FROM MULTIDIMENSIONAL
SCALING ANALYSIS FOR THE FIFTEEN
STIMULI COMBINATIONS (FIG. I)

1	1	−.315
2	6	.005
3	7	−.260
4	11	.289
5	12	−.070
6	13	−.480
7	16	.461
8	17	−.078
9	18	−.205
10	22	.275
11	23	.029
12	24	−.331
13	27	.439
14	28	.175
15	29	.066

The individual stimuli were distance to places where groceries could be purchased and the population size of these places. The latter is clearly a surrogate measure with many empirical studies confirming a strong relationship between functional complexity and town population size.

There have been criticisms of the construction of preference functions on the basis of such ad hoc hypothesizing of relevant attributes [1] as well as criticisms of the use of surrogates that are presumably several times removed from the more fundamental stimuli from which the true ''worth'' of any spatial alternative actually springs [7, 8]. The use of such ''intermediate'' stimuli, though, does allow the first step to be taken in characterizing objects by attributes and developing scales for the attributes that can be combined according to rules of combination to produce the real-valued utility function that is sought. If, through the chain of abstracting from unique objects to general properties, irrelevant attributes are introduced, vital ones ignored, or poor surrogates chosen, pairwise comparisons of alternatives will not yield a meaningful utility function. Research designed to identify relevant properties of alternatives that are related to the spatial choice decision thus becomes supportive of the research strategy described here [1].

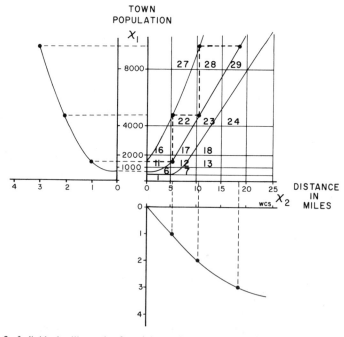

FIG. 2. Individual utility scales from joint-preference scale: Iowa grocery patterns, 1960

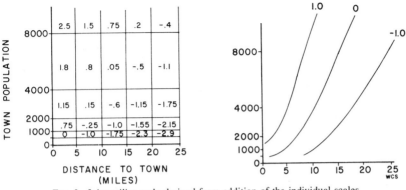

FIG. 3. Joint utility scale derived from addition of the individual scales

RESULTS

The Fishburn Graphical Method

Three isolines were interpolated from the scale values, and two were used as a basis for the individual scaling of the two stimuli variables, town size and distance to town (Fig. 2). The joint preference scale is "recovered" in Figure 3 by adding the individual utilities of the two stimuli.

Between each pair of the stimulus combinations the difference in utility values was computed, and these were correlated with the original paired comparison preference distances (Fig. 4). The correlation was .588, which compares with a correlation of .660 for the relation between the difference in MDS scale values and the original preference distances (Fig. 5). Since the MDS algorithm was designed specifically to compute scale values the rank order of which would be as close as possible to the rank order of the input preference distances without any constraint that the preference function should be a continuously defined real-valued function, the fact that the additive utility function fits the original values almost as well as the MDS scale fitted them is encouraging empirical evidence of the fruitfulness of this method of decomposing the joint-preference function.

Regression Analysis of the Scale Values

The stimulus values for the midpoints of the class intervals of the

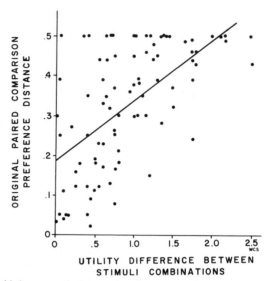

FIG. 4. Relationship between paired comparison distances (Table 1) and joint utility scale distances (Fig. 3)

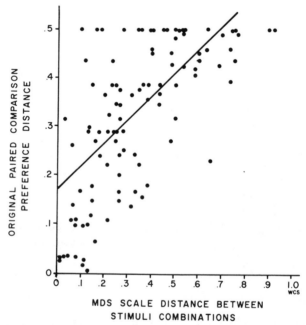

FIG. 5. Relationship between paired comparison distances (Table 1) and distances from MDS scale (Table 2)

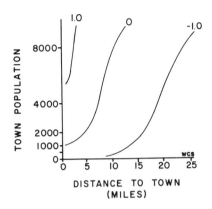

FIG. 6. Third-degree polynomial trend surface of MDS scale values (Table 2) with $r = 0.968$

fifteen stimulus combinations shown in Figure 2 were the independent variables in a regression analysis in which the fifteen MDS scale values were the dependent variable (Table 2). The TORSCA algorithm was used to compute the scale values [11]. The correlation coefficients for the first- through third-degree polynomial regression equations were .861, .930, and .968 respectively. The graph of the surface of computed values from the third-degree polynomial equation shows that the sample consumers made a rapid trade-off of distance to reach places that were larger than 4,000 population (Fig. 6). Most interesting is the sharp break around the 4,000 population mark, with the sample population being unwilling to travel farther to reach larger places. The difference in computed scale values between all pairs of the fifteen stimulus combinations used in the first method was computed, and the correlation with the original paired comparison preference distances was .582.

Conjoint Measurement Model

From the conjoint measurement model [12], scale values were computed for the stimulus combinations for the additive model on distance and town-size components (Kruskal's stress formula 2 [6] was .101). The separate effects are shown in Figure 7. For any particular stimulus combination, the separate effects are added to yield a joint-effects score. Differences between these scores correlated with the original observations with $r = .554$. For the multiplicative model, the differences correlated with $r = .577$.

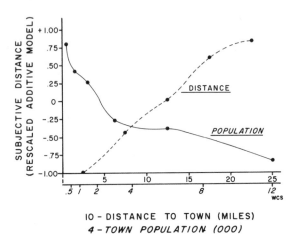

FIG. 7. Utility scales derived from polynomial conjoint measurement model (POLYCON)

CONCLUSION

Three methods of decomposing the joint-effects preference score for stimulus combinations in spatial choice data yielded very similar results when assessed against their capacity to reflect the original paired comparison observations. The Fishburn graphical method yielded scale score differences that correlated .588 with the original observations; the third-degree, trend-surface function yielded differences that correlated with $r = .582$; and the conjoint measurement, multiplicative model correlated with $r = .577$ with the original observed differences. The high degree of consistency among three quite different methods in this case illustrates the flexibility open to the researcher in this matter. Most interesting is the fact that little information is apparently lost in the move from the individually computed scale values to the values based on models that combine the individual stimuli through some arithmetic rule.

Particular interest is drawn to the graphical method in that it is based on a narrower region of the joint preference function than the remaining two methods examined here. This methodology, therefore, reduces the data requirements for empirical applications: only two trade-off functions are required. This reduced data need is beneficial both for the case where established methods are used for generating the space-preference function and the many other cases of procedures for generating the trade-off functions that, curiously, have not yet found application to the spatial choice problem. Fishburn, for example, reviews twenty-four methods of estimating additive utilities [3]. Other advantages can be noted. Where the number of stimuli becomes large (three or more), currently used methodologies (method of paired comparisons or factorial designs) for finding preference functions break down because of the explosive combinatorial problems that arise. But so long as the assumption of additivity of individual utility effects holds, the joint preference function can be computed by performing successive scale transformations in the manner described earlier. Because the methodology begins with the two trade-off functions defined, the manner in which they are found is externally decided. Accordingly, the individual researcher may decide to compute these either by the presentation of hypothetical alternatives or by the reconstruction of revealed preferences from actual choices. It seems to be a fact that researchers tend to be predisposed to one or the other of these approaches. The indifference of the decomposition method to this issue may thus be seen to be a distinct advantage in uniting such superficially different methodologies.

The methodology is, of course, more than a method of reconstructing and generalizing the empirical relations in a data set. It is this, but it is also a model of human behavior in that the assumption on which the method is constructed is a model of how human beings combine different stimuli to reach a choice decision. It is not obvious that simply adding the utilities attributed to individual stimuli will yield a net effect for all combinations that preserve their overall ordering. The explanatory power of such models would be significantly improved if this finding can be validated in new contexts and shown also to be valid in situations involving more than two stimuli, for the researcher would then be in a position to predict expected spatial behavior patterns for novel combinations of stimuli.

Irrespective of the success in validating this particular model, the goal of this research should continue to be pursued. The dependence on preference functions that have been independently calibrated for each occasion must be reduced. The overcoming of distance separation in response to opportunities of different degrees of attraction is a general problem and should not be solved by calibrating models for each case.

Spatial interaction models have failed in their generality from this cause, and if any lesson is to be learned from the history of model building in that area, it is that priority was given to satisfying goodness-of-fit criteria rather than attempting to ensure robustness of model parameters under varying conditions—perhaps accepting some loss in the degree of fit between model and data. Considering the totally different degrees of effort that have been expended in studying spatial interaction by entropy maximizing models and spatial preference models, the only justification for continuing the research in the latter area is the anticipation that the different ways in which distance effects are treated in the two types of models is more likely to lead to robust models in the spatial preference case. This is because distance separation in the preference model is not regarded as a variable that increases or decreases the likelihood of an interaction but rather as a (negative) stimulus contributing its part-worth to a person's evaluation of any spatial alternative. Knowledge of the person's system of attributing part-worths to distance and to other stimuli that are relevant to choice is knowledge that can be transferred from one spatial set of alternatives to another because it is knowledge that is independent of any one set of spatial alternatives. It is this independence that makes this knowledge more fundamental than, for example, the trip-attenuating function of a more traditional spatial interaction model that shows in contrast how a particular set of alternatives were judged. The judgmental process is a general process, and the task of model building is to extract from the particular judgments of a given context the general rules of evaluation that the people involved invoke whenever a new situation arises. It is knowledge internal to the subject that is applied to an ever-changing spatial pattern of opportunities. The result is spatial behavior. As researchers we have for too long been interested in the outcome of this choice process rather than with the pattern of decision-making by the subjects, which when applied to the unique set of alternatives generates the outcome we observe.

ACKNOWLEDGEMENTS

I would like to thank Mr. James A. Kohler for help with the computations and Dr. Stanley R. Lieber for his advice on the nonmetric conjoint measurement problem.

LITERATURE CITED

1. Burnett, P. "The Dimensions of Alternatives in Spatial Choice Processes." *Geographical Analysis*, 5 (1973), 181–204.

2. Fishburn, P. C. "Independence, Trade-offs, and Transformations in Bivariate Utility Functions." *Management Science*, 11 (1965), 792–801.

3. ———. "Methods of Estimating Additive Utilities." *Management Science*, 13 (1967), 435–53.

4. ———. "Utility Theory." *Management Science*, 14 (1968), 335–78.

5. Golledge, R. G., and G. Rushton. *Multidimensional Scaling: Review and Geographical Applications.* Technical Paper No. 10, Commission on College Geography, Association of American Geographers, Washington, D.C., 1972.

6. Kruskal, J. B. "Multidimensional Scaling: A Numerical Method." *Psychometrika*, 29 (1964), 115–29.

7. Lancaster, K. J. "A New Approach to Consumer Theory." *Journal of Political Economy*, 14 (1966), 132–57.

8. Quandt, R. E., and W. J. Baumol. "The Demand for Abstract Transport Modes: Theory and Measurement." *Journal of Regional Science*, 6 (1966), 13–26.

9. Rushton, G. "The Scaling of Locational Preferences." In *Behavioral Problems in Geography: A Symposium*, ed. K. R. Cox and R. G. Golledge, pp. 197–227. Northwestern University Studies in Geography No. 17, Department of Geography, Northwestern University, 1969.

10. Tversky, Amos. "Elimination by Aspects: A Theory of Choice." *Psychological Review*, 79 (1972), 281–99.

11. Young, F. W. "TORSCA-9: A FORTRAN IV Program for Nonmetric Multidimensional Scaling." *Behavioral Science*, 13 (1968), 343–44.

12. ———. "A Model for Polynomial Conjoint Analysis Algorithms." In *Applications in the Behavioral Sciences*, vol. 1, ed. R. N. Shepard et al., pp. 69–104. New York: Seminar Press, 1972.

CHAPTER 8

ROBERT L. KNIGHT, MARK D. MENCHIK

Conjoint Preference Estimation for Residential Land Use Policy Evaluation

I. INTRODUCTION

It is frequently useful to decompose preferences for a complex good (such as a transport mode or a residence) into preferences for each of its attributes. In addition to deepening understanding, the decomposition would help evaluate individuals' response to new transportation forms or residential environments, phrased as new combinations of existing elements [9, 12]. In this fashion, Quandt and Baumol [14] estimated the demand for a new transport mode by defining transport modes in general as combinations of the variable attributes of travel time, trip cost, and departure frequency. They estimated their abstract transport mode model with aggregate data on the use of existing modes.

Here, we are interested in decomposing individual preferences for alternative residential forms. A conjoint measurement procedure is used to estimate preferences using preference-based rankings obtained from questionnaire respondents. A variant of multidimensional scaling [3], conjoint measurement procedures are generally useful in the direct measurement of preferences for multiattribute items.

The empirical work described below was conducted to help evaluate the demand for new residential land use patterns designed for higher quality residential environments than are commonly the case, but with fewer negative environmental consequences. It may be useful to discuss our research motivation and its relevance to the procedure described. Great quantities of land on the peripheries of large metropolitan areas are currently being converted from rural to urban uses. Most of the new peripheral development follows a "spread" or "urban sprawl" development pattern with large home lots and uniformly low population densities. Not only are large quantities of land converted to urban uses, but land that is scenically valuable or ecologically vulnerable may be built upon. Additionally, this pattern is associated with extensive and automobile-based local travel, long utility lines, and, in general, heavy use of scarce resources.

On the other hand, it has been argued that a spread development pattern is inevitable given (among other things) generally weak and nonspecific land use controls and the limited offerings of new housing. This market currently offers few "nonstandard" alternatives such as clusters of small lots in otherwise sparsely settled areas. Some assert, however, that these limited offerings are consistent with existing public preferences. It is further said that there is a widespread preference for large amounts of privately owned space combined with naturally appearing environs and that large lots are a good way to satisfy such preferences.

The above reasoning works better in the small than in the large, however. As more and more people buy large lots, the natural environs everyone moved out to obtain are inevitably destroyed. An area completely divided into one-acre, or even larger, residential lots is hardly natural. An alternative to this pattern is the employment of land use controls to focus development (see, e.g. [18]). Appropriate siting and effective land use controls would guarantee a high level of natural environmental quality, in exchange for the necessary reduction in private space.

In this paper we attempt to contribute to the evaluation of the potential demand for residential land use alternatives such as various forms of clusters development. One may study persons living in such areas [10], but these proposals have not as yet been extensively executed (also see [11]). Instead, in this paper we use the expressed preferences of prospective home buyers to attempt such an evaluation. We define a residential bundle as containing all the characteristics pertinent to a resident's satisfaction with his house, its location, its surroundings, the neighbors, and so on. To assess alternative land use policies, some important attributes are those bearing on the private space used and the off-lot visual environmental quality. Thus, one way to compare preferences for the two general types of development patterns discussed above is to see whether people are willing to sacrifice the private space of the spread pattern for the high-quality natural environment of the alternative.

Preference measurement for such abstract and hypothetical alternatives is a difficult task, that of the remainder of this paper. Section 2 presents the attributes used to define the various residential bundles and discusses the phrasing of a general preference structure for them. There are severe practical problems in estimating this preference structure with common conjoint measurement algorithms. Instead, section 3 presents a more specialized preference model, estimated with the algorithm of the following section. Empirical results of this procedure are discussed in section 5. Estimated preference models are used in section 6 to simulate the choices of individuals for alternative residential environments. The final section summarizes and concludes the paper.

II. RESIDENTIAL BUNDLES AND THE STRUCTURE OF PREFERENCES

Let us define residential bundles according to the seven attributes of Table 1. The first two attributes, the views from the backyard and the front yard, are measures of off-lot visual environmental quality. Backyard size, side-to-side distance between houses, and the distance between the house and sidewalk (the next three attributes) are, in one sense, components of lot size. They may also be indicators of something very subjective—an individual's sense of privacy and spaciousness, as influenced by the space available for family activities, the physical separation from neighbors, and the separation from a public street. The number of floors is also space related, for building additional stories allows the ground area built upon to be reduced, given a fixed amount of interior space. The last attribute is the home's purchase price.

The list in Table 1 could surely be lengthened, and other attributes could replace the ones chosen. The attributes listed, however, were selected according to study purposes. These are to show individuals' relative preferences for off-lot visual quality, private space, and cost in enough detail to indicate, for example, whether persons are more willing to give up front or side separation.

TABLE 1

ATTRIBUTES OF RESIDENTIAL BUNDLES AND THEIR LEVELS

Attribute	Level
1. View from backyard	1. Wooded area just outside backyard 2. Other backyards nearby, wooded area four houses away 3. Other backyards only, no wooded area nearby
2. View from front yard	1. Open view of natural countryside 2. Other homes 3. Shopping center, medium sized
3. Backyard size	1. 50 × 80 feet (4,000 sq. ft.) 2. 30 × 65 feet (2,000 sq. ft.) 3. 20 × 25 feet (500 sq. ft.)
4. Distance between houses	1. 30 feet 2. 15 feet 3. Touching
5. Distance from house to sidewalk	1. 30 feet 2. 20 feet 3. 10 feet
6. Number of floors (not including basement)	1. One 2. Two 3. Three
7. Price of home (relative to price respondent expects to pay for next home)	1. $2,000 less 2. "Most likely" price 3. $2,000 more

We can further specify that each attribute is a discrete variable assuming one of the three levels of Table 1. Assuming discrete variation adds considerable generality and psychological realism to the problem. The "view from the backyard" cannot be measured simply as one continuous operational variable. One can, however, define it as a nominal variable (see [16]) so that there are three kinds of views. The ordering of attribute levels in Table 1 is arbitrary and does not prejudge the empirical determination of whether an individual prefers one backyard view over another. Preferences for perceived spaciousness and privacy are unlikely to be simple continuous functions of square footage and distance. As will be shown, phrasing attributes as discrete-valued variables allows us to estimate preferences on the attribute levels without assuming any functional form.

Any residential bundle may thus be defined in terms of a vector-valued variable, each of whose seven components represents an attribute, and with values indicating the level of that attribute. We can define a number of residential bundles thereby and have a person order them preferentially. If we specify a polynomial conjoint measurement model, as discussed by Tversky [17] and Young [19], it can be estimated by a nonmetric multidimensional scaling procedure. A moment's reflection, however, suggests that this procedure would not be practical for the scale of the problem defined by Table 1. Taking all combinations of attribute levels, there are 3^7 or 2,187 possible residential bundles. Even a small fraction of this number represents an unreasonable ranking task, and too small a quantity of residential bundles to be ranked may not provide sufficient information to estimate the rather general polynomial conjoint preference model. The high dimensionality of the preferential judgments required makes the ranking additionally difficult. Ranking twenty-five different combinations of backyard size and distance to the sidewalk is tedious, to be sure, but the individual is simply trading off one variable against another. Ranking whole residential bundles that can differ in any or all of seven attributes requires a much higher dimensional trade-off judgment to be made simultaneously. Human information processing capabilities are rather limited in general [13]; even a trade-off between two simple geometric dimensions may lead to surprising results, as Shepard [15] shows.

The generality of the implicit preference model makes the hypothetical task statistically unreasonable as well. Nowhere have we made restrictive assumptions on the decomposition of preferences, that is, how the "part-preference" for a given attribute or level of that attribute interacts with that for another attribute or level. Consider a child's preference for various quantities of jam, bread, and licorice. The relative preference for jam as against licorice (i.e., the rate at which he will sacrifice one for the other) depends on the quantity of bread, because the child presumably derives little satisfaction from breadless jam. Because of this particular interaction or complementarity between the preferences for jam and bread, a conjoint measurement approach would have to produce diet alternatives for ranking that simultaneously vary the quantities of the three foods. We cannot simplify the problem by trading off only pairs of foods; the nature of the preference structure will not allow it. Going back to the original preference problem, we therefore need an ordering of many multidimensionally heterogeneous bundles to estimate preference when such a potentially complex preference structure is allowed.

What is here loosely referred to as the "structure of preference" is precisely defined in the literature [1, 2, 5] discussing the general utility functions and the much simpler separable variants. There the utility or preference index is often defined as a continuous function of continuous variables, indicating quantities of each good consumed, but the difference between the continuous and discrete formulations in no way mitigates the conclusion that a general preference structure allows a wide range of preference interactions, at a great cost in mathematical complexity and proportionately greater data requirements.

III. THE SEPARABLE PREFERENCE MODEL

A more restrictive preference model will help make the problem feasible. In general the utility or preference function is of the form

$$U = U(q_1, q_2, \ldots, q_7) \tag{1}$$

where U is the (ordinal) utility level and $q_1, q_2, \ldots q_7$ are variables simply indicating the level by each of the attributes. Assume that the utility function is multiplicative-separable [1] in form so that it can be written as

$$U = \prod_{i=1}^{7} U_i(q_i). \tag{2}$$

Total utility can thus be written as the product of seven "part-utility" functions U_i, each defined on one and only one attribute so that the part-utility generated by one attribute is independent of the levels of all other attributes. Otherwise put, the trade-off between any two attributes is independent of any other attributes. This assumption has been called that of "want-independence" [2, p. 28]; it rules out the preference structure of the jam, bread, and licorice example.

The utility function (2) is called ordinal because it specifies only orderings along the utility level U. These orderings are unchanged by any monotonic transformation of both sides of (2), such as taking logarithms. This operation converts (2) to an equivalent additive-separable form.

Because attributes take on only discrete levels, we can set the function $U_i(q_i)$ equal to the constant p_{ij} when attribute i assumes level $j, j = 1, 2, 3$. The constant p_{ij} can be interpreted intuitively as the preference for level j of attribute i. Inserting in (2), find

$$U = \prod_{i=1}^{7} p_{ij} \tag{3}$$

where U is the preference for a residential bundle specified by the combination of the j subscripts.

Equation (3) is a simple preference model with, in our seven-attribute, three-level case, twenty-one easily interpreted parameters. Furthermore, with the method to be described here, the parameters can be estimated by a small number of simple preference orderings, each ordering trading off just one pair of attributes. In the case of two three-level attributes, nine such choices are possible. In the empirical work presented below, survey respondents indicated their preference rankings on trade-off matrices like Figure 1. Drawings as well as words (see Fig. 2) defined the levels of all attributes except price. Price levels

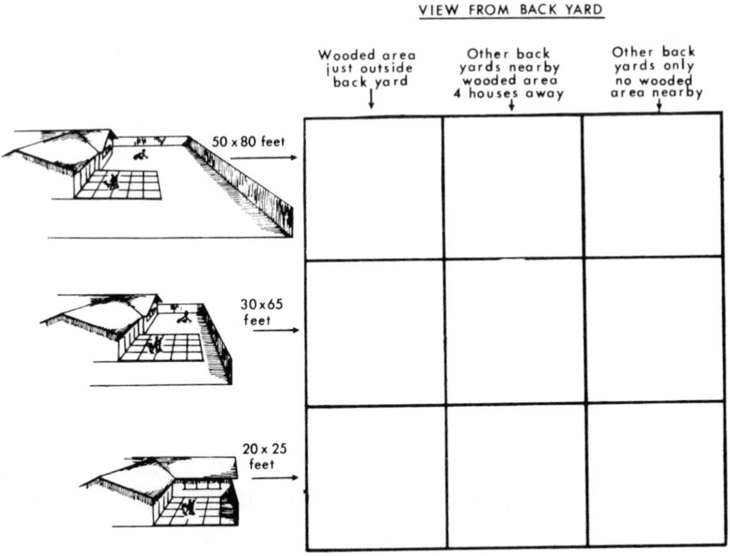

FIG. 1. Example of trade-off matrix

VIEW FROM BACK YARD

Other Yards   Wooded Area

VIEW FROM FRONT YARD

Other Homes   Open View

FIG. 2. Representations of some levels of environmental quality attributes

were phrased as $2,000 deviations from the price each prospective home buyer interviewed expected to pay for his new home. This both added psychological realism and allowed the same forms to be used for a wide range of expected house price levels.

With seven attributes, there are $1/2$ $(7)(6) = 21$ possible attribute pairs, but the algorithm used does not require all those trade-offs to be made. Twelve pairwise trade-offs were chosen so that each attribute appeared in three or four trade-off matrices as just described. The linkages of Figure 3 show the pairings of attributes traded off, and indicate that pairs not directly linked were linked indirectly with no more than one other attribute intervening.

Observe that the simplification of the preference model allows a single individual to provide enough data to estimate his preferences. If only "average" preferences of an assumed fairly homogeneous group are needed, each respondent's task can be reduced to a simple subset of the possible preference orderings, and a more complex preference

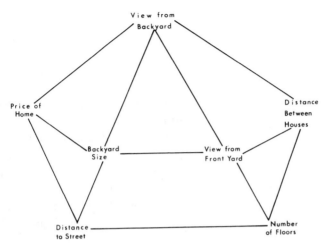

FIG. 3. Pairings of attributes used for trade-off matrices

model can be used. Green and Rao [4], for example, use block or random designs to allocate subsets of all possible combinations to the respondents. Estimating group preferences is less useful, however, in exploratory research with a heterogeneous population where there is little prior basis for groupings. The present approach may be used at an early stage of research to develop a tentative typology of groups with uniform preferences. Alternatively, one can test for associations between individual preferences and descriptive variables such as socioeconomic and demographic characteristics.

IV. THE ESTIMATING ALGORITHM

The conjoint measurement algorithm used was developed by Market Facts, Inc. [6] from Johnson's multidimensional scaling procedure [7]. Input data for the present example are the respondent's rankings from one to nine for the cells of each of the twelve trade-off matrices such as in Figure 1. The "one" cell is the most preferred. The algorithm calculates a matrix **P** of preference or part-utility parameters, P_{ij}. In this multiplicative model, estimated parameters are scaled so that for each attribute the preferences for the three levels sum to unity. This loses no generality.

At each iteration the algorithm multiplies together the provisional p_{ij} values corresponding to the pair of attributes in each of the trade-off matrices. These "predicted" utility values are compared with the actual rankings, by a "badness-of-fit" measure, ϕ. A gradient search procedure produces an improved estimate of $\mathbf{P}$ for the next iteration. The gradient search procedure computes a matrix of partial derivatives, $\mathbf{G}$, each of whose elements is the partial derivative of ϕ with respect to p_{ij}. As in the maximization or minimization problems of elementary calculus, these partial derivatives may be used to find a minimal value of ϕ, corresponding to the best fit of the preference parameters to the ranking data. This is done iteratively: the provisional estimates are changed in the way suggested by $\mathbf{G}$, producing an improved preference matrix whose badness of fit is calculated in the same way, and altered by another gradient search step, and so on.

The description below states the algorithm in a little more detail. It assumes the dimensions of the present problem, where all seven attributes have three levels. In general, though, the number of levels may vary across attributes. The steps are as follows.

1. Generate a random starting preference matrix $\mathbf{P}_1$, the subscript indicating preference values for the first iteration.

2. Consider a trade-off matrix using attributes h and i ($h, i = 1, \ldots,$ 7; $h \neq i$). Multiplying rows h and i of $\mathbf{P}_1$, compute the nine-element vector $\mathbf{x}'_{h,i}$ (understood to be for the first iteration) with

$$\mathbf{x}'_{h,i} = (x_{11}, x_{12}, x_{13}, x_{21}, \ldots, x_{33}). \tag{4}$$

The elements of that vector correspond to the cells in that trade-off matrix and are simply the product of the two appropriate elements of the $\mathbf{P}_1$ matrix. This vector contains the "predicted" utility values for that trade-off matrix.

3. For the same trade-off matrix the data vector (constant, of course, through all iterations) is

$$\mathbf{d}'_{h,i} = (d_{11}, \ldots, d_{33}), \tag{5}$$

whose elements are a permutation of the integers one to nine.

4. Let r and s signify particular cells in the trade-off matrix where $r, s = 1, \ldots, 9$ and $r \neq s$. Now,

a. Find the sign of the quantity

$$\frac{x_r}{x_s} - 1 \tag{6}$$

where x_r and x_s are the rth and sth elements of the vector $\mathbf{x}_{h,i}$. The computed sign indicates whether or not cell r is predicted as being preferred to cell s.

b. Find the sign of the similar quantity

$$\frac{d_r}{d_s} - 1 \tag{7}$$

where, as above, d_r and d_s are taken from the $\mathbf{d}_{h,i}$ vector, showing whether or not the respondent in fact prefers cell r to cell s.

c. The same signs in (6) and (7) indicate that the preference estimates *incorrectly* predicted the ordering of cells r and s. This is because a small value of d_r indicates a highly preferred or top-ranked cell, whereas a small value of x_r indicates just the reverse, being the product of two part-utility parameters. If the two signs are the same, calculate

$$\frac{x_r}{x_s} + \frac{x_s}{x_r} - 2 \tag{8}$$

and cumulate it into U_1, the subscript indicating the first iteration. This quantity is a metric measure of the predicted preference difference between cells r and s, being zero for equal predicted preferences and increasing as the ratio x_r/x_s grows larger or smaller than one.

d. Whether or not the signs of (6) and (7) agree, cumulate (8) into V_1.

e. Repeat steps 4a, b, c, and d for all pairs of distinct cells in the h, i trade-off matrix, cumulating the results into U_1 and V_1.

5. Repeat steps 2–4 for all pairs of attributes for which trade-off data were obtained, again cumulating calculated quantities into U_1 and V_1.

6. Let

$$\phi_1 = \frac{U_1}{V_1}$$

be a badness-of-fit measure for the first iteration, showing how poorly the provisional preference estimates reproduce the given rankings. ϕ is a metric analogue of the proportion of wrongly predicted ranking comparisons. The numerator, U_1, increases with the poorness of prediction as stated above.

7. Compute a gradient matrix $\mathbf{G}_1$ proportional to

$$\frac{\partial \phi}{\partial \mathbf{P}_1} = \frac{\partial \left(\dfrac{U_1}{V_1} \right)}{\partial \mathbf{P}_1} = \frac{1}{(V_1)^2} \left(V_1 \frac{\partial U_1}{\partial \mathbf{P}_1} - + V_1 \frac{\partial V_1}{\partial \mathbf{P}_1} \right) \qquad (10)$$

8. Compute a new and improved preference matrix $\mathbf{P}_2$ where

$$\mathbf{P}_2 = \mathbf{P}_1 - \phi_1 \mathbf{G}_1 \qquad (11)$$

so that $\mathbf{P}_1$ changes in the "direction" suggested by $\mathbf{G}_1$.

9. With the new matrix of preference estimates, begin a second iteration by returning to step 2. The whole process is repeated until iteration n, where ϕ_n indicates that a sufficiently good set of estimates has been obtained, or until a prearranged number of iterations has been performed.

V.   RESULTING PREFERENCE DATA

A random telephone survey conducted March and April 1973 in the Milwaukee metropolitan area yielded 220 self-identified potential home buyers. All except those refusing to divulge their address were visited, resulting in 123 complete interviews. The overall response rate of 59 percent was rather high considering the practical difficulties of telephone screening and respondents' likely suspicion of a sales effort. (See [8] for details on sampling and interviewing procedures.) All respondents were asked to complete the twelve trade-off matrices; one respondent, however, was removed from further analysis for having made only 3 of the 108 rankings. Inspection disclosed that responses, by and large, were intuitively "sensible." Respondents did in fact appear to be trading off among the two attributes.

The Market Facts algorithm appeared to perform quite well, converging in a modest number of iterations to acceptably low values of ϕ and

TABLE 2

Goodness of Fit Between Actual and "Predicted" Rankings

Kendall's Tau	Number of Respondents	Percentage of Respondents
.99–1.000	0	0
.97– .989	7	6
.95– .969	29	24
.93– .949	27	22
.91– .929	17	14
.89– .909	18	15
.87– .889	8	7
.85– .869	6	5
.83– .849	4	3
.81– .829	2	2
.79– .809	0	0
.77– .789	2	2
.75– .769	2	2
Below .75	0	0
Total	122	100

generating reasonable preference estimates. Another test involved computing the predicted utility value for the cells in each trade-off matrix by multiplying the two appropriate calculated utility values. For each respondent, predicted and actual rankings were compared using Kendall's tau, a rank-order correlation coefficient [16, pp. 213–23]. Tau can, of course, be viewed as a nonmetric analogue of ϕ the algorithm's goodness-of-fit measure. Table 2 shows the distribution of tau across the survey respondents.

Values of tau less than unity (the maximum) can be due to a variety of empirical imperfections. The respondent's original ordering can be "bad data" because of random measurement error or some other cause of test-retest ranking variation. Intransitive rankings would suggest internal "inconsistencies" or preferences that are probabilistic rather than deterministic, as was assumed. Similarly, a misspecification of the preference model would cause lack of fit. Finally, lack of fit could be a weakness of the estimating algorithm. Like any aggregate goodness-of-fit measure (e.g., R^2 for a regression model), tau cannot distinguish among the various error sources but seems a useful indicator of the "quality" of the resulting data.

Table 2 shows the preference estimates to be quite good by this standard. Experience with the algorithm suggests that individual preferences with tau values of 0.8 or higher are fully useful for analysis (John

Fiedler, personal communication). As virtually no tau values below this level were found, all 122 respondents were used for analysis.

There are many ways to analyze the large quantity of resulting preference information forming (for each respondent) twenty-one data points across the two dimensions of attributes and level of each attribute. Two nonmetric preference measures are the level of each attribute with the highest utility value and the preferential ordering of each attribute's levels. By and large, these correspond with the arrangement of attribute levels in Table 1, as was expected. For example, the backyard view of a wooded area had the highest utility value for 87 percent of the respondents. There were minority opinions, however, with each of the two other alternatives being preferred by 8 (7 percent) of the respondents.

The conjoint procedure used here, however, is most useful for metric preference measures, giving more information than just orderings. It is nor surprising that most people prefer a large backyard to a small one, and a view of woods to a view of others' backyards. It is the *magnitude* of these preferences that is necessary to indicate real-world choices, given current or future alternatives.

A moment's manipulation of the multiplicative preference model (3) shows that the magnitudes of preference differences are indicated by the ratios of the utilities for different levels of the same attribute. Alternatively, take logarithms in (3), obtaining an additive model. Then differences in log utility for various levels of an attribute have ratio scale properties [16]. Thus, depending on the data, one can make statements such as that an attribute's level 1 is preferred over level 3 by twice as much as it is preferred over level 2. Similarly, we can compare the magnitude of the preference difference between two levels of one attribute with that between two levels of another attribute. As an example, we might find that an individual prefers a front view of open space to one of other homes (two levels of attribute 2) and a 4,000 square foot backyard to a 2,000 square foot one (attribute 3). Suppose, however, that the magnitude of the preference difference is greater for the latter than the former attribute. Then, all else equal, one would prefer a home with a front view of other houses and a 4,000 square foot backyard to one with an open space front view and the smaller backyard.

Such preference comparisons are simply the discrete analogues of marginal or infinitesimal changes in the utility functions of classical consumer theory [5, chap.2]. Preference differences among levels of one attribute are equivalent to the marginal utility of infinitesimal increases in one commodity. A comparison of interlevel preference differences for two attributes is exactly the rate of commodity substitution, a ratio of marginal utilities for two commodities. These quantities show the results of hypothetical trade-off choices, indicating as in the example above, which residential bundle or combination of commodities would be chosen.

There is a lesson to be learned in the comparison of the two utility models. In the consumer theory one does not simply prefer one good to another; intercommodity preference comparisons are made only between specified changes in the quantities of the two commodities. In the present discrete model the simple question as to whether a person considers the quality of the front view more important than backyard size is similarly meaningless. This is because the result of any specific comparison of residential bundles depends on the "quantities" of view quality and backyard space being exchanged. It is indeed possible that given a 4,000 square foot backyard and a front view of a shopping center, one would *not* accept a reduction of 3,500 square feet for an open space view, but would accept a 2,000 square foot reduction for it. One cannot compare whole attributes, only specified changes in attribute levels.

VI. SIMULATING THE DEMAND FOR ALTERNATIVE RESIDENTIAL ENVIRONMENTS

To stimulate demand for residential alternatives, we must first specify the offerings in some hypothetical "market," simply several residential bundles defined as combinations of the attribute levels of Table 1. With an individual's estimated preference values, we compute the predicted utility values for each of the residential bundles and have the individual "choose" that one with the highest calculated utility. Performing this operation across all individuals, and summing, yields the number of individuals choosing each offering. This simple simulation procedure assumes that an indefinite quantity of each offering is available at the stated price. The quality of the simulation is, of course, dependent on the realism of the alternatives that are offered. The total demand, that is the number of persons buying houses, is assumed exogenous to the characteristics of the alternatives being considered. More precisely, it is market share that is being modeled.

The levels of all seven attributes might vary across the alternatives in a very general simulation. In the examples here, however, we are interested in exploring in simple fashion the likely response to a market alternative affording a higher quality environment than is commonly the case. (For other simulations, see [8].) This higher environmental quality is obtained by restricting construction from some of .the land in the subject house's view. All else equal, it is reasonable to assume that each household so benefited either must pay a higher price (i.e., for its share of the the land not developed) or, at the same price, must settle for less private space than otherwise. The simulations below evaluate the latter alternative, asking whether persons would willingly sacrifice a given component of private space for a stated change in off-lot visual environmental quality. For most persons, this latter change would be an improvement.

Each of the eight simulations presented is rather simple, offering two alternatives differing on two attributes. One of two environmental quality attributes (the view from the backyard or from the front yard) is traded off against one of four space-using attributes: backyard size,

TABLE 3

SIMULATIONS TRADING OFF BACKYARD VIEW
AGAINST SPACE-USING ATTRIBUTES

	SPACE-USING ATTRIBUTE			
	Backyard Size	Distance between Houses	Distance from House to Sidewalk	Number of Floors
First level	4,000 sq. ft.	30 ft.	30 ft.	1
Second level	2,000 sq. ft.	15 ft.	20 ft.	2
	PERSONS CHOOSING EACH HOUSE			
	No. %	No. %	No. %	No. %
A. "Conventional" house (view of other backyards and first-level attribute for that column)	32 26	44 36	23 19	24 20
B. "Alternative" house (view of wooded area and second-level attribute for that column)	90 74	78 64	99 81	98 80
Total	122 100	122 100	122 100	122 100

TABLE 4

SIMULATIONS TRADING OFF FRONT YARD VIEW
AGAINST SPACE-USING ATTRIBUTES

	SPACE-USING ATTRIBUTE			
	Backyard Size	Distance between Houses	Distance from House to Sidewalk	Number of Floors
First level	4,000 sq. ft.	30 ft.	30 ft.	1
Second level	2,000 sq. ft.	15 ft.	20 ft.	2
	PERSONS CHOOSING EACH HOUSE			
	No. %	No. %	No. %	No. %
A. "Conventional" house (view of other homes and first-level attribute for that column)	57 47	67 55	43 35	35 29
B. "Alternative" house (open view of countryside and second-level attribute for that column)	65 53	55 45	79 65	87 71
Total	122 100	122 100	122 100	122 100

distance between houses, distance from house to sidewalk, or the number of floors. The five remaining attributes (including price) remain constant for the two alternatives in each simulation.

Row A of Table 3 represents the "conventional" house with a back view of other backyards, and row B represents an alternative with a wooded area just outside the backyard. Each set of columns indicates the space-using attribute that is traded off against the backyard view. The leftmost hypothetical market of Table 3 shows that a home with a 4,000-square-foot backyard looking onto other backyards would be chosen by thirty-two persons while one with a 2,000-square-foot backyard fronting on a wooded area would be selected by the remaining ninety. The same construction is employed for the four simulations of Table 4, except that a front view of other homes in row A is compared with an open countryside view in row B.

Numerical results indicate that in all but one case a majority of potential homebuyers will give up a specified element of private space for the environmental quality features offered. This is not due to the respondents' market expectations—other survey questions showed them as both being interested in a rather conventional house (over available alternatives such as townhouses and duplexes) and expecting to buy one [8]. Notice, however, that the simulation asks for the sacrifice of relatively small fractions of the kind of private space indicated, in contrast with the extreme losses required by most presently available alternatives to the conventional house. The simulations also show that more persons are likely to respond to the offered improvement in the back view than the front view. Furthermore, for both Tables 3 and 4, respondents are more sensitive to specified reductions in side separation and backyard size than they are to the specified reduction in front yard depth and the increase in the number of house floors.

VII. SUMMARY AND CONCLUSIONS

In summary, the research discussed here defined a residential bundle as a combination of one of three levels of each of seven attributes. The attributes pertain to a residence's space-using characteristics, its off-lot visual environmental quality, and its price. Thus phrased, residential preferences may be estimated by general polynomial conjoint measurement procedures, but these are infeasible for the scale of the problem as defined. Instead, separability or "want-independence" is assumed for the underlying preference structure or utility function. Roughly speaking, in a separable utility function the quantitative changes in satisfaction associated with different levels of the same attributes are independent of whatever levels the other attributes take on.

A special-purpose algorithm, a type of nonmetric multidimensional scaling procedure, was used to estimate the preference parameters using preference data collected from 123 self-identified prospective home buyers. Each questionnaire respondent filled out twelve trade-off matrices. In each, a pair of attributes was traded off, with the respondent ranking the nine combinations of attribute levels. The algorithm sought those preference values that, when combined according to the preference model, best predicted the observed rankings. This was done by a gradient search technique, iteratively modifying the provisional parameter values to increase the fit between predicted and actual preference orderings.

The estimated preference models were used in eight simulations of persons' response to alternative residential bundles. The two alternatives in each simulation traded off a specific reduction in private space for an improvement in off-lot visual environmental quality.

In presenting conclusions, it may be helpful to separate methodological findings from substantive findings. From the first point of view, the authors believe that the work reported here has demonstrated the usefulness of conjoint measurement techniques for evaluating policy questions in environmental planning. We did not originate the estimating algorithm; indeed the most sophisticated applications of the technique have been made in marketing research. As shown, preference data for a highly multidimensional item may be collected by having respondents make a small number of simple and concrete trade-offs. The procedure used yields independent preference estimates for each respondent, avoiding assumptions involved in grouping preference data across individuals (e.g., ecological correlations), indicating who has which preferences and allowing direct investigation of relationships between, say, socioeconomic characteristics and preferences.

The good fits between the respondents' rankings and the estimated preference functions suggest the accuracy of the preference estimates and the underlying model. This is an important achievement for a difficult measuring task. Individual preference estimates are, furthermore, plausible, varying fairly widely across both individuals and attributes. Similarly, results of the simulations are intuitively appealing, varying sharply with the attributes traded off.

Once individual utility functions are estimated, one can easily perform a wide variety of demand simulations more complex and realistic than the ones presented here. A large number of residential alternatives could be used, varying among many (or all) attributes. It should be possible to relax the assumption (used in the simulations here) of unlimited supply of each alternative at the stated price. It should be possible to make the demand side of the simulation more realistic, for example, by allowing the potential home buyer to stay if none of the alternative residences is sufficiently appealing relative to the "stay" option. This avoids the assumed exogeneity of overall demand.

Substantively we feel that these results suggest support for residential land use policies achieving high environmental quality levels while reducing individuals' lot sizes. More precisely, the results indicate that large proportions of prospective house buyers will sacrifice specific elements of private space for specific improvements in off-lot visual environmental quality. In a policy sense, the quantities of persons making each choice are important. These vary, of course, with the items being traded off. For the eight simulations discussed the percentage of those choosing the "environmental quality" option ranged from a high of 80 percent willing to add another house floor (reducing ground coverage, but with approximately the same indoor space) to gain a backyard view of a wooded area, to a low of 45 percent willing to reduce the separation between neighboring homes for a front yard view of open countryside. This range suggests a considerable market if such increases in environmental quality can be achieved through modest (but definite) reductions in private space for single-family dwellings.

ACKNOWLEDGMENTS

This work was conducted at the Institute for Environmental Studies, University of Wisconsin—Madison. The authors are indebted to John Fiedler and Richard Johnson, of Market Facts, Inc., for generously running their algorithm on our preference data, and for the financial support of NSF Grant GI-29731

LITERATURE CITED

1. Fishburn, P. C. *Decision and Value Theory.* New York: John Wiley and Sons, 1964.
2. Goldberger, A. S. "Functional Form and Utility: A Review of Consumer Demand Theory." Workshop Paper 6703; Center for Systems Formulation, Methodology, and Policy; Social Systems Research Institute; University of Wisconsin; Madison; 1967.
3. Golledge, R. G., and G. Rushton. "Multidimensional Scaling: Review and Geographical Applications." Technical Paper No. 10, Commission on College Geography, Association of American Geographers, Washington, D.C., 1972.
4. Green, P. E., and V. R. Rao. "Conjoint Measurement for Quantifying Judgment Data." *Journal of Marketing Research,* 8 (1971), 355–63.
5. Henderson, J. M., and R. E. Quandt. *Microeconomic Theory: A Mathematical Approach.* 2nd ed. New York: McGraw-Hill, 1971.
6. Johnson, R. M. "Trade-Off Analysis: A Method for Quantifying Consumer Values." Working Paper, Market Facts, Inc., Chicago, 1972.
7. ———. "Pairwise Nonmetric Multidimensional Scaling." *Psychometrika,* 38 (1973), 11–18.
8. Knight, R. L., and M. D. Menchik. "Residential Environmental Attitudes and Preferences: Report of a Questionnaire Survey." Institute for Environmental Studies, University of Wisconsin, Madison, forthcoming.
9. Lancaster, K. *Consumer Demand: A New Approach.* New York: Columbia University Press, 1971.
10. Lansing, J. B., R. W. Marans, and R. B. Zehner. *Planned Residential Environments.* Ann Arbor: Institute for Social Research, University of Michigan, 1970.

11. Menchik, M. D. "Residential Environmental Preferences and Choices: Empirically Validating Preference Measures." *Environment and Planning,* 4 (1972), 445–58.

12. ———. "Transport Modal Characteristics, Modal Choice, and Aggregate Travel: A Behavioral Model." *Economic Geography,* in press.

13. Miller, G. A. "The Magical Number Seven, Plus or Minus Two: Some Limits on Our Capacity to Process Information." *Psychological Review,* 63 (1956), 81–97.

14. Quandt, R. E., and W. Baumol. "The Demand for Abstract Transport Modes: Theory and Measurement." *Journal of Regional Science,* 6 (1966), 13—26.

15. Shepard, G. "On Subjectively Optimal Choice Among Multiattribute Alternatives." In *Human Judgments and Optimality,* ed. M. W. Shelly and G. L. Bryan. New York: John Wiley and Sons, 1964.

16. Siegel, S. *Nonparametric Statistics for the Behavioral Sciences.* New York: McGraw-Hill, 1956.

17. Tversky, A. "A General Theory of Polynomial Conjoint Measurement." *Journal of Mathematical Psychology,* 4 (1967), 1–20.

18. Whyte, W. H. *Cluster Development.* New York: American Conservation Association, 1964.

19. Young, F. W. "A Model for Polynomial Conjoint Analysis Algorithms." In *Multidimensional Scaling: Theory and Applications in the Behavioral Sciences,* vol. 1., ed. R. N. Shepard et al., pp. 69–104. New York: Seminar Press, 1972.

CHAPTER 9

SUSAN HANSON

Spatial Variation in the
Cognitive Levels of Urban Residents

Recently there has been an increasing interest in studying individuals' spatial behavior within the context of decision-making. Researchers concerned with intraurban consumer travel behavior have found the disaggregate decision-making approach particularly useful because the complexity of the urban environment places severe limitations upon the effectiveness of the more traditional macroscale models in which the unit of study is the areal unit rather than the individual or household.

When consumer travel behavior is viewed as the outcome of a decision-making process, considerable attention must be given to the choice situation facing the decision-maker. Within the city there are a host of potential trip destinations that the consumer must evaluate in order to make decisions concerning which stores to patronize. However, these evaluations are inevitably made on the basis of the decision-maker's limited information about the available opportunities for shopping. Clearly, the concept of economic man making decisions on the basis of complete information cannot be retained if we are to understand the way in which travel destinations are selected. The need for insights into the information upon which travel decisions are based has been made evident in some of the recent work on destination choice [4].

Of particular importance is the spatial variability of the information upon which the consumer bases decisions. A person may know about various shops at different locations, but this information will be unevenly distributed over space because certain locations will be better known than others. The term "information level" (or "cognitive level") is used here to refer to the amount of information a person or group of people has about a particular location. The purpose of this paper is to investigate the spatial variation in the cognitive levels of a sample of urban residents so that we may learn something about just how much information people have on the urban environment in which they make daily travel decisions.

INFORMATION LEVELS

The process through which information levels are built is inextricably linked to the process by which discernible travel patterns emerge over a period of time: the individual gathers information in the course of traveling around the city, while at the same time information levels influence the choice of trip destination. This kind of mutual feedback process has been described by Maruyama [8] as a deviation-amplifying mutual causal process, in which two processes interact, each effecting change in the other. Either information about a place or a trip to a place can start the process off in a certain direction; the effects of this initial "kick" are amplified when the explorations are successful, and sub-sequent trips and information gain become concentrated in the same locations. As a result of this deviation-amplifying process, what was once a set of equally unknown stores will become highly differentiated as information is accumulated in varying amounts about a subset of the available opportunities. The set of stores about which the shopper has some information is referred to here as the individual's "cognitive opportunity set" and identifies that portion of the total opportunity set from which travel destinations can be chosen by that person.

Two types of information are identified as being relevant to the consumer's decision-making process. The first is information on the *location of the store*—its location relative to the residence, the work-place, the CBD, and other shops. The second type of information pertains to the *interior of a store*—its layout, the line of goods it carries, the level of service available, the approximate prices of the goods, and so on. Information about the location of a store should prove useful in the shopper's estimation of the efficiency of traveling to one store as opposed to another; information about the interior of a store should be useful in estimating the probability that one will find what is wanted in a given store. These two types of information will be referred to as "locational information" and "specific information."

MEASURING INFORMATION LEVELS

This paper reports some initial findings from a study carried out in the spring of 1971 in Uppsala, Sweden. The Uppsala study and a similar one [2] conducted in 1970 in Evanston, Illinois, represent preliminary efforts to measure the cognitive levels of urban residents.

In order to assess the cognitive levels of urban shoppers, measurements needed to be made on the amount of locational information and the amount of specific information that consumers had about a given set of opportunities. Because it was felt that consumers make decisions about potential trip destinations on the basis of their perceived familiarity with various locations, it was desirable that the measure employed should reflect the respondent's subjective evaluation of the amount of information possessed about a given place. Therefore, it was decided to measure the respondent's subjective assessment of his or her level of familiarity with each of a set of specific locations within the city. The specific places that the respondents were to evaluate were identified as clearly as possible (i.e., by store name, address, and brief description of location), so that errors due to respondents' recall ability would be minimized and so that the respondents would not be confused as to which store was in question.

The method used to measure people's information levels is successive-category scaling, developed by Torgerson [14] and based on Thurstone's law of categorical judgment [13]. Thurstone postulates a psychological continuum for the attribute under consideration—in this case, familiarity. When a subject is presented with a stimulus, the ability to discriminate enables the subject to place the stimulus at a point on the continuum.

The approach employed here falls into what Torgerson calls the "stimulus-centered" or "judgment" approach, in which the "systematic variation of the reactions of the subjects to the stimuli is attributed to differences in the stimuli with respect to a designated attribute" [14, p. 46]. This approach is in contrast to a subject-centered approach, where the variation in response is attributed to attributes of the subjects, and is also in contrast to the response approach, where the variability of reactions is attributed to variation in both the subjects and the stimuli. In this study the variability in the subjects' responses is viewed as a function of variation in the size of the store and its distance and direction from the respondent's residence.

The stimuli used in this study were the ninety grocery stores in Uppsala; the continuum was operationally presented as a seven-point ordinal scale. At each extreme the scale was anchored with the labels "completely unfamiliar" at one end and "extremely familiar" at the other; the five middle points on the scale were unlabeled. The task set the subject was to evaluate his or her level of familiarity with each grocery store by marking whichever one of the seven scale intervals best described how familiar he/she felt with the stimulus (store) in question.

The method requires that each subject evaluate the *same set* of stimuli. For a spatially oriented study this means that the respondents should be clustered as closely as possible around one point in space so that they are all located identically with respect to the stores. The cluster sample used in this study consists of ninety-three respondents from an area approximately 400 × 300 meters. The centroid of the area was taken as the common residence of all the cluster-sample respondents so that all the stores in the opportunity set are assumed to be located identically vis-à-vis every respondent; that is, all respondents in the cluster are assumed to be responding to a spatially identical set of stimuli. The location of the cluster sample vis-à-vis the opportunity set is given in Figure 1.

From the ordinal scale responses, a value on an interval scale can be obtained for each stimulus for any group of thirty or more respondents. The interval-scale value obtained for each grocery store is called the familiarity score and represents a mean group information level for the store in question. Two familiarity scores were obtained for each stimulus—one measuring the respondents' familiarity with the location of the store, the other indicating the respondents' familiarity with the store characteristics related to the interior of the store. The locations of the category boundaries on the interval scale are also recovered via this scaling technique. To obtain the interval-scale values from the ordinal data, analytical procedures developed by Diederick, Messick, and Tucker [5] were used.

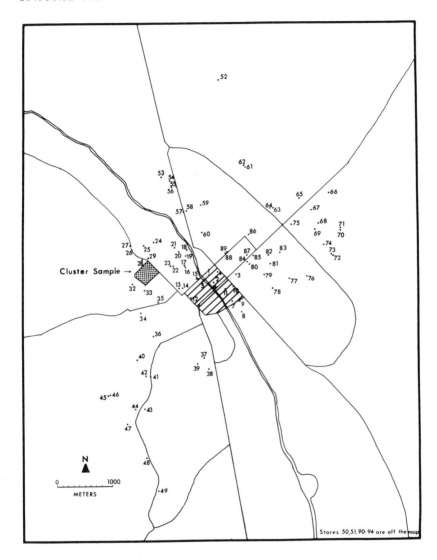

Fɪɢ. 1. Location of cluster sample and grocery stores

The analysis is broken into two parts. The first examines the *extent* of the respondents' familiarity—how many stores are known to each of the respondents and how well each store is known to the sample as a whole. The second part deals with the *spatial variation* in the group's information levels—how familiarity varies with distance and direction from the respondents' place of residence.

EXTENT OF FAMILIARITY

The ordinal data may be used to examine the differences among individuals' extent of familiarity; once the ordinal data has been converted to an interval scale it is not possible to study the variation in cognitive opportunity sets from individual to individual. When the focus is simply on whether or not a store is known, familiarity is taken simply as a dichotomous, rather than a continuous, variable. A response in the first category on the ordinal scale indicates the respondent's total lack of familiarity with the store in question, and responses in categories two through seven mean that the individual has some information, no matter how slight, about the store. Responses in category one are therefore taken to identify unknown stores, and responses in categories two through seven identify known stores.

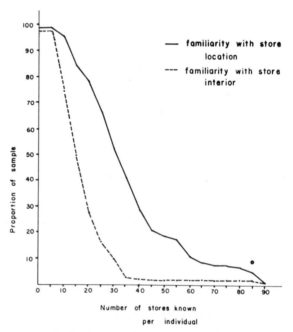

FIG. 2. Number of food stores known per individual

The simplest question concerning the extent of people's familiarity is how many stores do people have some information about? How many stores are in people's cognitive opportunity set? The cumulative graph in Figure 2 shows the proportion of the sample knowing a given number of stores. For instance, 79 percent of the sample respondents have some degree of familiarity with the location of twenty stores, whereas only 22 percent of the sample know about the location of as many as forty-five stores (50 percent of the opportunity set). As expected, people have some *locational* information about more stores than they have *specific* information about; only 19 percent of the sample had some information about the interiors of twenty stores. These data suggest that people's information is far from complete, and that individuals make decisions based on knowledge of only a limited number of available opportunities. Moreover, there does seem to be a noticeable difference in the respondents' knowledge of the locations of stores and their knowledge of the interiors of stores, indicating that people's trips around the city for purposes other than food shopping do make them aware of the locations of stores that they may never have patronized.

To examine how the *intensity* of the respondents' familiarity varies from place to place, an interval scale was recovered from the ordinal data; each store's position on the interval scale reflects the level of information that the group of respondents has about the store. In Figures 3 and 4 the frequency distributions of the scale scores are given for each

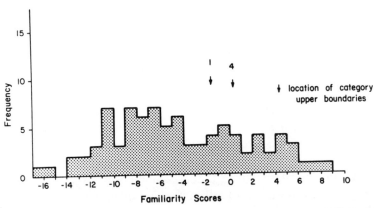

FIG. 3. Frequency distribution of scale scores for familiarity with location of food stores

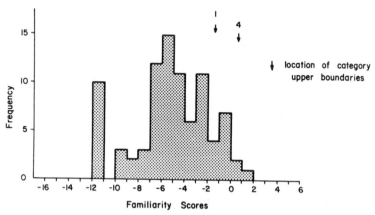

FIG. 4. Frequency distribution of scale scores for familiarity with store interiors

of the two familiarity scales (familiarity with store location and familiarity with store interior).

The distribution of familiarity scores for respondents' locational information is rather flat, spread out and without any distinct mode, indicating that though the locations of many stores were unfamiliar, there were also many store locations that the group knew fairly well. In fact, sixty-one stores fall in category one on the interval scale, and sixteen fall in category seven, implying that while sixty-one stores were very unfamiliar, sixteen store locations were extremely familiar to the group.

The distribution of familiarity scores for specific information is more peaked, and more stores fall toward the lower end of the scale. Seventy-five stores lie in the lowest category, and the interior of *no* store in the city is extremely well known to the group as a whole; that is, no store falls in category seven.

These distributions indicate startlingly low levels of information for the group. It seems evident that individuals cease the search for shopping alternatives long before they have explored a substantial portion of the opportunity set. Since often only limited search is undertaken for grocery stores [7], perhaps one should expect such restricted cognitive opportunity sets. Also, given the large number of food stores in Uppsala, generally low levels of information might be anticipated because, as the number of alternatives increases, the cost of complete search becomes prohibitive, and the consumer tends to concentrate on gathering information on only a few opportunities [1, 12]. Nevertheless, it is surprising that for the group as a whole so few stores are even moderately well known.

SPATIAL VARIATION IN INFORMATION LEVELS

Not only are the information levels of the sample distinctly limited as we have seen above, but they are also likely to be spatially biased. Since search usually begins at, and remains centered upon, the home place and is costly in time and effort, we might expect a residence-centered distance bias in information levels, whereby stores located close to home are better known than the more distant stores. There is also reason to believe that large stores will be better known than smaller ones [3].

These two independent variables—distance and store size—are expected to contribute the most to an explanation of the spatial form of the group's information levels. Figures 5 and 6 plot the distribution of the familiarity scores against distance; both graphs suggest a decline in familiarity with distance. Figures 7 and 8 graph the familiarity scores

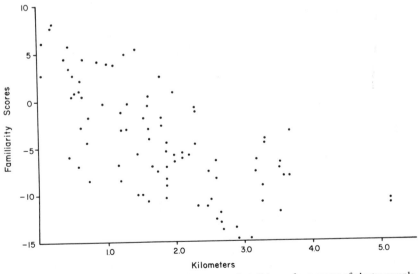

FIG. 5. Familiarity with location of grocery stores against distance from center of cluster-sample area

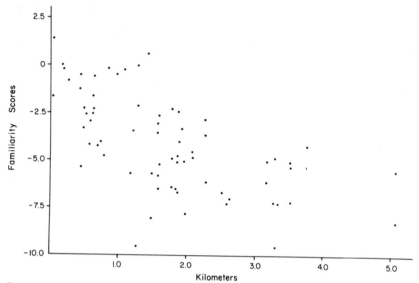

FIG. 6. Familiarity with interior of grocery stores against distance from center of cluster sample area

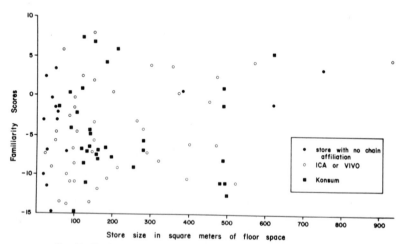

FIG. 7. Familiarity with location of grocery stores against store size

against store size; a positive but much weaker relationship seems to exist between the scale scores and store size. Figures 7 and 8 include the chain affiliation of the stores and indicate that there does not appear to be any

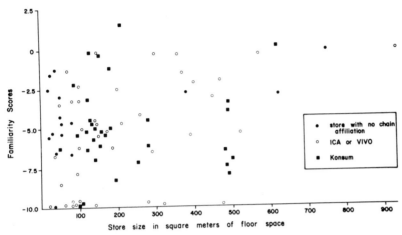

FIG. 8. Familiarity with interior of grocery stores against store size

relationship between the scale scores and chain affiliation of the food stores; subsequent statistical analysis confirmed this lack of relationship.

To examine the relative importance of distance and store size to familiarity, the data were fitted to the following linear regression model:

$$\hat{F}_i = a + bD_i + cS_i + \varepsilon$$

where

$\hat{F}_i$ = estimated group familiarity with ith store

D_i = distance in kilometers of the ith store from the center of the cluster

S_i = size of the ith store in square meters of floor space

a, b, c = constants

ε = error term

The model was applied to each of the two kinds of familiarity scores corresponding to locational information and specific information. The results of fitting the data to this model via standard stepwise regression

TABLE 1

RESULTS OF REGRESSION OF FAMILIARITY SCORES

DEPENDENT VARIABLE	COEFFICIENTS				
	INTERCEPT	DISTANCE TO STORE	STORE SIZE	CHAIN	R^2 VALUE
Familiarity with store location	2.12	−3.53 (.438)*			.43
	.12	−3.85 (.39)	.01 (.002)	.57	
Familiarity with store interior	−2.17	−1.61 (.26)			.31
	−3.28	−1.79 (.24)	.007 (.001)		.46

*Numbers in parentheses are standard errors of the regression coefficients.

techniques show the expected negative relationship of familiarity with distance and the expected positive relationship with size (see Table 1).

The R^2 values indicate that although distance and size influence both kinds of familiarity, the impact of distance is greater than that of store size. More interesting is the evidence that distance is a better predictor of locational information than of specific information. It is suggested that this reflects the large number of stores with extremely low scores for familiarity with interiors at all distances of more than one kilometer from the cluster. The other point of interest indicated by these regressions is that store size bears the same relationship to both kinds of familiarity; size seems to have the same impact on people's familiarity with store location as on their familiarity with store interiors.

A major problem with the regression equations is that, since each scale is derived from a conceptually different underlying psychological continuum, the two interval scales (familiarity with store location and familiarity with store interior) may not be directly compared, nor can the two regression lines be plotted on any one scale for comparison of how the two types of familiarity may decay differentially with distance. In order to compare the distance-decay rates of the two types of familiarity, a different approach had to be taken: the proportion of the total opportunity set known at each distance was calculated. A store is considered to be "known" if its scale score falls above the upper limit of the first category boundary, as in Figures 3 and 4.

The proportion of opportunities known by the group at each distance is given in Figures 9 and 10. It is evident that locational information does

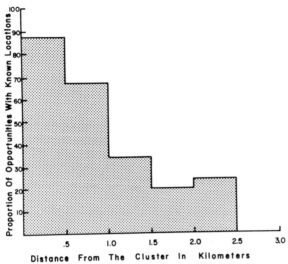

FIG. 9. Proportion of the opportunity set with known locations at each distance from cluster sample

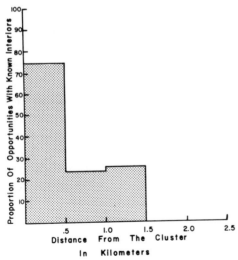

FIG. 10. Proportion of the opportunity set with known interiors at each distance from cluster sample

not decay as rapidly with distance as specific information does. The
locations of a greater proportion of opportunities are familiar to the

group at a given distance than are the insides of stores. Beyond two and a half kilometers, locational information drops to zero, and the group's specific information about food stores is virtually nonexistent beyond one and a half kilometers from the cluster.

The residuals from the regressions were mapped to see if any spatial patterning in familiarity could be observed when distance and store size were held constant. The pattern of positive residuals confirmed expectations that familiarity will generally be highest in the area between the cluster and the CBD, in the CBD itself, and in other areas with a high level of retail activity. This directional bias in the familiarity levels was investigated next.

Higher levels of familiarity might be expected in the direction of the CBD (that is, between the location of the sample and the CBD) for several reasons. First, and most simply, the measurement technique used to assess familiarity levels will automatically register zero familiarity for any area where grocery stores are lacking. Moore [9] has shown that for residents living any distance from the CBD, the majority of the opportunities for person-to-person contact lie in the direction of the CBD if a circular normal distribution of the city's population is assumed. A similar situation obtains with respect to grocery opportunities for the cluster-sample respondents in Uppsala. Few food stores are located west, northwest, or southwest of the cluster; most lie to the east, in the direction of the CBD.

A second reason for expecting higher familiarity levels in the direction of the CBD and in the CBD is also related to the distribution of the stores. Rogers [11] and Bowlby [2] have suggested that when the effect of distance from the residence is removed, stores that are spaced closely together (in high density commercial areas) should be better known than those that are more widely spaced in low density commercial areas. They reason that where the density of stores is high, search will be encouraged since the effort involved in going from store i to store j in a cluster of stores is less than when the stores are spaced farther apart. Following this line of reasoning, one might expect to find high levels of information, again where the effect of distance from the residence is controlled, for those stores located in areas with high levels of retail activity such as the CBD. Furthermore, if trips to the CBD, either for purposes of work, entertainment, or general shopping are made frequently, each opportunity in the CBD may be visited more often than stores lying away from the CBD. We would expect this kind of behavior to build high levels of familiarity with store interiors as well as with store locations. Finally, if people make frequent trips to the CBD, we might expect stores located between the cluster and the CBD to be passed by often and therefore to have higher scale scores than stores located in other sectors of the city.

A seemingly reasonable method for testing the hypothesis of directional bias would be to compare the regression equations of (1) familiarity as it varies with distance in the CBD-oriented sector with (2) familiarity as it varies with distance in all other sectors. One would expect the two equations to have different coefficients. However, because of the spatial distribution of Uppsala food stores vis-à-vis the location of the cluster sample and the CBD, the group's familiarity with these stores would have to be compared with their familiarity with five stores at similar distances from the cluster but not located toward the CBD.

Since regression techniques may not be used for comparing such small samples, an alternative method, similar to an approach taken by Moore and Brown, was used [10]. This approach involves placing a grid over the study area, defining x- and y-axes, and then calculating marginal frequency distributions with respect to each of the axes. The grid is placed in such a way that the location of the cluster sample and the CBD lie on a straight line, parallel to the x-axis (see Figure 11).

To obtain the marginals for familiarity, first the mean of the familiarity scores for the stores in each cell are calculated for each of the two types of information considered; these means are then summed for each row (marginal distribution with respect to y) and each column (marginal distribution with respect to x). For familiarity scores, the marginal frequency distributions with respect to the y-axis are expected to form a normal distribution centered on the cluster-sample location. But since higher levels of information are expected in the CBD and in the corridor connecting the cluster with the CBD, the distributions with respect to the x-axis are expected to be skewed, with higher levels of familiarity occurring toward the CBD. Marginal frequency distributions are calculated for grocery stores as well as for familiarity scores since information levels are expected to be related to the distribution of opportunities.

From Figures 12 and 13, which give the marginal frequency distribu-

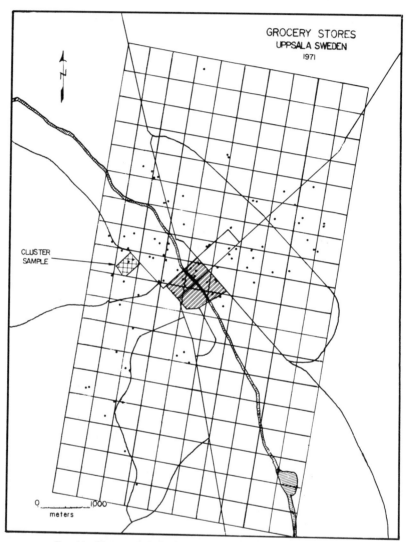

Fig. 11. Placement of grid for calculation of cell counts and marginals

tions for grocery stores in the city, it is evident how uneven is distribution of grocery stores in Uppsala. In Figures 14 and 15 the marginal distributions for familiarity with the location of stores are given; Figures 16 and 17 show the marginal distributions for the respondents' familiarity with store interiors.

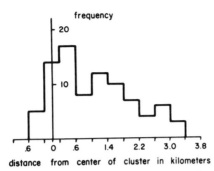

FIG. 12. Marginal frequency distribution with respect to *x* for grocery stores

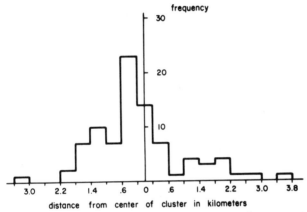

FIG. 13. Marginal frequency distribution with respect to *y* for grocery stores

When marginals for familiarity are compared with the store distributions, a striking similarity between the distributions is evident (compare Figures 12, 14, and 16; 13, 15, and 17). Familiarity levels are closely tied to the distribution of stores. There are several additional points of interest, however. The distributions with respect to the *x*-axis show high levels of familiarity near the location of the cluster sample. The familiarity scores are also skewed in the direction of the CBD, which is located in the interval 1.4 to 1.8 kilometers from the cluster sample; familiarity with store location is particularly high in the interval that includes the CBD. Both the distance-biased component and the direction-biased component are observable in the marginals with respect to the *x*-axis. The evidence in Figures 12, 14, and 16 would seem to indicate the effect

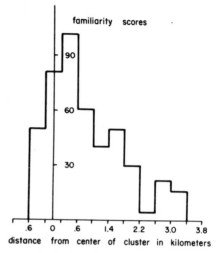

FIG. 14. Marginal frequency distribution with respect to x for familiarity with the location of grocery stores

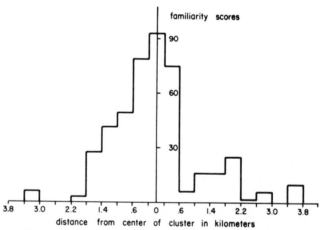

FIG. 15. Marginal frequency distribution with respect to y for familiarity with location of grocery stores

of high store density on raising the consumers' cognitive levels, with stores in areas such as the CBD enjoying greater familiarity than would be expected on the basis of a simple distance decay in information levels.

The distributions with respect to the y-axis show extremely high

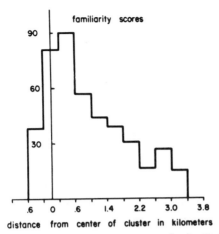

FIG. 16. Marginal frequency distribution with respect to x for familiarity with grocery store interiors

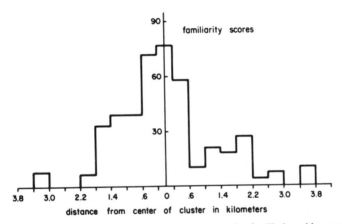

FIG. 17. Marginal frequency distribution with respect to y for familiarity with grocery store interiors

familiarity levels in the immediate vicinity of the respondents. Since this interval contains the location of the CBD as well as the location of the cluster sample, this peak in information levels is a composite of (1) the high familiarity associated with stores in the neighborhood of the residence and (2) the high familiarity associated with stores in the CBD. The marginals taken with respect to the y-axis do not separate these two components to be observed separately.

CONCLUSION

When the spatial variation in consumers' cognitive levels is examined, it is clear that consumers make shopping decisions on the basis of incomplete information about shopping alternatives, and this information is unevenly distributed over urban space. Familiarity does decline with increasing distance from the residence, but this decline is not symmetrical about the home place. The distribution of stores is shown to have a marked effect on information levels, with stores in areas of high store density (such as the CBD) enjoying greater levels of familiarity than would be expected on the basis of a simple distance decay in information levels.

The scaling method used here for estimating people's information levels has proven to be an effective way of determining the cognitive levels of a group of respondents. Furthermore, elsewhere the study design has been found to be applicable to a randomly located sample of respondents as well as to a spatially clustered sample [6]. An extension of this research that is currently under way involves incorporating the characteristics of the respondents so that cognitive levels are explained not only in terms of the spatial relationship of the subject to the stimuli, but also in terms of the socioeconomic characteristics of the subject. The question is whether different social groups exhibit different levels of information about the urban environment.

Perhaps the most interesting extension of the research reported here is to explore the relationship between individual's cognitive levels and their choice of travel destinations. That is, what is the relationship between people's limited information and their spatial behavior? This question has been examined elsewhere [6], and it is evident that an understanding of consumer's information levels is a necessary first step in understanding consumer choice behavior; it is also necessary, however, to incorporate notions regarding the quality as well as the quantity of information possessed and notions of individuals' preference functions.

ACKNOWLEDGEMENTS

This research was conducted while the author was supported by a National Science Foundation Dissertation Fellowship, and the data collection was supported in part by Grant No. GS-27721 from the National Science Foundation. My thanks to Jack Vitek for drawing the figures and to Duane

Marble and Perry Hanson for their help in Evanston, Uppsala and Buffalo. Sophia Bowlby, too, was a valuable collaborator at many stages of this study.

LITERATURE CITED

1. Anderson, L., J. Taylor, and R. Holloway. "The Consumer and His Alternatives: An Experimental Approach." *Journal of Marketing Research,* 3 (1966), 62–67.
2. Bowlby, S. R. "Spatial Variation in Consumers' Information Levels." Ph.D. dissertation, Department of Geography, Northwestern University, 1972.
3. Bucklin, L. "The Concept of Mass in Intra-urban Shopping." *Journal of Marketing,* 31 (1967), 37–42.
4. Burnett, P. "The Dimensions of Alternatives in Spatial Choice Processes." *Geographical Analysis,* 5 (1973), 181–204.
5. Diederick, G., S. Messick, and L. Tucker. "A General Least Squares Solution for Successive Intervals." *Psychometrika,* 22 (1955), 159–73.
6. Hanson, S. "Information Levels and the Intraurban Travel Patterns of Swedish Households." Ph.D. dissertation, Department of Geography, Northwestern University, 1973.
7. Katona, G. "Rational Behavior and Economic Behavior." *Psychological Review,* 60 (1953), 307–18.
8. Maruyama, M. "The Second Cybernetics: Deviation Amplifying Mutual Causal Processes." In *Modern Systems Research for the Behavioral Scientist,* ed. W. Buckely. Chicago: Aldine, 1968.
9. Moore, E. "Some Spatial Properties of Urban Contact Fields." *Geographical Analysis,* 2 (1970), 376–86.
10. Moore, E., and L. A. Brown. "Urban Acquaintance Fields: An Evaluation of a Spatial Model." *Environment and Planning,* 2 (1970), 443–54.
11. Rogers, D. S. "The Role of Search and Learning in Consumer Space Behavior: The Case of Urban In-migrants." Master's thesis, Department of Geography, University of Wisconsin, 1970.
12. Schneider, C. "Transportation and Individual Spatial Search in the Urban Environment." Ph.D. dissertation, Department of Geography, Northwestern University, 1972.
13. Thurstone, L. L. "Psychological Analysis." *American Journal of Psychology,* 38 (1927), 368–89.
14. Torgerson, W. S. *Theory and Methods of Scaling.* New York: John Wiley and Sons, 1958.

CHAPTER 10

MICHAEL F. GOODCHILD

Perception, Preference, and Geometry
A Commentary

One significant side effect of recent work on spatial preferences using the techniques of multidimensional scaling has been an upsurge of interest in geometry. Such terms as *metric* and *non-Euclidean* take on new significance, and questions that could once be dismissed as irrelevantly abstract have a new substantive base. In the last decade or so, geometrical discussion in geography as been dominated by Tobler's work of the early sixties [10], with a recent contribution by Angel and others [1]. Much of that work took the form of proofs of existence. It is, for example, possible to stretch and distort a map of population in such a way as to produce a new map of uniform population density. But though one can prove that such a possibility exists, it is clearly quite another matter to actually produce the distortion. The tools of calculus are limited to those cases where densities can be described by simple algebraic functions, which is to all intents and purposes never (although see [6]). Examples such as Harris's map [7] showing the United States distorted to give a uniform density of retail trade or Getis's work [4] on Tacoma have been constructed by rather lengthy trial and error, by fitting together pieces with known area but variable shape so as to preserve the contiguity and conformality of the real world.

The conceptual break between these early, rather laborious attempts and the facility with which Golledge and others are able to construct distorted maps of their subjects' mental knowledge of their city lies in the dichotomy between a continuous and a discrete view of space. Their problem is manageable because they attempt to fix the locations of a finite number of points from knowledge of the interpoint distances, and interpolate the rest of the space around them with grid lines, rather than seek a continuous transformation of the whole space. In a similar way, Rushton [9] has been able to produce maps of trade areas on nonuniform population density surfaces by calculating the appropriate distances between sellers and then using these to recover the seller locations and thence the trade area boundaries. There is a striking similarity here with location theory, where the classical approach based on continuously distributed demand has received a corresponding impetus by exploiting the potential of location/allocation models of discretely distributed demand. Here, too, the elegance of calculus has been replaced by practical, algorithmic methods.

Multidimensional scaling, in both its metric and nonmetric forms, clearly provides the key to the practical construction of spaces by locating points given distances between them or rankings of those distances. At the same time, it raises a host of questions about the nature of geometries and abstract spaces [3], if we take anything more than Kant's purely classificatory view of space.

It is usual to think of the locations of points in space as real and the distances between them as something more related to convention. In the experiments of Golledge and others on space as perceived, reality is reversed. Although the distances have undoubted empirical worth, the existence of a corresponding space can only be hypothesized. The space might be regarded more as a model; the locations of points, coupled with an agreed upon means of measuring distance between them, can be used to regenerate distances at will. The model is useful, for the representation of n points in a space of m dimensions requires a mere mn pieces of information, whereas the number of pairwise distances will be much greater at $n(n-1)/2$.

Viewed as a model, however, it is by no means clear that the space need exist. In fact, to hypothesize its existence requires some rather strong assumptions about the perception of distance. First, there is the question of the metric. Nonmetric MDS programs allow some choice in the way distance is measured between points in reconstructing a space. Often the choice lies in a control over the R parameter in Minkowski's generalized metric. But suppose that the perception of distance corresponds to a hyperbolic, or Lobachevskian, geometry as Roberts and Suppes suggest [8]. It would be impossible to structure such a space with a Minkowski metric; or, stated another way, attempting to do so would create a certain residual stress due only to the mischoice of metric. The problem is directly analogous to standard geographical projections, which can be seen as forcing a Riemannian two-space into a Euclidean metric, the inevitable distortion corresponding to stress.

There would appear to be a considerable empirical evidence to support the notion that the relationship between perceived and physical distance is not linear. In experiments like this, where distances are measured between many dispersed origins and destinations, it is inevitable that the most appropriate geometry will be non-Euclidean. There is some interesting work to be done here in modifying MDS routines to select both best-fit locations and the best-fit metric, chosen from some geographically interpretable set.

Besides the metric itself, reality allows considerable choice in the path over which distance is measured. MDS routines, on the other hand, will assume that distance is measured by some prescribed path, usually straight. If this assumption is untrue, the deviation will appear as a contribution to the overall stress.

We have identified two sources of the inherent stress that will be encountered in attempting to recover perceived spaces, the first due to an inappropriate choice of metric and the second to differences between actual paths and the model's assumed straight lines. A third, perhaps more important, lies in the error introduced by the subject. Consider the pair of distances AB and CD, and suppose that in reality AB is greater than CD. Within the experimental design used by Golledge and others, it is quite conceivable that a subject would either give equal scores to AB and CD or even reverse the ordering. The likelihood of either occurring is presumably a function of the relative magnitudes of AB and CD, of the subject himself, and perhaps also of the magnitudes of all the other distances in the task set.

The consequences of statistical error in the initial data can be considered in two ways. First, if one admits that such error exists, then one ought to be able to establish confidence limits for the points in the final recovered space. Unfortunately there appears to be no general principle by which one can relate probabilistic models of the original choice data to probabilistic models of point location. Ideally, there would be statistical models of standard error, distribution, and so on, but it appears that MDS is rather like factor analysis in this respect; statistically speaking, it is not particularly tractable or well behaved.

An alternative statement of the problem might be as follows. Nonmetric MDS is formulated for the perfect case, requiring the recovery of a set of point locations such that the interpoint distances are in a prescribed order. Should such a set of locations not be recoverable in a given number of dimensions, then we require the routine to find that set which results in the minimum amount of disordering, measured by a stress value.

Suppose that such a case has arisen by a small, probabilistic disordering of a perfectly scalable set of distances. In recovering a space with minimum stress, it by no means follows that we recover a set of point locations minimally displaced from the optimum set. It is not clear whether the effect will be to displace each point or to concentrate the displacement on one or two points. Since the perfect set of locations is in any case unknown and hypothetical, it may well be that the recovered set of locations is a distortion of some quite different perfect set.

In short, the data supplied to an MDS analysis are invariably subject to statistical error, yet very little is known about the effect of such error on the analysis. It would be useful if studies such as this and Rushton's were to examine the effect of probabilistic distortion of the raw data on the recovered space, so as to gain some impression of the standard errors of the results, if only by crude simulation.

In such an analysis, with considerable residual stress, there is some ambiguity in the final recovered space. Locations depend to a large extent on the precise MDS method used, starting values, and so on. Although quite small movements in point locations would alter the ordering of distances, quite extensive rearrangements would be possible without appreciably increasing stress. For these reasons, it would seem useful to be able to recover that set of locations which represents the minimum distortion from some hypothesized set, rather than that set with minimum stress per se. One approach would be to use the true locations as a starting point for MDS iterations.

Similar problems arise in measuring goodness of fit between recovered and true point locations. With stress present, there is also no guarantee that there is not some other set of recovered locations with the same stress but with a better fit. Using the true locations as the starting points would improve the guarantee. But a more direct measure would compare the perceived distances with the true rank ordering by a rank correlation coefficient.

There are several other points on which one might argue that a test of distances is more direct than a test of a recovered space. The first two of Golledge and others' four general comments on the observed space distortion concern distances rather than locations. But a more fundamental point is raised here. Hart and Moore are quoted as defining spatial cognition as "the internalized reflection and reconstruction of space in thought." To return to a point made earlier in these comments, it is the distances that are revealed in dealing with problems of space perception, both in action and in response to interview. The space can only be inferred as a model for those distances in the mind of the individual. We have discussed some of the problems of metric and statistical uncertainty if such a model is hypothesized. The major problem that this kind of research must tackle concerns the relative importance of distances and associated models, both in their respective roles in spatial cognition and as tools for the analyst.

Rushton, Hanson, Knight, and Menchik are all concerned with conjoint analysis, with the identification of the basic dimensions of choice, and with the way in which those dimensions are combined in a preference function. The difficulty in this kind of analysis lies in the infinite variety of possible functions and possible weighting schemes. Once a function has been identified, it is possible to identify weights either deterministically or by some least-squares fit, as Rushton shows; but this leaves the choice of function largely to chance, as many alternatives seem intuitively acceptable. One might place the Rushton and Knight and Menchik studies together as having a highly identified model (Rushton additive, and Knight and Menchik multiplicative) and thus distinguish them from the rather lower identification in the Hanson study.

Young [11] presents a taxonomy of combinatorial rules, many of them special cases of a polynomial conjoint model. He presents the basis of algorithms for polynomial conjoint analysis, in which the stimuli are scaled into a space defined by the basic dimensions. By an appropriate choice of metric, it would be possible to arrange that the "distances" between points be in the same order as the differences in preferences between corresponding pairs of stimuli. Such algorithms would in effect be the answer to the problems of interpreting dimensions noted by Golledge and Rushton [5, pp. 25–26] and by Burnett [2] in scaling preferences by MDS.

The wide range of intuitively reasonable conjoint models argues for a rather different approach to analysis. Algorithms working in batch mode, out of any control of the user, are rather cumbersome in an area where a loose trial-and-error format is desirable. In addition, we are concerned with the identification of algebraic combinations of interval data, to explain essentially ordinal observations, so that an infinite selection of weights and functions is capable of fully explaining a given set of data, even if the size of that set tends to infinity. A great deal is to be gained by proceeding interactively, in a medium in which the researcher can to some extent control the choice of functions and weights, thereby retaining the work of decision-making, but leaving the heavy computational effort to the machine. A modest example is discussed below to illustrate such a methodology.

Consider a set of stimuli, each with two attributes, A and C, and associated utility values $U(A,C)$. With little loss of generality we can define U as

$$\sum_{i=0}^{\infty} \sum_{j=0}^{\infty} a_{ij} A^i C^j$$

and regard the problem of conjoint analysis as that of finding the coefficients a_{ij} (a_{00} can be ignored, since any test will involve an ordering of U values only). Now suppose that a set of paired comparisons of stimuli is available. Any pair will be correctly predicted if the relative U values, given a set of a_{ij}'s, are in the same order as the revealed preferences. So the problem resolves to finding a set of a_{ij}'s such that all paired comparisons are correctly predicted.

If enough polynomial terms are included, it is possible to derive a utility function wholly consistent with any finite set of choice pairs and perfect as a predictive device. But such a function would be excessively complex and specific to the data set, and therefore unacceptable. The parsimony principle is conveniently expressed by limiting the terms in the expansion of U:

$$U = \sum_{i=0}^{MA} \sum_{j=0}^{MC} a_{ij} A^i C^j$$

where MA and MC are the highest exponentiation of A and C respectively.

Each choice pair in which stimulus 1 is preferred to stimulus 2 can be written

$$\sum_{i=0}^{MA} \sum_{j=0}^{MC} a_{ij} A_1^i C_1^j > \sum_{i=0}^{MA} \sum_{j=0}^{MC} a_{ij} A_2^i C_2^j.$$

Reducing i and j to a single subscript and writing

$$A_1^i C_1^j - A_2^i C_2^j = T_{12}^{ij} = T_{12k}, \qquad a_{ij} = a_k,$$

we have

$$\sum_{k=1}^{n} a_k T_{12k} > 0 \tag{1}$$

where

$$n = (MA+1)(MC+1) - 1.$$

The problem reduces to finding the vector of a_k's such that the maximum number of these inequalities is satisfied, given a matrix of T values from empirical observations.

The problem can be viewed as one of optimization, in which the objective is to maximize the number of correctly predicted choice pairs. A dialogue between investigator and computer, in an interactive system, combining the human's power of intelligent selection of functional forms with the rapid computation of the machine provides a feasible form of solution. In the technique described here, the T values are computed first and held on disk. Coefficient values are then examined in turn. Consider the ith term a_i. Equation (1) may be rewritten

$$a_i > - \frac{\sum_{k \neq i} a_k \, T_{12k}}{T_{12i}} \quad \text{for} \quad T_{12i} > 0;$$

$$a_i < \frac{\sum_{k \neq i} a_k \, T_{12k}}{T_{12i}} \quad \text{for} \quad T_{12i} < 0.$$

As each term is considered, the value of

$$L_{12i} = - \sum_{k \neq i} a_k \, T_{12k} \, / \, T_{12i}$$

is computed for each choice pair and stored in core, together with the sign of T_{12i}. The investigator then suggests various values for a_i, and these are examined by the system, which reports a tabulation of the numbers of choice pairs satisfied, that is, for which $(a_i - L_{12i}) \, T_{12i} > 0$. Once an optimum value has been determined for a_i, the investigator moves to the next coefficient a_j, retaining the new value for a_i. Commands allow a specific a_i to adopt values that are automatically incremented between given limits by a given step size.

The objective function has local minima, so that examination of coefficients in a different sequence will give different end results. But since the data are qualitative, it is clear that a wide range of utility functions can give essentially similar predictions. Although the sequence of examination of coefficients affects their final values, it has very little effect on the degree of prediction achieved.

The system has been tested on spatial behavior data. A consumer patronizing a certain grocery story out of the NS available to him is assumed to have rejected all other $(NS - 1)$ stores in the system, and thus to have implied $NS - 1$ pair comparisons. Observation of the behavior of NC customers will thus generate $NC(NS - 1)$ pair comparisons. Following Rushton and others, the A and C attributes are identified as the attraction of the store (measured in this case in floor area) and the inverse of distance between customer and store (see for example [5, pp. 61–71]).

Because of core restrictions, only 7,440 choice pairs have been analyzed, from data on 120 customers and their choices among sixty-three stores. Fairly simple utility functions can be found, involving up to ten terms, that are in agreement with nearly all of these choice pairs.

After a series of trials, the following function was chosen as achieving a high agreement with the data, while involving only five terms:

$$U = C + 0.0085A + 2.0AC + 0.00001A^2 + 0.06A^2C.$$

It is in agreement with 93.19 percent of the 7,440 pairs. Further terms, such as AC^2, A^2C^2, and A^3, do not appreciably improve on the objective.

One incidental advantage of the formulation of the utility function in polynomial terms is that it is possible to test the additivity of the model, the degree to which utility is a simple addition of part utilities of attraction and distance. Additivity is expressed in the polynomial expression by the disappearance of all terms combining A and C, $a_{ij} = 0$ unless $i = 0$ or $j = 0$.

The predictive power of additive terms alone is almost as great as that of general terms. The five-term additive expression

$$U = 1.0A - 0.05A^2 - 0.105A^3 + 151C - 2910C^2$$

is in agreement with 93.09 percent of the choice pairs.

A useful test of the procedure is the degree to which a known utility function can be recovered from artificially generated consumer behavior. An assistant was asked to select a function and generate a set of data consistent with it. The interactive analysis was then used to recover a utility function in ignorance of the original, and the two were then compared. There is little difficulty in recovering a function completely in agreement with the data in a few minutes: the function recovered is not the same as the original, but generally is in a monotonic relationship to it.

In summary, the four papers point to a variety of interesting areas for further research. Golledge and others' paper suggests a deeper examination of the geometrical underpinnings of perceived space. With Rushton's, it also prompts a greater concern for the performance of MDS under statistical perturbation of the basic data. Finally, the three papers on the dimensions of choice suggest a need for greater flexibility in the methods used to identify and fit conjoint models. Perhaps if all of these problems have a common theme it is that methods adopted from the techniques of psychological measurement now require significant extension if they are to serve adequately the needs of spatial analysis in the future.

LITERATURE CITED

1. Angel, S., and G. M. Hyman. "Transformations and Geographic Theory." *Geographical Analysis,* 4 (1972), 350–67.

2. Burnett, P. "The Dimensions of Alternatives in Spatial Choice Processes," *Geographical Analysis,* 5 (1973), 181–204.

3. Degerman, R. L. "The Geometric Representation of some Simple Structures," in Shepard, R. N., A. K. Romney and S. B. Nerlove, *Multidimensional Scaling: Theory and Applications in the Behavioral Sciences.* New York: Seminar Press, 1972, 194–212.

4. Getis, A. "The Determination of the Location of Retail Activities with the Use of a Map Transformation." *Economic Geography,* 39 (1963), 14–22.

5. Golledge, R. G., and G. Rushton. *Multidimensional Scaling: Review and Geographical Applications.* Technical Paper No. 10, Commission on College Geography, Association of American Geographers, Washington, D.C., 1972.

6. Hägerstrand, T. *Innovationsforloppet ur korologisk synpunkt.* Lund: G. W. K. Gleerup, 1953.

7. Harris, C. D. "The Market as a Factor in the Localization of Industry in the United States." *Annals, Association of American Geographers,* 44 (1954), 315–48.

8. Roberts, F. S., and P. Suppes. "Some Problems in the Geometry of Visual Perception." *Synthese,* 17 (1967), 173–201.

9. Rushton, G. "Map Transformation of Point Patterns: Central Place Patterns in Areas of Variable Population Density." *Papers and Proceedings, Regional Science Association,* 28 (1972), 111–32.

10. Tobler, W. R. "Geographic Area and Map Projections." *Geographical Review,* 53 (1963), 59–78.

11. Young, F. W. "A Model for Polynomial Conjoint Analysis Algorithms." In *Multidimensional Scaling: Theory and Applications in the Behavioral Sciences,* ed. R. N. Shepard et al., pp. 69–104. New York: Seminar Press, 1972.

PART III
Specific Problems and Applications

CHAPTER 11

STANLEY R. LIEBER

A Comparison of Metric and Nonmetric Scaling Models in Preference Research

INTRODUCTION

One of the goals of scientific investigation may be considered to be the decomposition of complex phenomena into sets of basic factors according to some specified rules of combination. In perception research, the basic conceptualization of geographical phenomena (spatial opportunities) has been one in which the spatial stimuli are assumed to be extremely complex. The research strategy then followed is one of data reduction in that complex phenomena are factored into their basic components [5, 8, 10, 7]. Multidimensional scaling models, both metric and nonmetric, have been used in geographic research because of their ability to uncover the essential dimensions and structure of the relationships among stimuli. The models have, in addition, been used to scale the stimuli given only the subjective judgments of individuals about the stimuli. Nonmetric scaling models have grown in their popularity as a scaling tool because of their ability to recover metric scale values on the dimensions of the stimuli from information that is only ordinal in nature.

Briggs and Demko [4] have pointed out that attention needs to be paid not only to scaling the stimuli but also to the form of the scaling model used in scaling the stimuli. Indeed, if the form of the scaling model is inappropriate, then the resulting scale values for the stimuli as well as the interpretation of the dimensions of the stimuli may be meaningless. The purpose of this paper is to compare two methods, one metric and one nonmetric, in terms of their ability to scale stimuli and to find the form of the function (behavioral rule) that best relates the levels of the attributes possessed by spatial stimuli to the overall judgment response of an individual for particular spatial stimuli. To this end, this paper departs from past research in space preference modeling in that the functional form of the space preference function is a central issue.

The first method, functional measurement [2], provides simple techniques for determining the functional form operating on the attributes of stimuli while simultaneously scaling the attribute and response dimensions. However, it is limited in its applicability by assumptions that require a continuous response capability of the individual decision-maker; assumptions that require laboratory-type controls. The second method, polynomial conjoint measurement [20], is less restrictive in terms of the response capability of the individual decision-maker in that only ordinal responses are required. Polynomial conjoint measurement is, therefore, less restrictive in terms of the situation in which responses are made, but these models have problems related to their ability to distinguish between scaling model forms without prior knowledge of the form of the model. These two scaling models complement each other in that the weakness of one model is the strength of the other. It is the thesis of this paper that their complementary use, in both controlled laboratory-like situations and uncontrolled survey situations, provides researchers with a valid avenue for studying the organization of consumer preference structures, choice patterns amongst spatial stimuli, and the perceptual tradeoffs amongst the attributes of spatial stimuli.

THE MEASUREMENT PROBLEM

It is often the case that perceived attributes of geographical situations or spatial purchasing opportunities are not physically observable or independently measurable. Sometimes only the joint order of the attributes of spatial stimuli are observable or measurable on a continuum such as likeableness or preference or desirability. This is the basic idea behind Wolpert's [21, p. 161] conception of "place utility" and Rushton's [16, p. 203] notion of preference for "locational types." In such a situation, it would be desirable to reduce the complex phenomena to their basic factors (the attributes of the situations) and simultaneously obtain a measurement of these factors such that the combination of them accounts for the order of the observation. This measurement problem is called the "conjoint measurement problem," and the rule relating the components that make up the observable order of the stimuli is known as the "conjoint measurement model." In psychology this measurement rule is often referred to as a "composition" rule [13,19]. The conjoint measurement model must be some specified series of sums, differences, and products of the factors. Such a rule can be a polynomial function. Before discussing the particular metric and nonmetric approaches to the conjoint measurement problem, the form of the data and its collection procedure will be illustrated.

FACTORIAL DESIGN

Suppose the purchase of gasoline from different service stations in an area is conceived of as a series of alternatives in which the desirability of each purchasing opportunity is a function of two or more attributes of the product and the location of the service station relative to a consumer's home. Further, it is assumed that people discriminate among service stations by the price per gallon of gasoline and the distance of the service station from their home and that consumers perceive no qualitative differences in the various brands of gasoline on the market or in the level of service at the various gas stations. In an experimental context, subjects could be instructed to disregard these factors in their evaluation of purchasing opportunities. Suppose, also, that the choice situation is one in which the decision-maker is at home and is going out solely to purchase gasoline for a trip to be made the next day and that the purchase is to be a cash transaction. The subjects could then be presented with all possible combinations of travel time to the service station and price per gallon of gasoline. These treatment combinations of travel time to a service station and price per gallon of gasoline would be considered by the subjects as purchasing opportunities to be evaluated on a line scale anchored with the phrases "extremely favorable" and "extremely unfavorable." The responses could be coded on a continuous scale with a meter stick or ruler and constitute preferential response data of the single-stimulus type as described by Coombs [6, pp. 21, 28].

The problem is to decompose the subjective favorableness or likeableness responses into subjective scale values for each different travel time to the service station and price per gallon while simultaneously finding the conjoint measurement model that best reproduces the pattern of responses for the spatial purchasing opportunities.

FUNCTIONAL MEASUREMENT

Functional measurement is a numerical rather than axiomatic approach to the study of composition rules in psychology. It attempts to scale the stimulus attributes and response measures simultaneously in order to determine the composition rule that relates the two. Its main features are reliance on factorial design of treatment combinations, quantitative responses, and a rescaling procedure for the responses that are monotonic.

Models of averaging, adding, subtracting, and multiplying information serve as the substantive theory [1, 2, 3]. The general form of the model as a weighted sum is

$$R = \Sigma \, w_i \, s_i + C \tag{1}$$

where s and w are the scale values and weights respectively, C is a bias or scaling term, and R is a theoretical response assumed to be on a continuous numerical scale. The particular operator, in this case addition, occurs over all stimuli. The type of operator indicates the functional form of the information utilization model. By differentially interpreting weight and scale value, the model is applicable to single-stage [17] and multistage [18] decision situations. Consider the factorial design in which rows correspond to the stimuli $P_1, P_2, \ldots$ (prices per gallon of gasoline) and the columns of the design correspond to other stimuli $T_1, T_2, \ldots$ (travel time in minutes from a decision-maker's home to a service station). Equation (1) becomes

$$R_{ij} = w_1 P_i + w_2 T_j \tag{2}$$

where the R_{ij} is the theoretical preference response to some spatial purchasing opportunity which is characterized by some attribute pair (P_i, T_j) which is combined with w_1 and w_2 as the weights of the two attributes. It is assumed that there is no context effect and that the weights (w_1, w_2) are variant over all rows and columns of the factorial design.

Since the equation above implies that the row-by-column interaction is zero and nonsignificant, analysis of variance (ANOVA) can be used to test the fit of the model. If the interaction is nonsignificant, the model is supported and subjective values of the row and column components of the purchasing opportunity can be estimated. Significant interactions occur when the model is violated or the response scale is invalid, possibly because the response measures constitute only an ordinal scale. The approach then calls for the transformation of the response measures to eliminate significant interactions, but this requires some a priori knowledge of the form of the model. Kruskal [9] has developed a suitable computing subroutine for this rescaling of response measures. With the absence of a suitable transformation, the model fails. The opposite is also true—the finding of a suitable transformation implies support for the model.

Functional measurement provides general and simple techniques for testing the additive model and scaling the stimulus variables at the level of the individual decision-maker. When verified, it provides interval scales for the responses and attribute components. More significantly, it treats a wide variety of single-stage and multistage decision tasks. For an example of the use of this technique in geographic research, see [12].

POLYNOMIAL CONJOINT MEASUREMENT

Polynomial conjoint measurement models in psychology may be considered to be analogues of the functional measurement metric procedure. These models take as their paradigm that the ordering of a dependent variable is obtained under different combinations of two or more independent variables. A simple axiomization in terms of the ordinal properties of the joint effect of two or more factors yield an interval-scale measurement of the additive type [13].

Let $T \times P$ be a data matrix M with typical elements $(a, p), (b, g)$, with a, b in T (travel time to service station) and p, g in P (price per gallon of gasoline) where $M(a, p)$ is some ordinal preference or likeableness measure of the (a, p) treatment combination. The matrix is additive if there exists functions f, g, and h defined on T, P, and M such that

$$h(a, p) = f(a) + g(p) \tag{3}$$

$$h(a, p) \geq h(b, g) \text{ iff } M(a, p) \geq M(b, g) \tag{4}$$

A matrix is additive if its cell entries can be rescaled such that their order is preserved and every rescaled entry is expressed as the sum of its row and column components. If such a representation exists, the factors can be regarded as independent in that they contribute independently to produce the joint effect. In testing for a significant interaction, one asks whether a *given* treatment combination response can be decomposed into an additive combination of row and column scales. In polynomial conjoint measurement one asks whether a *given* treatment combination response value can be *monotonically transformed* such that the model (additivity) will be satisfied. Polynomial conjoint measurement models, therefore, *search for order-preserving transformations* while maintaining a data requirement (monotonicity). Besides additive models, polynomial conjoint measurement models can treat averaging, subtracting, and multiplying frameworks. McClelland [14] gives the algebraic proofs for additive, averaging, and multiplying models, and Young [22] discusses the computational problems of this methodology and its relationship to nonmetric multidimensional scaling.

In analyzing preferential response data, this methodology is not as clear-cut as functional measurement in distinguishing between measurement model forms. This point is illustrated in Figures 1 and 2. Both figures portray hypothetical sets of continuous response data for treatment combinations of gasoline prices per gallon and travel times to a service station. The vertical axes represent the likeableness values for the various treatment combinations. The lines of each graph represent constant travel time. The prices per gallon of gasoline are thirty-three, thirty-five, and thirty-seven cents, and the travel times vary from two to seventeen minutes. In an analysis of variance, an additive model would exhibit a characteristic parallelism in the plot of the travel time lines; the lines should differ by a constant since an additive model would have a nonsignificant interaction term. In a multiplying model, the travel time lines should exhibit a converging-diverging pattern since the interaction term of the analysis of variance should be significant and the variables affect each other at all values. In Figure 1, portions B and C represent two possible plots of additive models. Plot A represents a converging-

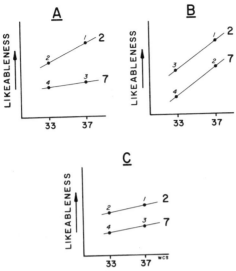

FIG. 1. Plots of hypothetical responses for four treatment combination factorial design

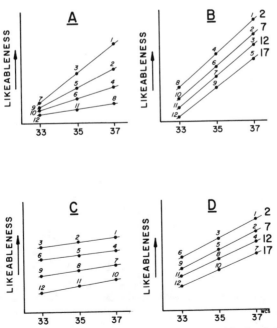

FIG. 2. Plots of hypothetical responses for twelve treatment combination factorial design

diverging pattern of lines and is characteristic of a multiplying model. The points (treatment combinations) are rank ordered according to their preference or likeableness values. Note that plots A and C have different rank orders while plots A and B have the same rank order of points. In Figure 2 none of the additive plots (B, C, D) have the same rank order as the multiplicative plot. Why should one set of plots (Fig. 1) be unable to lead one to distinguish clearly between measurement models while another set of graphical plots (Fig. 2) shows a clear distinction between additive and multiplying formulations? The answer must lie in the relationship between the number of ordinal constraints in the plots relative to the number of points. Obviously, the more points (treatment combinations) in a particular problem, the more ordinal relationships will exist among points. The more ordinal relationships that exist in a particular problem, the harder it becomes to make more than one model give a good fit to the ordinal data. One can see that twelve points put many more ordinal restrictions upon the location of points relative to each other than do four points. And by doing so, the form of the best fitting model becomes more distinct.

Because of the fact that there is some difficulty in distinguishing among forms of the measurement model, a large number of treatment combinations need to be used. One way of getting around the problem is to gather several replications of the data. In the same way that functional measurement uses replications of data to obtain an estimate of error, replications of data for the nonmetric polynomial conjoint measurement models increase and solidify the ordinal structure of the relationships among the treatment combinations of the design.

GOODNESS OF FIT

The test of goodness of fit in functional measurement for a particular model is not the amount of common variance (R^2) between the independent variables and dependent variable but the significance and structure of the residual unexplained variance. In the factorial design, replications of each treatment combination can be gathered from the subjects. Theoretically, from each subject, the response to the same treatment combination should be identical in terms of the subject's response on the line scale mentioned earlier. Thus, for each subject, the replication mean sum of squares can be considered to be an estimate of true error in the data. By utilizing the between-variables mean sum of squares and the replication mean sum of squares, validity of the additive model in analysis of variance can be tested. If the F-value is significant, even though the main effects (travel time to service station and price per gallon) are significant, the additive model is rejected. If the linear-by-linear component of the sum of squares in the polynomial orthogonal breakdown of the sums of squares is very large, a multiplying model is implied [3, p. 180]. After performing a log transform or some other type of nonlinear transformation such as a square root transformation and then reapplying the analysis of variance, the disappearance of significant between-variable interaction terms implies support for a log additive model that is identical to a multiplying model for the original raw data. Taylor [19] discusses the types of transformations that might be applicable to achieve the best approximation to linearity. The row and column marginal means of the factorial design are estimates of the subjective scale values of the components of the spatial purchasing opportunity when the form of the model and the response scale are validated.

Regression coefficients from a fixed effects log additive regression, in which the fixed effects are the marginal means (subjective scale values), can be interpreted as the subjective weights for the individual or the exponents the subject attaches to each variable in a multiplying model.

For the polynomial conjoint measurement model there are two measures of goodness of fit. The first, called "stress," has meaning in terms of the structural relationships among the data [22, pp. 80–83]. When comparing stress values from different measurement models for the same data set, an ordinal comparison of the values indicates which measurement model is most appropriate. In addition to stress values, the coefficient of determination between the raw data responses to treatment combinations and the treatment combination values derived via a *specified* measurement model serves as an adequate measure of a certain model's ability to reconstruct the relationship among the treatment combinations. The higher the coefficient of determination, the more appropriate is the chosen measurement model. This is especially true since some knowledge of the form of the model will have been gathered by way of the functional measurement approach.

DATA

Data were gathered for the full factorial design for the gasoline purchasing situation mentioned earlier. Three gasoline prices per gallon and four travel times to the service station formed the basis of the design. The prices of gasoline were thirty-three, thirty-six, and thirty-nine cents per gallon. The travel times in minutes to the service station were two, seven, twelve, and seventeen. In addition to these twelve treatment combinations of the factorial design, two additional treatment combinations were included in each replication of data. These two additional treatment combinations formed reference points or "fillers" for the presentation of the stimuli [2, p. 157]. The components of these two additional treatment combinations were thirty cents per gallon and less than one minute in travel time and forty-two cents per gallon and twenty-two minutes in travel time. Four replications of responses for each treatment combination were presented to twelve separate subjects, with the first replication being used to acquaint the subjects with the values of the various treatment combinations. Only the last three replications of data were included in the analysis so that no learning bias would enter the response pattern and analysis. To avoid a serialization effect, the treatment combinations were randomized within each replication.

RESULTS

Table 1 portrays the between-variable F-values and the probability of this F-value being due to chance. The probability values indicate that all of the subjects, with the possible exception of one, cannot be best described by a model that is additive or linear in form. In each of the individual's orthogonal components breakdown, a very large proportion of the residual sum of squares was concentrated in the linear-by-linear component. Furthermore, the between-variables F-values were nonsignificant when the raw data were log transformed and reanalyzed by analysis of variance. For all twelve subjects, the log additive model proved most appropriate, thus implying a multiplying formulation rather than an additive or linear one for each individual's raw data. The one subject for which the analysis was inconclusive (subject four) had extreme variation in the response pattern of his data. That is to say that the cell variances fluctuated greatly from cell to cell. This wide fluctua-

TABLE 1

ANALYSIS OF VARIANCE FOR
FACTORIAL DESIGN EXPERIMENT

Subject	Between-Variable F-Value	Probability of F-Value Having Arisen by Chance
1	4.48	.01<
2	20.06	.01<
3	7.63	.01<
4	1.03	NS
5	2.42	.06
6	2.93	.05<
7	1.71	.25
8	1.91	.12
9	4.22	.01<
10	3.14	.05<
11	1.98	.11
12	2.20	.08

tion in the response set makes the analysis of the data set and the derivation of a functional relationship between the variables problematic.

The same data sets of the twelve subjects, after being analyzed and validated in a multiplying format according to the functional-measurement–ANOVA paradigm, were then scaled according to their rank order properties by polynomial conjoint measurement procedures utilizing an algorithm developed by Young [23]. The stress values for all twelve subjects indicated that a multiplying model was most appropriate. The vertical axis in Figure 3 represents the likeableness ratings of the raw data or the rescaled likeableness ratings derived from the polynomial conjoint measurement algorithm. The horizontal axis is travel time to the service station. The combinations are plotted with lines representing constant prices per gallon of gasoline. Table 2 presents the coefficients of determination for each subject between the raw data and the derived additive and multiplicative responses to the price and travel time treatment combinations. It is clear that the multiplying model approximates the structure of the data for each individual more closely than the linear additive model.

Extreme variations in the response sets of subjects four and twelve account for the closeness of fit of both the additive and multiplying models. Additional replications of the data might have eliminated this

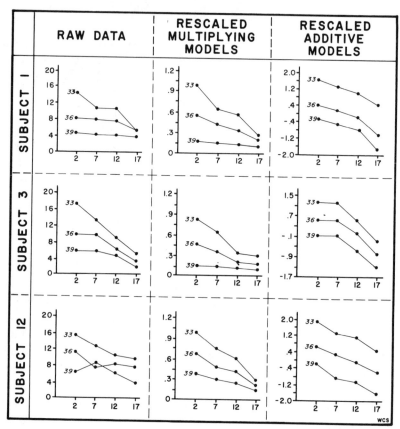

Fig. 3. Plots of three subjects for raw data, rescaled multiplying model, and rescaled additive model

closeness of fit of both models for these two subjects. The polynomial conjoint measurement scaling procedures, nevertheless, consistently scaled the treatment combinations such that over 90 percent of the structure of the response data was recovered from ordinal responses. They also distinguished between the linear additive model and the multiplying model.

Table 3 presents the subjective scale values (marginal means of the factorial design) of the raw data and additive and multiplying configurations for three of the twelve subjects. The comparability of the subjective scale values for the raw data and the two scaling models was

TABLE 2

COEFFICIENTS OF DETERMINATION FOR
RAW DATA AND VARIOUS CONJOINT
MEASUREMENT MODELS

Subject	Multiplying Model	Additive Model
1	.95	.76
2	.89	.74
3	.90	.83
4	.98	.97
5	.92	.88
6	.91	.59
7	.95	.90
8	.92	.76
9	.93	.84
10	.96	.78
11	.91	.86
12	.87	.84
Group Model	.99	.81

achieved by arbitrarily choosing two levels of each variable as the zero and unit references for a scale and interpolating the remaining values with respect to the reference points of the scale. For example, two minutes and seventeen minutes were the levels of the travel time variable that received the most extreme ratings in terms of the marginal means of the factorial design. These values defined a range of ratings, and the endpoints of that range were assigned zero and unit values. The remaining levels of the travel time variable, seven minutes and twelve minutes,

TABLE 3

SCALE VALUES FOR THREE SUBJECTS

	SUBJECT No. 1			SUBJECT No. 10			SUBJECT No. 12		
	RD[a]	ADD[b]	MULT[c]	RD	ADD	MULT	RD	ADD	MULT
Objective travel time in minutes									
2	1.00	1.00	1.00	1.00	1.00	1.00	1.00	1.00	1.00
7	.63	.78	.64	.60	.56	.60	.55	.56	.55
12	.54	.43	.55	.27	.33	.27	.36	.42	.36
17	.00	.00	.00	.00	.00	.00	.00	.00	.00
Objective price per gallon									
33	1.00	1.00	1.00	1.00	1.00	1.00	1.00	1.00	1.00
36	.46	.40	.46	.57	.53	.56	.47	.37	.47
39	.00	.00	.00	.00	.00	.00	.00	.00	.00

[a]RD   =Raw data with fixed zero and unit
[b]ADD   =Rescaled values for additive model with fixed zero and unit
[c]MULT =Rescaled values for multiplying model with fixed zero and unit

had ratings that fell within the range of the extreme values. Their relative distance (in terms of ratings) could be compared to the total range of ratings (the difference in ratings between the extreme values), and they could be interpolated onto a scale with a fixed zero and unit. This simple procedure made the scales standardized for comparative purposes.

In comparing the scale values, the multiplying model's scale values were almost identical with those of the raw data while the additive model's scale values were not. The subjective appraisals of the objective stimuli are not as equally spaced as the objective values themselves, indicating the presence of some kind of perceptual distortion or bias within the individual. It is obvious that the form of the scaling model strongly affects the bias in scale value estimates and that it is not sufficient to assume that a linear model or additive model is valid.

An analysis was also done for all the subjects' data as a group. The design became four (travel time) by three (gasoline price per gallon) by thirty-six (twelve subjects by three replications) replications. The F-value for the analysis of variance for the interaction term of the model was significant beyond the .01 significance level. The linear-by-linear component was very large and indicated a multiplying model for the group data. Additive and multiplicative polynomial conjoint measurement models were fit to the rank order of the data, and the stress values clearly indicated that the appropriate measurement model was a multiplicative one. The coefficient of determination for the raw data and the rescaled additive model was 0.81 (81 percent) while the multiplicative model and raw data had a coefficient of determination slightly above 0.99 (over 99 percent). Again, a nonlinear multiplying model is clearly more appropriate.

Two months after the original data elicitation, five of the original twelve subjects were contacted. They were presented with all the treatment combinations simultaneously and asked to rank order the treatment combinations according to the same kinds of considerations as in the first experiment. No subject's rank order correlation was lower than 0.88. Such high rank order correlations indicate a consistency by subjects in their pattern of trade-offs between the two variables; that is to say, the subjects' preference patterns remained essentially the same despite a two-month time lag and whatever changes might have occurred in their purchasing environment.

DISCUSSION

Three types of error can occur in attempting to describe behavioral choice processes. The first type of error is the error of incorrectly specifying the form of such a model. This type of error can lead to models that vary in functional form and to an inability to make useful predictions. The second type of error is in the estimation and variability of parameters for models that describe behavioral choice processes. Errors in correctly specifying the functional form of the model can lead to errors and spurious variability in estimating model parameters. The third type of error is usually inescapable and it is measurement error. The problem with most gravity and distance formalizations of movement models is that the source of variability in the parameters of such models cannot be pinpointed since they are derived from aggregated data. Olsson [15] has extensively reviewed the literature on distance interaction models, and his criticisms are often related to these three sources of modeling error and the inability of movement research to untangle them. Is the variability in gravity-type movement models due to errors in specifying the form or forms of the individual decision-making model? Is it due to changes in environment or differences in interpersonal perceptions or purchasing opportunities? Or is it measurement error? In this research, the form of the individual preference functions is invariant: a multiplicative form is the best form for the general decision-making rule of the individual subjects. The group model for the same subjects' data has also been shown to be a multiplying model. In order for the group model to be internally consistent with the data from which it was derived, the group model had to be identical in form to the individual preference functions. Any inability of the group model to predict each individual's data would be a function of interpersonal variability in the group model parameter estimates and not an error in specifying the form of the decision-maker's evaluation rule. Therefore, any description of behavioral choice processes must, of necessity, consider the form of the scaling model as critical to the scaling of spatial opportunities and any predictive or policy use that the scaled stimuli might possess.

The data-gathering techniques utilized here have required fairly strict controls, as in any laboratory experiment, in order to obtain metric responses to treatment combinations. In large-scale surveys, these controls are usually absent, and the best that can be hoped for is a consistent rank ordering of the stimuli by the individual subject. It has been shown that both the metric and nonmetric approaches to uncovering the form of the relationships that is operating on the attributes of spatial stimuli were very successful in describing the form of the model and in scaling the levels of the attributes used in the experiment. Even though the follow-up sample was small, some evidence has been given to show that a simple ranking procedure from a questionnaire yielded high rank correlations with the original controlled experimental data. This correspondence occurred despite a two-month time period between responses.

The main purpose of this paper has been to show the importance of utilizing scaling methods that consider the central question of preference function form. These methods also do more than an adequate job in scaling the variables. What has developed out of the comparison of the metric and nonmetric approaches to the functional form and scaling issue might be a complementary research strategy. The first part of such a research project would be to find the function that best describes individual choice patterns among variables that are perceived to be part of a common set of attributes of the stimuli. This could be done through personal interviews and functional measurement scaling procedures. The second part of the research strategy would be to gather rank order responses to the same treatment combinations from a wide variety of individuals. Polynomial conjoint measurement procedures could then be utilized to find out if there is any form variability and its extent. Once this has been done, treatment combinations of real-world spatial stimuli should be chosen and developed in a questionnaire format in order to gather rank response data. Individuals responding to the design could then be grouped, possibly by Q-mode principal components analysis or by some type of cluster or nonmetric grouping procedure. This should insure that group models or a group model would be representative of the data from which it came. Calibration of scale values could then be accomplished based upon the ordinal data requirements of the nonmetric scaling procedures and the previous knowledge of the form of the model determined through functional measurement and polynomial conjoint measurement procedures.

LITERATURE CITED

1. Anderson, N. H., and J. B. Sidowski. "Judgments of City-Occupation Combinations." *Psychonomic Science,* 8 (1967), 279–80.

2. Anderson, N. H. "Functional Measurement and Psychophysical Judgment." *Psychological Review,* 77 (1970), 153–70.

3. ———. "Integration Theory and Attitude Change." *Psychological Review,* 78 (1971), 171–206.

4. Briggs, R., and D. Demko. "A Model of Spatial Choice and Related Operational Considerations." *Proceedings, Association of American Geographers,* 3 (1971), 49–52.

5. Burnett, P. "The Dimensions of Alternatives in Spatial Choice Processes." *Geographical Analysis,* 5 (1973), 181–204.

6. Coombs, C. H. *A Theory of Data.* New York: John Wiley and Sons, 1964.

7. Golledge, R. G., and G. Rushton. *Multidimensional Scaling: Review and Geographical Applications.* Technical Paper No. 10, Commision on College Geography, Association of American Geographers, Washington D.C., 1972.

8. Gould, P. R. "On Mental Maps." Discussion Paper No. 9, Department of Geography, University of Michigan, 1966.

9. Kruskal, J. B. "Analysis of Factorial Experiments by Estimating Monotone Transformations of the Data." *Journal of the Royal Statistical Society Association,* (1965), 251–63.

10. Lieber, S. R. "A Joint Space Analysis of Preferences and Their Underlying Traits." Discussion Paper No. 19, Department of Geography, University of Iowa, 1971.

11. Louviere, J. "A Psychophysical Experimental Approach to the Modeling of Spatial Behavior." Ph.D. dissertation, Department of Geography, University of Iowa, 1973.

12. ———. "After MDS; or, the Role of Mathematical Behavior Theory in the Analysis of Spatial Behavior." Paper read at the Symposium on Multidimensional Scaling at the Annual Meetings of the Association of American Geographers, Atlanta, Georgia, 1973.

13. Luce, R. D., and J. W. Tukey. "Simultaneous Conjoint Measurement: A New Type of Fundamental Measurement." *Journal of Mathematical Psychology,* 1 (1964), 181–91.

14. McClelland, G. "Nonmetric Tests of Composition Rules in Impression Formation." Paper 72-7, Michigan Mathematical Psychology Program, Department of Psychology, University of Michigan, 1972.

15. Olsson, G. *Distance and Human Interaction.* Philadelphia: Regional Science Research Institute, 1965.

16. Rushton, G. "The Scaling of Locational Preferences." In *Behavioral Problems in Geography: A Symposium,* ed. K. R. Cox and R. G. Golledge, pp. 197–227. Northwestern University Studies in Geography, no. 17, Department of Geography, Northwestern University, 1969.

17. Shanteau, J. C., and N. H. Anderson. "Test of a Conflict Model for Preference Judgments." *Journal of Mathematical Psychology,* 6 (1969), 312–25.

18. Shanteau, J. C. "An Additive Model for Sequential Decision Making." *Journal of Experimental Psychology,* 85 (1970), 181–91.

19. Taylor, P. "Distance Transformation and Distance Decay Functions." *Geographical Analysis,* 3 (1971), 221–38.

20. Tversky, A. "A General Theory of Polynomial Conjoint Measurement." *Journal of Mathematical Psychology,* 4 (1967), 1–20.

21. Wolpert, J. "Behavioral Aspects of the Decision to Migrate" *Papers and Proceedings of the Regional Science Association,* 15 (1965), 159–69.

22. Young, F. "A Model for Polynomial Conjoint Analysis Algorithms." In *Multidimensional Scaling: Theory and Applications in the Behavioral Sciences*, ed. R. N. Shepard, et al., pp. 69–104. New York and London: Seminar Press, 1972.

23. ———. "Conjoint Scaling." Technical Report No. 118, L. L. Thurstone Psychometric Laboratory, University of North Carolina, April, 1973.

CHAPTER 12

JORDAN J. LOUVIERE

Information-processing Theory and Functional Form in Spatial Behavior

INTRODUCTION

This paper is concerned with the application of theory and methodology developed in human information-processing to the study of spatial behavior. Spatial behavior is defined as any form of human behavior that involves or exhibits an interaction between the individual (or group) and one or more points in space. By definition, therefore, there are a number of different but related behaviors of potential interest to geographers because they possess one or more of the following characteristics: (1) a spatial variable is considered by the individual in the judgment process; (2) the response, that is, the behavior of interest, is spatial (e.g., a movement); or (3) one or more of the consequences of the response are spatial. Viewed at this conceptual level, there is little to distinguish what geographers have come to term ''spatial behavior'' from the judgment behavior studied in human information-processing in psychology. Topics such as evaluation of spatial alternatives, choosing among spatial alternatives, decision-making with respect to spatial alternatives, and the like, therefore, would be subsumed under a broad umbrella that might be termed ''spatial judgment behavior'' [53]. Despite this specific focus, the potential extension of the methodology to other areas of geographic concern should be apparent.

A general model for psychological judgment behavior, therefore, might be regarded as a general model for ''spatial judgment behavior.''

Such a model may be expressed as follows:

$$B_{it} = f(s_{kt})$$ (1)

$$s_{kt} = g(S_{kt})$$ (2)

$$B_{it} = h(S_{kt}).$$ (3)

Equation (1) states that any particular judgment B_{it} (at some point in time t) is some function (f) of an individual's *subjective* evaluation of a set of stimuli s_{kt}. Equation (2) indicates that these subjective estimates are in turn a function g of their objective counterparts, the S_{kt}. Equation (3) states that h is a composite function of equations (1) and (2). Although conceptually attractive, a simultaneous solution to these equations has eluded researchers, and solutions to the individual functions (f, g, h) remain controversial in psychology and elsewhere [1, 2, 4, 5, 7, 54, 55].

SCALING THEORY

Psychophysics and scaling deals with equation (2). Commonly referred to as the "psychophysical function," equation (2) may also be termed the "scaling function" because a model or correspondence rule is established to relate objective and subjective stimulus values. For example,

$$s = kS^n$$ (4)

is such a model. Despite considerable concern regarding single-stimulus scales in psychophysics and scaling [2, 10, 11, 53, 54, 55] evidence is mounting to suggest that estimates of scale values and weights vary as a direct function of the number and nature ("relevance" to context of task) of additional stimuli being evaluated, judged, and so forth [5, 10, 42].

Thus, the scales values estimated for single stimuli or the scaled values estimated from paired comparisons of stimuli cannot necessarily be directly employed in equation (1). This is because there is considerable controversy regarding whether paired- or single-stimulus scaling procedures can yield valid subjective scales for stimuli that are being simultaneously evaluated together with more than two additional stimuli. Hence, the judgmental response to some stimulus a may differ if it is presented singly, paired with a second stimulus or tripled, quadrupled, and so forth, with others. Furthermore, the scale value and also the worth (weight) of a may depend upon the context of the task. For example, price and availability of gasoline may have completely different weights in the context of the journey to work as compared with a journey across country.

The weight and scale value parameters, therefore, depend not only upon the context of the behavior under examination but also upon the number and the nature of stimuli involved in the evaluation, judgment, or the like. Because of this, theories have been developed to consider explicitly the problem of conjoint measurement, that is, the problem of modeling the subject's response to the presentation of multiple-stimulus items. Such theories are the concern of various paradigms in human information-processing. They are reviewed in several places (e.g. [7, 9, 14, 17]), and this paper will apply experimental and analytical methodology from two of the most widely accepted theories to two problems of potential relevance to studies of spatial behavior.

HUMAN INFORMATION-PROCESSING

Much of the literature in spatial behavior reads "as if" the authors were actually concerned with estimating the joint effects of the occurrence of multiple-stimulus items on spatial behavior (equation (1)). A typical assumption held by many authors is contained in the following phrases: it is assumed that a set of attributes (variables, stimuli, and so on) that the individual(s) trade off in the evaluation of alternatives; if the evaluation function can be determined, then it will describe the nature of the trade-offs; knowledge of such functions would presumably permit prediction of spatial behavior.

Human information-processing is concerned with the estimation of algebraic functions that account for the effects of the joint presentation of multiple-stimulus items. In particular, most paradigms in human information-processing are concerned with mathematical description of the manner in which individuals act "as if" they integrate (that is, functionally combine) various items of information (stimuli) in order to judge or to evaluate some person, object, or event. Although there are several competing paradigms in this area, this paper limits itself to the experimental application of theory and methodology derived from two: stimulus integration theory (e.g. [38, 42]) and judgment policy-capturing (e.g. [12, 23, 25, 56]).

STIMULUS INTEGRATION THEORY

There are two central concepts in integration theory: weight and scale value. Scale value is the location of any particular stimulus along the dimension of judgment, and weight is the importance of worth attached to any particular stimulus or stimulus dimension. For a single stimulus the relationship between weight and scale value may be expressed as

$$R = ws$$

where R is the numerical response to stimulus $S(s = g(S))$, and w is the weight of the stimulus s in the judgment R. The concept of weight and scale value can be extended to any number of stimuli and the multiplicative relationship will remain constant.

Experimental Method

Experimental tests of integration theory normally entail the use of a complete or a fractional factorial design [7, 28, 49]. Such designs are logically consistent with the conception that the judgment in any particular behavioral context depends upon the processing of combinations of items of information (stimuli) ''relevant'' to that behavior in that context. Although any experimental design in which the stimulus item could be arrayed in multiple-item combinations could be employed, only with a full factorial design is it possible to test all of the terms in algebraic models. Because stimulus integration theory depends upon algebraic expressions as theoretical models of judgment, such designs are mandatory to this paradigm. Where possible, they also offer the advantage of providing the most complete information regarding experimental effects.

The paradigm follows a "within-subjects" format to guard against ecologically fallacious inferences in model-building. Because such effects frequently occur in judgmental experiments [7], the hypothesized model is tested at both the level of the single subject and of the group. The formal design, therefore, is a "within-subjects, repeated measures" experiment. The error term is the effect-by-replication interaction for single subjects, and the effect-by-subjects interaction for group data. At the group level, therefore, the design is mixed, consisting of both "within" and "between" subject terms. Thus, sufficient degrees of freedom are available to provide individual descriptions of each subject's "judgment policy" (that is, the functional descriptions of the data), as well as to provide a description of the group data. Departures from the functional form of the group data and differences among parameter estimates can therefore be tested. Thus, the methodology permits one to observe and to account for real individual differences, should they exist.

Analytical Method

Because each subject judges the same stimulus combinations several times, sufficient degrees of freedom are available for an analysis of variance. The analysis of variance can serve two functions: it can provide insight into an algebraic form that might be fit to the data; or it can serve as a goodness-of-fit test for a hypothesized algebraic model.

Analysis of variance provides a test of fit of a hypothesized model. Consider an algebraic expression of the form:

$$R_{ij} = s_i + t_j + e_{ij} \qquad (5)$$

where R_{ij} is the mean response to cell ij; s_i and t_j are, respectively, the row and column factors (stimuli); and e_{ij} is an error term. Equation (5) predicts that the st interaction term in an analysis of variance should be zero in theory and nonsignificant in practice. Likewise, consider a model of the form

$$R_{ij} = s_i \times t_j + e_{ij} \qquad (6)$$

where R_{ij}, s_i, t_j, and e_{ij} are defined as above. This model, in contrast to equation (5), predicts that the st interaction term should be nonzero in theory and significant in practice. Furthermore, it predicts that all of the variance in the interaction effect should be concentrated in the linear-by-linear component. An exact statistical test is available for this effect [50].

In addition, a graphical test of fit is usually employed. Because equation (5) predicts that the differences between each row of each column of data will be constant, the marginal means of the respective rows or columns plotted as a function of their corresponding experimental values should plot as a series of parallel lines. In contrast, equation (6) predicts that the difference between each row or column will not be a constant, but will differ by slopes corresponding to s_i for rows to t_j for columns. This predicts that the data will plot as a series of diverging straight lines. Departures from either form would disconfirm a hypothesized expression. Likewise, these characteristic forms of the plotted data can provide a clue to algebraic models that might be fit to data, if the experimental data are so plotted.

Thus, plotting of data permits visual assessment of form. Each univariate, bivariate, and so on, plot of the means corresponds exactly to one of the terms in a complete ANOVA [2, 3]. Without plots of data, spuriously significant terms may be given interpretations unwarranted by the data. Thus, random response errors and scale effects cannot be detected in the absence of data plots. Thus, ANOVA and graphical plots are truly complementary in that each provides a bit of information that the other is unable to convey.

If a model can be fit to the data satisfactorily, it can be used to derive subjective scales for the stimuli, and, by substitution, can assist in the solution to equations (1) and (3). For example, consider the following equation derived by averaging over columns in equation (5):

$$R_{i.} = s_i + k + e_{ij} \tag{7}$$

where $r_{i.}$, s_i, and e_{ij} are defined as before; and k is a constant. Equation (7) shows that the marginal mean $(R_{i.})$ for any row i provides an estimate of the subjective scale value of stimulus s_i up to a linear transformation. Consider equation (6), averaged over columns in the same fashion:

$$R_{i.} = ks_i + e_{ij} \tag{8}$$

where R_i, s_i, and e_{ij} are defined as before; k is a constant. The marginal mean of row i (R_i) will therefore provide an estimate of s_i up to multiplication by a constant. Model 5, therefore, if fit, provides interval scales; and model 6 provides ratio scales.

Once the s_i are known, one can plot them as a function of the S_i (objective, experimental values) to obtain an estimate of the function g (equation [2]). A polynomial trend analysis will complement this graphical plot with an exact statistical test for the form of function g [2, 4]. Equations (1) and (2) then can be estimated in theory; and by substituting equation (2) into equation (3), one can simultaneously solve all three equations. Thus, by basing the acquisition of scale values on a theory of behavior, rather than on an isolated measurement operation, integration theory claims to be able to solve simultaneously the equations that have eluded solution to date.

Policy Capturing

Beginning with Brunswick [12] and continuing with the works of Hoffman [31], Hursch, Hammond, and Hursch [33], Goldberg [25, 26], and Stewart and Gelberd [56], to name only a few, considerable attention has been focused upon the quantitative description of subjects' judgment policies. That is, the idiosyncratic manner in which individual subjects act "as if" they weigh and combine different items of information (stimuli) into a single quantitative judgment.

Although a number of models have been proposed for the analysis of the responses to presentations of multiple items of information (cues), by far the most popular is the multiple linear regression model (Slovic and Lichenstein [53]). Although nonlinear models have been employed [7, 23, 26, 32], little evidence exists to refute Yntema and Torgerson's [61] decade-old proof that whenever independent variables are monotonically related to a dependent variable, the linear model will give quite accurate predictive ability, even in truly nonlinear cases.

Reliance upon multiple regression procedures provides considerable design flexibility in the construction of experiments. Complete (full) or fractionated factorial designs are no longer mandatory because only the "main effects" are of interest under a strictly linear assumption. The parameters of the regression equation, of course, are equivalent to the estimates of the main effects in the ANOVA. Formally, therefore, a random-effects regression model is employed to analyze data derived from "representative designs" [12]. Such designs need only capture a sample of the possible combinations of stimuli (items) from the experimental environment; hence, considerable flexibility is gained both in terms of the number of factors that may be examined and the number of combinations that are necessary to reliably estimate the regression parameters.

If one suspects that the linear model is theoretically inadequate, or where the emphasis is upon theory construction rather than practical prediction, full factorial designs provide significant advantage. Information regarding higher-order interaction terms is sacrificed in designs that are incomplete. Of course, regression models can be used to analyze data from complete factorial designs; in this instance the correct model is the "fixed effects" form. For the most part, however, regression has not borne the analytical responsibility for theoretical work in judgmental analysis. Rather, it has been the direct estimation of algebraic models via maximum-likelihood procedures that has been employed. As will be shown in the applications section of this paper, maximum-likelihood approaches in the estimation of parameters and the comparison of measures of goodness-of-fit. The remainder of this paper will deal with empirical applications of both stimulus integration theory and policy-capturing approaches to the analysis of behavioral data.

EMPIRICAL APPLICATIONS

The results of a judgment experiment provide a hypothesis that must be tested in the real world. This hypothesis represents an estimate of the behavior one would expect to obtain under conditions in the real world corresponding to those examined in the laboratory. It is testable at both the level of the group and of the single individual. Experiments that can be interpreted in real-world contexts constitute a major research problem because the real world most often contains a host of influences that must be artificially held constant in the laboratory. However, if results from repeated laboratory experiments are consistent, one can proceed from observed regularities to model-building to empirical testing in a manner similar to that frequently practiced in the physical sciences.

Two recent applications of judgment theory and methodology have been chosen to represent its potential [37, 38, 39]. The first application is a description of the manner in which sample individuals' responses vary as a function of systematic manipulations of public transportation system variables. This question is clearly amenable to experimentation: by direct manipulation of the system parameters of interest; by simulation experimentations; or by paper-and-pencil experimentation. Clearly, the first alternative is the most desirable but is usually not possible, and simulation models presume prior knowledge of functional form—usually not known. The paper-and-pencil alternative, therefore, was selected as a focus for study to test the applicability of information-processing methodology to the analysis of judgments about bus systems.

The "bus" experiment focused upon changes in the subjective likelihood of taking a bus as a function of changes in fare, frequency of service, and walking distance to the bus stop. Twenty-seven combinations of experimental stimuli were varied in a 3^3 factorial design. Each stimulus combination was printed on a half-sheet of typewriter paper with a response scale placed immediately beneath. The response scale was labeled "probability of taking a bus."

Subjects were instructed that each stimulus combination represented a different hypothetical bus system, and that the experimenters were interested in the likelihood that they would take the bus described by each particular combination of characteristics. Subjects were told to interpret the "probability" scale as that "proportion of the time that they would choose to use the described system as against any other transportation alternative."

Judgments were made on 150 millimeter line scales anchored on one end by 0 and on the other by 100. Subjects were instructed that judgments of 0 and 100 represented absolute certainty that they would *never* or *always*, respectively, under all conceivable circumstances, take a bus possessing the characteristics described. Subjects responded by marking a slash mark in pencil across the scale (line) at that point which "best estimated their feelings" about the combination of stimuli. Responses were measured with a millimeter ruler to the nearest ½ millimeter, and then transformed to range between 0 and 100 so that they might be interpreted as "subjective probabilities."

In addition to the experimental values (Table 1), end anchors were provided. End anchors are stimulus combinations that are more extreme than those actually under investigation. Their purpose is to provide a

TABLE 1

STIMULUS VALUES

		15¢	30¢	45¢
½b	15 min.			
	30 min.			
	60 min.			
3b	15 min.			
	30 min.			
	60 min.			
9b	15 min.			
	30 min.			
	60 min.			

The fare is 15c
The bus passes the closest stop every 30 minutes
The closest bus stop is 3 blocks away

0 ————————————————————————————————— 100

FIG. 1. Sample experimental item

frame of reference within which judgment might be couched and to guard against nonlinearities in scale usage. Specifically, subjects are instructed that the end anchors represent the *most extreme* combinations that will be encountered. It is also suggested to them that these combinations might represent scale values close to 0 and 100 (Fig. 1).

Twenty-one subjects participated in two separate experimental sessions, and each received a remuneration of $10.00 for their participation. Ten subjects participated in an initial experiment and eleven in a follow-up session. One subject was removed from the study for failure to follow directions. Subjects attended two one-hour sessions, during each of which they judged six replications of the design, for a total of twelve replications in each of the two experimental sessions. Following the usual practice in judgmental analysis, the first replication at the beginning of each session is treated as practice and not analyzed. Analytical results, therefore, are based upon data from ten replications.

Specific Results from the Bus Experiment

Group data are plotted in Figure 2. The three-way plot (fare × frequency × walking distance) is omitted because it is in more than two dimensions. Only group data are presented because all of the single

TABLE 2

SUMMARY TABLE FOR THE ANALYSIS OF VARIANCE
AT THE GROUP LEVEL

Source of Variation	Sums of Squares	Degrees of Freedom	Mean Squares	F-Values & Posterior Probabilities
R	6,813.19	9	757.02	$2.26P=0.020^a$
B	565,568.29	2	282,784.14	$53.39P=0.000^b$
F	65,983.30	2	32,991.65	$16.29P=0.000^b$
BF	11,459.08	4	2,864.77	$9.99\ P=0.000^b$
M	777,793.00	2	388,896.50	$57.1\ P=0.000^b$
BM	112,124.63	4	28,031.15	$33.15P=0.000^b$
FM	17,083.21	4	4,270.80	$10.73P=0.000^b$
BFM	8,799.70	8	1,099.96	$8.93\ P=0.000^b$
(The remaining terms have been omitted.)				
Total	3,458,279.96			

R = Replications Factor
B = Walking Distance (Blocks)
F = Frequency of Service (Frequency)
M = Fare (Money)
[a] Probability of an F this large occurring by chance is less than 0.05.
[b] Probability of an F this large occurring by chance is less than 0.01.

subjects' data were similar in form. This implies that all of the subjects followed the same combination rule in putting the stimuli together to arrive at a judgment (at least they acted "as if" they did!). Formally, this is a mixed design: "between" and "within" subjects. Each graphical plot corresponds to one of the terms in the analysis-of-variance table (Table 2).

All ANOVA terms were statistically significant (Table 2), and the plotted data confirm this result (Fig. 2). This suggests that the best-fitting model for both the single subjects and the group should be nonlinear. This hypothesis is examined by means of linear and log-linear regression and by maximum likelihood estimation of the following general function forms:

$$R_{ijk} = s_i + t_j + u_k + e_{ijk} \qquad (9)$$

$$R_{ijk} = s_i \times t_j \times u_k + e_{ijk} \qquad (10)$$

where R_{ijk} is the observed numerical response in cell ijk; s_i, t_j, and u_k are the respective row, column, and surface stimuli; and e_{ijk} is an error term assumed additive with mean 0, unit variance. Maximum likelihood estimation [7, 40] should provide a better test of fit than R^2 because the parameters of the models and the measure of goodness of fit can be estimated directly from the raw data, rather than relying upon a log

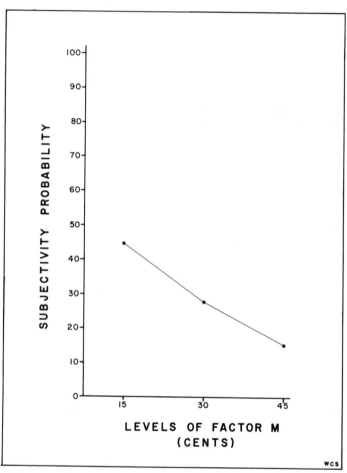

FIG. 2a. Average sample response to levels of fare with walking distance and frequency of service held constant

transformation in the case of the regression approach. It is well known that R^2 is highly dependent upon the distribution of the data, and Birnbaum [9] has shown that it can easily take on a higher value for the wrong model as compared with the right model in an example employing contrived data. Moreover, the likelihood of the model given the data—a quantitative expression—provides a superior test of fit because a log transformation theoretically violates the normality assumptions of

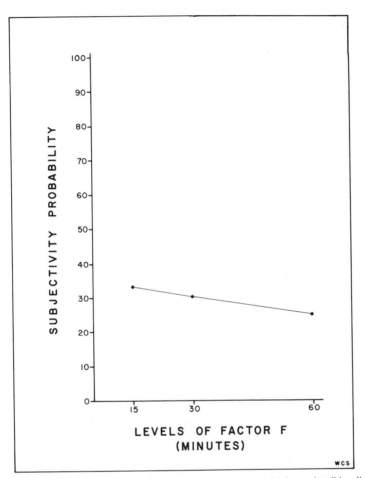

Fɪɢ. 2b. Average sample response to levels of frequency of service with fare and walking distance held constant

multiple regression and further complicates interpretation because multiple R is dependent upon the frequency distribution of the observations (see [9, 40, 42]). Transforming these observations to log form clearly alters that original frequency distribution.

By estimating the general forms of the two equations, (9) and (10), the likelihood expressions can be directly compared without transforming the raw data. For example, under homogeneous variance assumptions

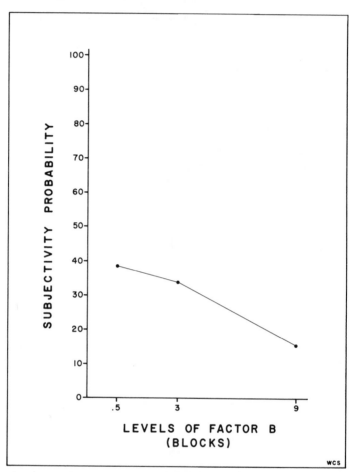

Fig. 2c. Average sample response to levels of walking distance with fare and frequency of service held constant

(also the regression assumption), least-square solutions are maximum-likelihood solutions [40]; hence, the reduced sum-of-squares in a direct numerical estimation procedure should be the maximum-likelihood solution—provided a unique solution exists. Such numerical estimation procedures are common in psychological model-building, and extended discussions may be found in [7, 9, 10, 18, 49, 58]. In this instance, the cell variances were found to be heterogeneous [42], and therefore,

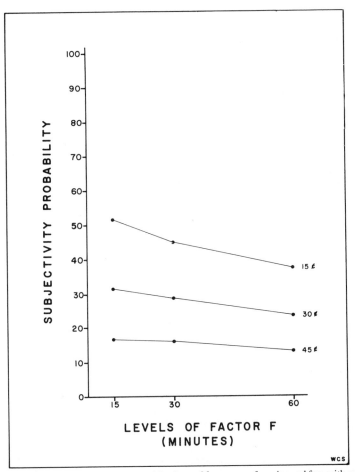

Fig. 2d. Average sample response to combinations of frequency of service and fare with walking distance held constant

Norman's [40] maximum-likelihood approach to estimation and goodness of fit for the heterogeneous variance, normal distribution function assumptions was employed in data analysis and estimation.

The results of the regression and maximum-likelihood estimations are listed in Tables 3A and 3B. The best-fitting model is clearly the multiplying model, equation (10), despite the higher correlation of the linear regression model with data from most single subjects and the group. On

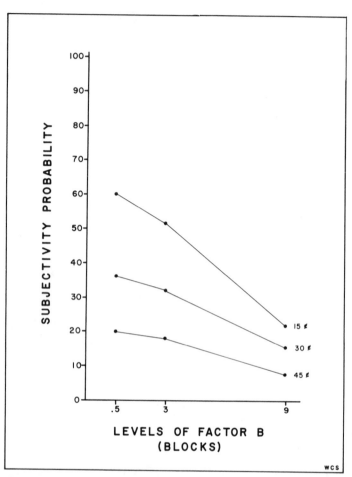

FIG. 2e. Average sample response to combinations of fare and walking distance with frequency of service held constant

the basis of correlation alone, therefore, one would have concluded that the linear model was the best model. Maximum-likelihood estimation, however, reveals that few individual subjects or the group data are fit as well with a linear equation. It appears that Birnbaum's "devil" is clearly at work here [9].

The results of the analysis of variance (Table 2) agree with these findings and illustrate the power of ANOVA as a test of fit for algebraic

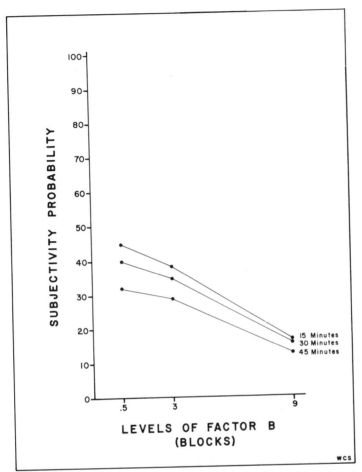

FIG. 2f. Average sample response to combinations of walking distance and frequency of service with fare held constant

models. The ANOVA indicates a significant three-way interaction for almost all the individual subjects and for the group data. Linear regression disagrees with this prediction. The multiplying model, however, is confirmed by maximum likelihood procedures. In this instance the multiplying model is clearly the best model for describing the judgments.

This model only applies to laboratory data, however, and is subject to

TABLE 3A

DIRECT LEAST-SQUARES ESTIMATION OF MODEL
PARAMETERS AND REDUCED SUM OF SQUARES

| Observed Data | THEORETICAL PREDICTIONS | |
	Linear Model	Multiplying Model
71.01	57.97	68.56
59.84	53.10	59.50
23.41	34.22	26.06
60.20	54.85	60.75
52.14	49.98	52.73
22.71	31.10	23.10
49.00	49.49	50.00
42.28	44.62	43.39
19.50	25.74	19.00
40.72	41.29	42.05
35.56	36.42	36.50
17.63	17.53	15.00
37.68	38.17	37.27
32.16	33.30	32.34
16.12	14.41	14.17
29.66	32.81	30.66
28.05	27.94	26.62
13.33	9.05	11.66
21.81	28.65	23.30
19.38	23.78	20.22
8.50	4.89	8.86
20.79	25.53	20.65
19.98	20.66	17.92
8.43	1.77	7.85
18.82	20.17	16.99
15.14	15.30	14.74
5.50	−3.59	6.46
Reduced sum of squares	3,632.77	3,589.75

considerable limitations. It has not been tested in the real world, although work is proceeding to do so. Because complete results of extensions are not available at the time of this writing, nothing further will be said. A discussion of the technical details of the study may be found in [37], and a treatment of maximum likelihood and a comparison with regression approaches is available in [42].

The Recommendation of Trout Streams

Conceptually, the problem may be outlined as follows: stream-evaluation behavior is assumed to be a learning process in which two basic components are acquired—*how* to fish and *where* to fish. These components are not independent of one another, and in the early stages

TABLE 3B

STANDARDIZED REGRESSION PARAMETERS FOR THE BUS DATA

	RAW DATA MODEL				LOG DATA MODEL			
	Fare b_1	Frequency b_2	Distance b_3	R^2	Fare b_1	Frequency b_2	Distance b_3	R^2
Grpi-	−0.703	−0.205	−0.600	.90	−0.731	−0.171	−0.527	.84
(1)	−0.609	−0.113	−0.607	.75	−0.514	−0.078	−0.661	.71
(2)	−0.857	−0.161	−0.204	.80	−0.940	−0.134	−0.217	.95
(3)	−0.696	−0.138	−0.472	.73	−0.670	−0.096	−0.443	.66
(4)	−0.861	−0.021	−0.178	.77	−0.967	−0.042	−0.114	.95
(5)	−0.664	−0.089	−0.546	.75	−0.584	−0.041	−0.485	.58
(6)	−0.851	−0.066	−0.201	.77	−0.983	−0.041	−0.122	.98
(7)	−0.093	−0.154	−0.977	.99	−0.114	−0.193	−0.834	.75
(8)	−0.103	−0.421	−0.862	.93	−0.092	−0.378	−0.724	.67
(9)	−0.750	−0.287	−0.435	.84	−0.716	−0.278	−0.332	.70
(10)	−0.881	−0.128	−0.202	.83	−0.953	−0.081	−0.099	.93
(11)	−0.512	−0.585	−0.286	.69	−0.482	−0.659	−0.194	.71
(12)	......	......	......		......			
(13)	−0.662	−0.070	−0.497	.69	−0.720	−0.002	−0.580	.86
(14)	−0.977	−0.059	−0.104	.97	−0.948	−0.050	−0.120	.92
(15)	−0.167	−0.150	−0.940	.94	−0.147	−0.118	−0.880	.81
(16)	−0.779	−0.156	−0.511	.89	−0.740	−0.156	−0.414	.74
(17)	−0.456	−0.015	−0.807	.86	−0.268	−0.002	−0.790	.70
(18)	−0.252	−0.230	−0.861	.86	−0.177	−0.184	−0.762	.65
(19)	−0.862	−0.075	−0.415	.92	−0.799	−0.094	−0.384	.80
(20)	−0.830	−0.228	−0.414	.91	−0.769	−0.174	−0.347	.74
(21)	−0.561	−0.152	−0.681	.80	−0.481	−0.141	−0.645	.67

of "learning" stimuli from both components are assumed to influence stream choice. If one assumes that an individual learns "how" to fish more quickly than he learns "where" to fish, then one would have the situation depicted in Figure 3.

Thus, individuals are shown "learning" how to fish more quickly than where to fish (Fig. 3). This is conceptually attractive because during a single stream trial, an individual can experience a large number of how-to-fish trials. Thus, a far larger number of trials should be required to learn *where* as compared with *how* to fish.

Meanwhile, factors important during the early stages of the "learning" process may become more or less important and may even serve as constraints in the sense that the individual "learns" not to choose a stream possessing too little of this or too much of that. In theory, therefore, the individual would simply eliminate from consideration all alternatives outside of the constraint set [57]. The constraints are assumed to become more numerous over time as the individual becomes increasingly expert; hence, the set of possible alternatives would be

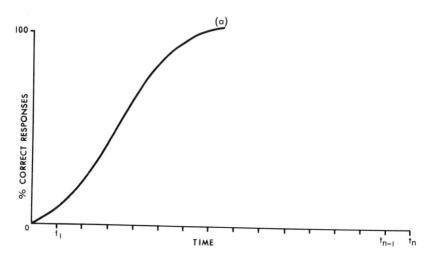

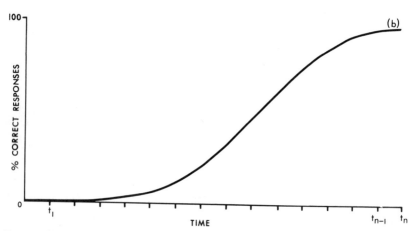

FIG. 3. Hypothetical learning curves. Curve (a) corresponds to "how to fish"; curve (b) corresponds to "where to fish." Percent correct is some measure of the individual's evaluation of his own achievement, i.e., his satisfaction or feedback from learning trials.

likewise narrowed by the increasing constraints imposed upon choices. In theory, therefore, the individual may be viewed as maximizing or minimizing some subjective evaluation function subject to a set of constraints.

At some stage in the "learning" process, say t_{n-1} (Fig. 3b), the individual will have learned about as much as he ever will (if these functions are "true") about *where* to fish. Choice of stream, therefore, can be assumed to be restricted to the set of alternatives, say $\{A\}$, where $\{A\}$ is a subset of $\{T\}$, the set of all possible streams. Choice behavior, therefore, devolves into picking a_i from $\{A\}$ rather than t_k from $\{T\}$, although someone on the outside may view the situation as the latter. This, of course, is only likely for those types of spatial behavior in which the $\{T\}$ remain fairly constant over time. Trout fishing is one of those types of spatial behavior. This assumption may not be reasonable, especially in the long run, for other types of spatial behavior such as grocery shopping. The $\{T\}$ for grocery shopping may change quickly over time and have possibly significant effects on observed spatial behavior. However, because little is known about the length of time required for spatial "learning" in any behavioral context other than Rogers' pioneering study [44], such speculation is strictly academic.

It is hypothesized that to choose a_i from $\{A\}$, the individual employs an evaluation function in which quantities of variables attractive in each stream are evaluated against travel effort. It is assumed that trout streams possess various values of attraction attributes; the "learned" set, $\{A\}$, share common constraint attributes, but differ in attraction values and values of travel effort. This, of course, is a gravity model hypothesis. To confirm its reasonableness, the following experiment was devised.

Specific Details of the Trout Experiment

A $5 \times 4 \times 4$ factorial design was employed: number of trout and travel time were varied (see Table 4 for their experimental values) systematically in each of four complete replications. Different orders of presentation were used in each replication. This design was based on similar experiments in psychology [7, 50], the bus experiment reported above, and extensive pilot work. More technical detail can be found in [37].

In addition to the experimental combinations, end anchors and filler items were employed. Fillers are combinations that are more extreme in value than those combinations under experimentation and are randomly distributed throughout the design. They are not analyzed because their purpose is to ensure that subjects recognize that there are more extreme

TABLE 4

VALUES OF STIMULI EMPLOYED IN TROUT EXPERIMENT

TRAVEL TIME (MINUTES)	NUMBER OF TROUT				
	2	14	26	38	50
15					
60					
105					
150					
195					

combinations than the combinations of interest and to guard against nonlinearities in scale use. Such procedures are commonly employed with line-mark response scales. A sample experimental item is illustrated in Figure 4.

Subjects were instructed to imagine that they had recently moved to a new state with which they were unfamiliar and had acquired a fishing buddy at work who was known to be an "expert" trout fisherman. This friend supplied the subject with information regarding all the trout streams in the new state that he personally considered to be "quality" water. "Quality" was defined to mean that all of the subject's maximum and minimum requirements beyond numbers of fish and travel time were met in each stream that was described.

Subjects were required to judge each combination on a "recommendation" scale. That is, they "recommended" that any particular stream (described by a combination of the experimental stimuli) be included in the set of streams to be *fished* or *not fished* in the coming fishing season. Subjects were instructed that the "strength" of this recommendation was desired; it was to be indicated by marking a slash mark between the end labels (see Fig. 4) at that point which "best represented the strength of their feelings." Therefore, "recommendation" for inclusion in the choice set is assumed isomorphic to actual choice.

The set of all hatchery personnel who were also trout fishermen at each of the three state-owned trout hatcheries in Iowa constituted the

There are 26 trout per 1/4 mile on the average in this stream
It takes 1 hour and 45 minutes to drive to the stream

Strong
rec not
to fish

Strong
rec to
fish

FIG. 4. Sample item for trout task

research subjects. These individuals are truly "experts" because they know all of the streams within their jurisdictions both professionally and personally. They therefore have information available to them regarding both experimental variables. Furthermore, the judgment task is a natural one for them because they are called upon daily by the public to "recommend" various streams for fishing trips. To control for possible multiple purpose behavior, subjects were asked to assume that all of their hypothetical trips were for a single day, exclusively for trout. Further, they were asked to assume that all of their requirements for stream "quality" were met, exclusive of trout and travel time (see above).

Results

The experimental data are graphed in Figures 5 and 6 (S1 to S10). Figure 5 contains the group data and Figure 6 the individual data. At the group level all main effects were highly significant, but the interaction effect was not. Figure 5 confirms this result because the data curves are nearly parallel. This result did not carry over to the single-subject data because nearly all individual subjects' data exhibited significant interactions (Table 5). The graphs in Figure 6 support these results, although it is evident that there is a considerable amount of linearity in the general trends of the curves. Examining the subjects' replication-by-replication responses revealed considerable response fluctuation that might be attributed to inattention, unfamiliarity with psychological judgment tasks, or other random effects. Furthermore, far fewer replications were

TABLE 5

Summary of the Individual ANOVAS

	Source of Variation		
Subject	Travel Time	No. of Trout	Time × Trout
S(1)	$F=88.4, p=.000$	$F=28.7, p=.001$	$F=5.84, p=.000$
S(2)	$F=40.1, p=.000$	$F=9.8, p=.010$	$F=2.31, p=.030$
S(3)	$F=75.4, p=.000$	$F=10.8, p=.008$	$F=1.01, p=.468$
S(4)	$F=20.4, p=.000$	$F=13.1, p=.005$	$F=2.21, p=.048$
S(5)	$F=20.4, p=.000$	$F=36.5, p=.000$	$F=3.82, p=.003$
S(6)	$F=24.1, p=.000$	$F=14.5, p=.004$	$F=0.67, p=.762$
S(7)	$F=25.8, p=.000$	$F=95.1, p=.000$	$F=2.25, p=.004$
S(8)	$F=17.5, p=.001$	$F=19.7, p=.002$	$F=0.97, p=.500$
S(9)	$F=6.4, p=.013$	$F=23.5, p=.001$	$F=2.90, p=.013$
S(10)	$F=8.2, p=.006$	$F=15.8, p=.003$	$F=3.74, p=.003$

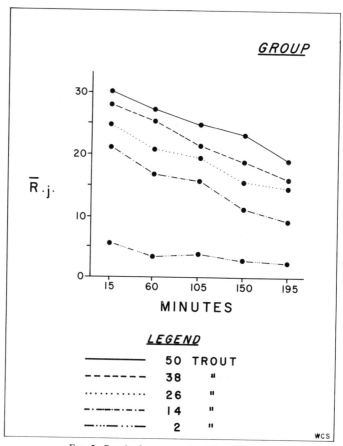

FIG. 5. Results from group level 5 × 5 design

collected as compared with the bus study; hence there are fewer degrees of freedom in the tests and fewer trials for the subjects' responses to stabilize.

After the fashion of the bus study, data were analyzed with regression and maximum likelihood procedures. Because Norman's [40] algorithm was unavailable at the time of analysis, Chandler's subroutine STEPIT was employed to minimize the sum of squares around the best-fitting general linear and multiplicative forms (see equations (9) and (10)). Under normal, homogeneous variance assumptions, regression and least-squares should provide equivalent results. The primary difference

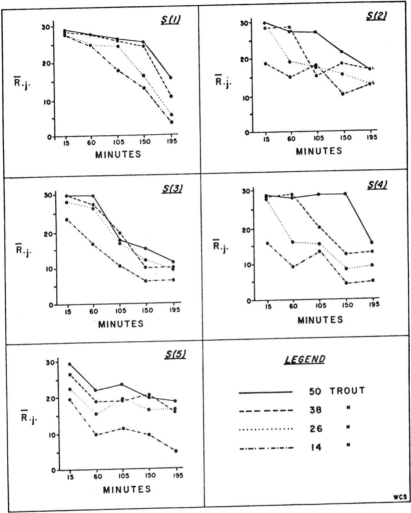

FIG. 6. Graphical plots of single subject data (4×5) a–j

is that more parameters are being fitted in the general forms (nine in each); nonetheless, the reduced sum of squares for both the linear and multiplicative case should provide a superior test of fit over R^2. Results (Table 6) indicate that the linear model does better than the multiplicative for seven of the ten subjects. The group model is clearly linear (Figure 5). These results disagree with the ANOVA results (Table 5):

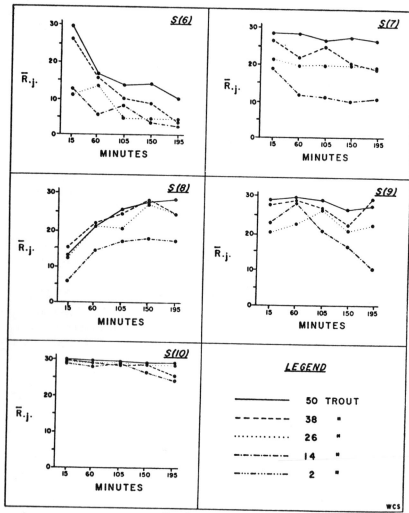

FIG. 6. (*continued*)

significant interactions occurred for most subjects. Although the evidence suggests that the interactions may have no real psychological interpretation other than random response error (see preceeding paragraph), one possibility is that the "true" model is a differentially weighted averaging model of the form.

TABLE 6

MODEL COMPARISONS FOR SINGLE SUBJECTS

	LINEAR MODEL		MULTIPLYING MODEL	
SUBJECT	Reduced SS	R^2	Reduced SS	R^2
1	494.03	0.816	673.58	.483
2	1,112.20	0.809[b]	1,080.36	0.810
3	681.73	0.905[a]	678.48	0.798
4	1,699.16	0.849	1,865.43	0.835[b]
5	584.83	0.783	670.11	0.828[a]
6	930.96	0.791[a]	699.09	0.735
7	285.76	0.900	336.44	0.898[b]
8	495.20	0.740	497.49	0.894[a]
9	1,084.60	0.589	1,133.72	0.474
10	72.20	0.581	74.10	0.492

[a] Means R^2 is higher for the statistically "wrong" model.
[b] Means R^2 for the statistically "wrong" model is very close to that for the "right" model.

$$R_{ij} = \frac{w_1}{w_1 + w_2 + \ldots + w_n} s_i + \frac{w_2}{w_1 + {}_2 + \ldots + w_n} s_2 \ldots$$
$$+ \frac{w_n}{w_1 + w_2 + \ldots + w_n} t_5 \qquad (11)$$

where R_{ij} is the response to the ij treatment combination; $s_1, s_2, \ldots, t_5$ are the four s treatments and five t treatments; and $w_1, w_2, \ldots, w_n$ are n (in this case $n = 9$) weight parameters, one for each of the n treatment (subjective value) parameters. This model predicts an interaction, despite its apparent linear form.

The practical predictive ability of equation (11), however, is limited, unless one can estimate each and all w's uniquely. To date, such unique solutions exist only under several restrictive conditions, although a novel experimental procedure for obtaining an estimate of them has been proposed by Norman [41]. Therefore, although one may find that one general form fits the data better than another, for extrapolation or practical prediction purposes, such models have limited utility. Thus, the regression equations, because they possess rate-of-change parameters, can be employed for such predictive purposes. Furthermore, these models appeared to yield satisfactory fits to the data, although not as satisfactory as the likelihood forms. Therefore, the regression functions are retained as first approximations for an additional analysis.

However, the substantial departures from linearity at the single-subject level are important (Table 6, Fig. 6). They illustrate the difference between theory and practical prediction—the "true" theoretical

Bloody Run Creek

a. Why did you rate Bloody Run as you did?
b. Would you estimate the following?
  1. How long does it take to drive to Bloody Run?
  2. How many trout are there per 1/4 mile of Bloody Run?

FIG. 7. Sample item and question format for phase two

form should be able to account for these observed discrepancies. Such discrepancies would be impossible to detect, of course, in the absence of a "within-subjects" design. Thus, the linear model would have been accepted as the "true" model with a high degree of confidence, given only the regression analysis of the pooled (group) data. Yet, it fits some individuals poorly. This, of course, is an example of the ecological fallacy with behavioral data. Despite recognition of the discrepancies at the individual level, no ready explanation for aggregate linearity can be advanced, save that of an artifact of averaging. This is surely a phenomenon that deserves more attention because it seems certain that some studies have been confronted with it and likely that others in the future will encounter it. It is also exemplary of one of the big disadvantages of working with survey data in which each individual (subject) constitutes a single replication. Unless one has a procedure for studying individual differences, ecologically fallacious inferences are a real danger.

A Second Trout Experiment

Because it is of interest to know how well the regression functions estimated in the experiment can predict real data, a second experiment was designed. This second experiment asked the hatchery personnel to evaluate a sample of real Iowa trout streams. As a sequel to the experiment described above, the subjects completed a questionnaire that required them to list their five (or less) favorite Iowa trout streams and then rate each of these "favorite" streams on the same "recommendation" scale employed in the experiment discussed above. As the subjects rated their favorite stream, second favorite, and so on, they were asked to state the reason why they so rated each stream. Subjects finally estimated for each stream (1) the number of trout per ¼ of a mile the stream contained and (2) the driving time from their residence to the stream. The format of this design is illustrated in Figure 7.

After rating their *favorite* streams, subjects were asked to provide the same information for a set of ten streams randomly chosen from the Iowa trout program. Because subjects were solicited from each of the three hatcheries in the state, any particular subject could be expected to be most familiar with those streams under his/her jurisdiction and less familiar with those outside. Hence, fewer than ten ratings were completed in this section by subjects who had no information (familiarity) about certain streams.

The rationale for this phase of the study is the assumption that if the models derived from the information-processing experiment can predict real stream choices, they should also be able to predict evaluations of real streams with which the subjects (potentially, at least) interact. To test this hypothesis, the various experimentally derived functions were employed to derive theoretical scores by substituting the subjects' estimates of trout and travel time (see Fig. 7) in these equations. Tests were conducted at the level of the single individual over all streams and at the level of the single stream over all individuals. Questionnaire estimates of the range of values were used to test correspondence between predicted and actual ratings on the real streams.

TABLE 7

MODEL PREDICTIONS OF INDIVIDUAL DATA
(Correlations of Models with Data)

	INDIVIDUAL PREDICTIONS TO STREAMS (MODELS DERIVED FROM EXPERIMENTAL DESIGN)		PREDICTIONS TO STREAMS USING SUBJECTS' OWN ESTIMATES (FIG. 7)
	Individual Linear Model	Group Linear Model	(Linear Regression)
All questionnaire streams	0.45	0.37	0.47
Streams with subjective estimates within the experimental domain	0.42	0.31	0.45
All favorite streams	0.47	0.47	0.58
Favorite stream with subjective estimates within experimental domain	0.35	0.32	0.52

Model parameters are available from the author upon request. Their general forms are:

$$R_{ij} = a + b_1 \text{ trout} - b_2 \text{ travel time} + e_{ij} \qquad (i)$$

$$\log R_{ij} = a + b_1 \log \text{trout} - b_2 \log \text{travel time} + e_{ij} \qquad (ii)$$

These data are obtained directly from the questionnaire (Fig. 7)

TABLE 8

MODEL PREDICTIONS OF STREAM DATA
(Correlations of Models with Data)

GROUP MODELS		SUBJECTIVE ESTIMATES	
Linear	Log	Raw	Log
0.668	0.752	0.474	0.856

Model forms are the same as in Table 7.
These data are obtained by averaging all subjects' responses to each real stream (12) in the questionnaire (Fig. 7).

Results (Tables 7 and 8) indicate that the aggregate linear model does as well as the individual linear models in predicting the evaluations of all the subjects over all streams. Furthermore, the predictions are in the expected direction. The models do significantly better for the average rating (over all individuals) given to each stream, but this is to be expected. Interestingly, the log-linear equation correlates significantly better than does the linear model for the twelve streams under consideration. The same result obtains when the subjects' estimates (see Fig. 7) are employed to estimate linear and log-linear functions from the questionnaire evaluation data. That is, the log-linear model again fits better in a correlative sense.

Now this is an interesting finding: the subjects' individual functions were primarily linear; yet data aggregated over subjects (average rating for each stream) suggests a definitely nonlinear relationship. This may be a result (artifact) of averaging; however, no ready explanation for this is apparent. Linearity as an artifact of averaging is well understood; but log-linearity resulting from the averaging of predominantly linear functions suggests no straightforward interpretation. The most immediate observation, of course, is that it is consistent with findings from the literature on spatial interaction [33, 43, 59, 60].

CONCLUSIONS

The results reported above are subject to considerable limitation—both in terms of design and of generality. Hence, they should be viewed as extremely exploratory ventures into the analysis of spatial behavior from an information-processing standpoint.

One limitation is that no attempt was undertaken to determine whether these results generalize to bus patronage behavior or stream choice behavior in the real world. Such testing would require extensive follow-up and/or monitoring of sample behavior. This is both expensive and time-consuming, but not impossible. In the case of the bus study, the actual testing might be tantamount to an experiment. Thus, it may be more convenient over the long run to design and conduct experiments that will yield data of the type needed for predictive models of mode choice.

A second issue concerns the manner in which the theoretical concerns in equations (1) and (2) were resolved. In particular, the linear model demands a linear assumption in the arguments for each of the independent variables. The great wealth of available evidence suggests that the function in equation (2) is nonlinear [10, 54, 55]. As demonstrated by Yntema and Torgerson and expounded upon by Dawes and by Dawes and Corrigan [16, 17, 61], the linear model will do well whenever the independent and dependent variables are related to one another in some monotonic fashion. Hence, departures from linearity are probably not serious, especially when one's goal is practical prediction, rather than a theoretically "true" equation.

No attempt was made to estimate equation (3), although many psychologists would argue that the regression of the experimental values on the response was precisely that. Equation (3) for geographers, however, would probably be regarded as the estimation of a function-relating response behavior to a set of objectively measurable stimuli: real travel times and numbers of trout; real bus fares, real walking distances, and real frequencies of service. Data for such an analysis were not available in a form amenable to estimation; hence, these functions could not be estimated.

The stream evaluation study suggests that gravity-type functions can be directly estimated from empirical observations, which is the usual practice. An important consideration, however, would seem to be the choice of a measure. If one pauses for a moment to reflect upon the relatively large number of possible measures for distance and attraction, it does not take a mathematician to realize that goodness of fit is related to measurement as well as to functional form; if the number of possible factors is large and there are several possible measures for each of these, then the number of possible equations to be fit to data is very large, given a linear functional assumption. When one also considers the very large number of possible equation forms, the task of finding the "right" model quickly becomes overwhelming. Working directly with single subjects can reduce the number of possible measures to only those that one elicits from the subject; "within-subjects" designs can provide insight into functional forms to be fit to data. Potentially, therefore, these types of analytical studies (if the models prove to have predictive ability) can considerably reduce the specification problem.

Granted that spatial behavior is a dynamic process: it changes in response to internal changes in the state of the actor, the alternatives, or the environment within which the behavior occurs. If one defines "learning" as a reduction-in-choice variability over some observation period, then more should be known about "learning" effects in spatial behavior. In essence, the results of these empirical studies reflect the end state of the individuals' choice or evaluative behavior over some period of time. The theoretically "true" model should be able to predict the observed data from the two empirical applications as the outcome of a process operating over time.

Because statics should probably be deduced from dynamics, some of the current work in dynamic learning models in signal detection theory [18] and by Dyreson [19, 20, 21] in simulating spatial adjustment and learning might prove useful. Despite the attractiveness of the concept of "learning," no one has yet shown that humans "learn" in any spatial context, despite Rogers' initial attempt in Madison, Wisconsin. As Rushton [45, 46, 47, 48] has argued, the distribution of opportunities has adjusted as much to behavior as behavior has adjusted to the distribution of opportunities. The continual accretion of new facilities and the deletion of old facilities probably contribute to a continual state of disequilibrium. Furthermore, changes in the environment of the system can provide substantial influence on behavior. When this paper was originally conceived, there was no energy shortage. Now the price and availability of gasoline is having profound effects upon public transportation patronage in this country. These effects could not have been predicted, nor could current methods of estimating travel demand handle these changes; yet, the methodology described and applied in this paper could be employed to derive estimates of changes in demand as a function of manipulation of cost and availability of fuel. Hence, the restriction to static formulations, though theoretically troublesome, may present no problem for short-run prediction. Until these models are actually tested, however, such speculation is academic.

Theoretical and methodological structures developed in human information-processing appear useful for the analysis of static behavior at both the individual and the group level. The paradigms described in this paper are not an isolated set, as there are several others also in this general area. They are reviewed in Slovic and Lichenstein [53].

The laboratory responses of individuals and aggregates thereof were described mathematically "as if" they corresponded to a gravity model when evaluating trout streams. This is an interesting finding because if it obtains under repeated research, it provides a theoretical rationale for the regularities inherent in the spatial interaction results. That is, individuals can be represented "as if" they make judgments in a manner mathematically similar to a gravity model. Individual differences as reflected in parameter differences might then be the next focus of study if the models can be first shown to fit real data. Both the range of variance and any systematic relationships that may obtain with environmental and/or personal characteristics of the individual might then become important. Such differences, however, cannot be detected in the absence of "within-subjects" designs.

In any event, these empirical applications have resulted in the generation of hypotheses that must now be tested in the real world, as well as in repeated studies in quasi-laboratory contexts. It is hoped that these results have stimulated sufficient interest to permit a large number of the questions raised to be more fully investigated.

A final and important possibility is that the models described herein are wrong. Each paradigm in psychology argues that the others fail to account for data in various experiments, while the accused paradigms "explain" such deviations by appeal to various factors. Thus, these methodologies have both proponents and opponents. Most are reviewed in Slovic and Lichenstein [53].

Perhaps geographers can assist in the development and testing of psychological theory by remaining open-minded to various developments, by recognizing the problems and limitations attendant to the borrowing of psychological theory, and by providing empirical evidence and possibly theoretical extensions of their own.

244   SPECIFIC PROBLEMS AND APPLICATIONS

LITERATURE CITED

1. Anderson, N. H. "Averaging versus Adding As a Stimulus Combination Rule in Impression Formation." *Journal of Experimental Psychology,* 87 (1967), 158–65.
2. ———. "Functional Measurement and Psychophysical Judgment." *Psychological Review,* 77 (1970), 153–70.
3. ———. "Information Integration Theory: A Brief Survey." *CHIP 24,* Center for Human Information Processing, U.C.S.D., La Jolla, April, 1972.
4. ———. "Cross Task Validation of Functional Measurement." *CHIP 26,* Center for Human Information Processing, University of California, San Diego, June, 1972.
5. ———. "Looking for Configurality in Clinical Judgment." *Psychological Bulletin,* 78 (1972), 93–102.
6. ———. "Cognitive Algebra: Integration Theory Applied to Social Attribution." *CHIP 31,* Center for Human Information Processing, U.C.S.D., La Jolla, December, 1972.
7. ———. "Algebraic Models in Perception." In *Handbook of Perception,* vol. 2, ed. E. C. Carterette and M. P. Friedman. New York: Academic Press, 1974.
8. Bechtel, G. G. "The Analysis of Variance in Pair-wise Scaling." *Psychometrika,* 32, (1967), 47–65.
9. Birnbaum, M. H. "The Devil Rides Again: Correlation as an Index of Fit." *Psychological Bulletin,* in press.
10. Birnbaum, M. H., and C. T. Veit. "Scale Convergence as a Criterion for Rescaling Information Integration with Difference, Ratio, and Averaging Tasks." *Perception and Psychophysics,* in press.
11. Bock, R. D., and L. B. Jones. *The Measurement and Prediction of Judgment and Choice.* San Francisco: Holden-Day, 1968.
12. Brunswick, E. *Perception and the Representative Design of Experiments.* Berkeley: University of California Press, 1956.
13. Burnett, P. "The Dimensions of Alternatives in Spatial Choice Processes." *Geographical Analysis,* 5 (1973), 181–204.
14. Cliff, N. "Scaling." *Annual Review of Psychology* (1973), 473–506.
15. Curry, L. "Central Places in the Random Spatial Economy." *Journal of Regional Science,* 7 (1967), 217–38.
16. Dawes, R. M. "A Case Study of Graduate Admissions: Application of Three Principles of Human Decision-Making." *American Psychologist,* 26 (1971), 180–88.
17. Dawes, R. M., and B. Corrigan. "Linear Models in Decision-Making." *Psychological Bulletin,* in press.
18. Dorfman, D. D., and D. Biderman. "A Learning Model for a Continuum of Sensory States." *Journal of Mathematical Psychology,* 8 (1971), 264–84.
19. Dyreson, D. "Control Theory and the Spatial Dynamics of a Settlement System." Paper presented to the Southwest Division of the Association of American Geographers, San Antonio, April, 1972.
20. ———. Conceptualizing Settlement Systems as Sets of Learning Monads." Paper presented at the Conference on Formal Methods in the Analysis of Regional Systems, N.S.F. Board on the Use of Mathematics in the Social Sciences, 18–20, October, 1973.
21. ———. "Simulating Spatial Avoidance Behavior: Robbers, Cops, and Stochastic Automata." *Proceedings, Association of American Geographers Meetings,* Atlanta, 1973, 64–66.
22. Downs, R. M. "The Cognitive Structure of an Urban Shopping Center." *Environment and Behavior,* 2 (1970), 13–39.

23. Einhorn, H. J. "Use of Nonlinear, Noncompensatory Models in Decision-Making." *Psychological Bulletin,* 73, (1970), 221–30.

24. Fishbein, M. *Readings in Attitude Theory and Measurement.* New York: Wiley, 1967.

25. Goldberg, L. R. "Simple Models or Simple Processes? Some Research on Clinical Judgments." *American Psychologist,* 23, (1968), 483–96.

26. ———. "Simple Models of Clinical Judgment: An Empirical Comparison between Linear and Nonlinear Representations of the Human Inference Process." *Organization Behavior and Human Performance,* 6 (1971), 458–79.

27. Golledge, R. G. "The Geographical Relevance of Some Learning Theories." In *Behavioral Problems in Geography: A Symposium,* ed. K. R. Cox and R. G. Golledge. Northwestern University Studies in Geography, no. 17, Department of Geography, Northwestern University, 1969.

28. Hahn, G. J., and S. S. Shapiro. *A Catalog and Computer Program of the Design and Analysis of Orthogonal Symmetric and Assymmetric Fractional Factorial Experiments.* T15 Rep. No. 66-C-165. Schenectady, N.Y.: General Electric Co., 1966.

29. Hammond, K. R. "New Directions in Research on Conflict Resolution." *Journal of Social Issues,* 21 (1965), 44–66.

30. Harvey, D. *Explanation in Geography.* London: Edward Arnold, 1969.

31. Hoffman, P. J. "The Paramorphic Representation of Clinical Judgment." *Psychological Bulletin,* 57 (1960), 116–31.

32. Hoffman, P. J., P. Slovic, and L. G. Rorer. "An Analysis of Variance Model for the Assessment of Configural Cue Utilization in Clinical Judgment." *Psychological Bulletin,* 69 (1968), 338–49.

33. Hursch, C., K. R. Hammond, J. L. Hursch. "Some Methodological Considerations in Multiple Cue Probability Studies." *Psychological Review,* 71 (1964), 42–60.

34. Lampel, A. K., and N. H. Anderson. "Combining Visual and Verbal Information in an Impression-Formation Task." *Journal of Personality and Social Psychology,* 9 (1968), 1–6.

35. Louviere, J. J. "An Empirical Analysis of Individual Preferences for Selected Attributes of Grocery Stores and Their Relationship to Selected Socioeconomic Characteristics." Paper presented to the West Lakes Division of the Association of American Geographers, October, 1971.

36. ———. "Final Report on a Before and After Transit Innovation Study." Technical Report No. 10, Institute of Urban and Regional Research, University of Iowa, January, 1973.

37. ———. *A Psychophysical-Experimental Approach to Modeling Spatial Behavior.* PhD. dissertation, Department of Geography, University of Iowa, July, 1973.

38. ———. "Predicting the Evaluation of Real Stimulus Objects from Abstract Evaluation of Their Attributes: The Case of Trout Streams." Submitted to *Journal of Applied Psychology.*

39. Louviere, J. J., L. L. Beavers, K. L. Norman, and F. C. Stetzer. "Theory Methodology and Findings in Mode Choice Behavior." Working Paper No. 11, Institute of Urban and Regional Research, University of Iowa, July, 1973.

40. Norman, K. L. "A Method of Maximum Likelihood Estimation for Information Integration Models." *Psychometrika,* in press.

41. ———. "Dynamic Processes in Stimulus Integration Theory: The Effects of Feedback on Motor Movements." *Journal of Experimental Psychology,* in press.

42. Norman, K. L., and J. J. Louviere. "Integration of Attributes in Bus Transportation: Two Modeling Approaches." Submitted to *The Journal of Applied Psychology.*

43. Olsson, G. "Distance and Human Interaction: A Bibliography and Review." Bibliography Series No. 2, Regional Science Association, 1965.

44. Rogers, D. S. *The Role of Search and Learning in Consumer Spatial Behavior: The Case of Urban Immigrants.* M. S. thesis, Department of Geography, University of Wisconsin, 1970.

45. Rushton, G. "Analysis of Spatial Behavior by Revealed Space Preferences." *Annals, The Association of American Geographers,* 59 (1969), 391–400.

46. ———. "Temporal Changes in Space Preference Structures." *Proceedings, The Association of American Geographers,* 1 (1969), 129–32.

47. ———. "The Scaling of Locational Preferences." In *Behavioral Problems in Geography: A Symposium,* ed. K. R. Cox and R. G. Golledge. Northwestern University Studies in Geography No. 17, Department of Geography, Northwestern University, 1969.

48. ———. "Behavioral Correlates of Urban Spatial Structure." *Economic Geography,* 47 (1971), 49–58.

49. Shanteau, J. C. "An Additive Model for Sequential Decision Making." *Journal of Experimental Psychology,* 85 (1970), 181–91.

50. Shanteau, J., and N. H. Anderson. "Integration Theory Applied to Judgments of the Value of Information." *Journal of Experimental Psychology,* 92 (1972), 266–75.

51. Sidowski, J. B., and N. H. Anderson. "Judgments of City Occupation Combinations." *Psychonomic Science,* 7 (1967), 279–80.

52. Slovic, P. "Analyzing the Expert Judge: A Descriptive Study of a Stockbroker's Decision Processes." *Journal of Applied Psychology,* 53 (1969), 649–744.

53. Slovic, P., and S. Lichenstein. "Comparison of Bayesian and Regression Approaches to the Study of Information Processing in Judgment." *Organizational Behavior and Human Performance,* 6 (1971), 649–744.

54. Stevens, S. S. "The Surprising Simplicity of Sensory Metrics." *American Psychologist,* 17 (1962), 29–39.

55. ———. "Neural Events and the Psychophysical Law." *Science,* 170 (1970), 1043–50.

56. Stewart, T. R., and L. Gelberd. "Capturing Judgment Policies: A New Approach for Citizen Participation in Planning." *Proceedings, U.R.I.S.A.,* 1972.

57. Tversky, A. "Elimination by Aspects: A Theory of Choice." *Psychological Review,* 79 (1972), 281–99.

58. Weiss, D. J. "Averaging: An Empirical Validity Criterion for Magnitude Estimation." *CHIP 26,* U.C.S.D., La Jolla, June 1972.

59. Wilson, A. G. "Models in Urban Planning: A Synoptic Review of Recent Literature." *Urban Studies,* 5 (1968), 249–76.

60. ———. *Entropy in Urban and Regional Modeling.* London: Pion Press, 1970.

61. Yntema, D. B., and W. S. Torgerson. "Man-Computer Cooperation in Decisions Requiring Common Sense." *IRE Transactions of the Professional Group on Human Factors in Electronics,* HFE 2(1), 1961, 20–26.

CHAPTER 13

G. O. EWING

Environmental and Spatial Preferences of Interstate Migrants in the United States

INTRODUCTION

The mathematical modeling and prediction of interregional migration has been one of the more extensively researched themes in spatial interaction analysis [1, 3, 4, 7, 8, 12, 13, 16, 17, 18, 19, 20, 21, 23, 24, 27, 29, 30, 32, 33, 34, 35, 36, 38, 39, 40]. The typical goal of these studies has been to identify the factors accounting for variations in the flow of migrants between different places and to determine the relative weights of these factors. Invariably, migration has been assumed to be explicable in terms of the characteristics of the chosen destination, including its distance from the origin, or in terms of differences between characteristics of the origin and destination. No notion of choice between alternative destinations is contained in these models. This paper posits an alternative model that considers migration as the outcome of a choice between alternative possible destinations. Specifically it considers some of the methodological problems inherent in spatial choice models, and, assuming a particular form of choice model, the model determines the relative effect of various attributes on a destination's chance of being chosen.

TRADITIONAL GRAVITY MODELS OF MIGRATION

Although there are many variants of the typical mathematical model of interregional migration, the following is a common general form:

$$m_{ij} = c \prod_{k=1}^{r} V_{jk}{}^{a}{}_{k} D_{ij}{}^{b}$$ (1)

where

c = an empirically estimated constant of proportionality

V_{jk} = the score of place j on the kth variable, or a measure of the difference between, or ratio of, i and j's scores on the kth variable

D_{ij} = the distance from i to j

R = the number of variables included in the model

$a_k,(k = 1, 2, \ldots r)$ and b = weighting factors on each variable whose values are typically estimated by solving the log linear transformation of equation (1) using linear regression

m_{ij} = the migration rate from i to j, normally defined as $M_{ij}/P_i P_j$, where M_{ij} = gross migration from i to j, and $P_i P_j$ = the populations of i and j respectively.

In some studies the dependent variable in the above gravity model is M_{ij} or $m_{ij} = M_{ij}/P_i$, whereas in others, referred to as "intervening opportunity" models, D_{ij} is replaced by O_{ij}, the number of alternative destinations (opportunities) as close or closer to i than j [1, 4, 8, 13, 23, 29, 38, 39, 40]. In studies where M_{ij} is the dependent variable [13, 16, 17, 19, 27, 35, 36, 38], the percentage variance explained by only a few variables is consistently quite high; for example, in Lowry's *Migration and Metropolitan Growth*, 68 percent is "explained" by P_i, P_j and D_{ij} [27]. In fact, 51 percent is explained by the two population figures, leaving only 17 percent accounted for by distance and even smaller percentages by other variables. Inevitably, the number of migrants leaving a place increases in proportion to the population of the place, whilst the larger the number of jobs and housing units in a destination, the larger is the number of immigrants to that place likely to be, other things being equal. In general, in studies where gross migration, M_{ij}, is the dependent variable, the largest partial correlations are with P_i and P_j presumably reflecting in large part a simple multiplier effect. In contrast, when this multiplier effect is removed by defining the dependent variable to be the migration rate, $m_{ij} = M_{ij}/P_i P_j$, the value of r^2 in those studies [16, 18, 21, 24] is markedly lower. There are several possible explanations of this decrease in r^2. Heteroscedasticity in the dependent variable, M_{ij} or log M_{ij}, which is typical of interaction data where the frequency curve of M_{ij} is positively skewed, is one cause of large r^2 values. The skewness in the distribution of the interaction rate, in this case $m_{ij} = M_{ij}/P_iP_j$, is typically much less severe, and an associated decrease in r^2 results. Also, in a model where the data are subject to a significant sampling error or where the model is incorrectly specified, a higher value of r^2 is obtained by using absolute flows rather than per capita rates of flow.

Also, where the gravity model is calibrated using data on interaction from different origins, the value of r^2 is typically lower than if data for only one origin are used. Thus, in one study [24], when m_{ij} is regressed against certain variables for each origin separately, r^2 ranges from .42 to .80, but when m_{ij} for all origins is considered simultaneously in one regression, the coefficient falls to .23. It might be concluded from this that the traditional gravity model, which by definition incorporates only characteristics of the origin and destination chosen, is not designed to predict movement in cases where the spatial distribution of alternatives changes, as it must when the location of the origin changes. For example, for any destination, j, and distance, D_{ij}, the traditional gravity model predicts a single value of m_{ij}, without reference to the distance to alternative opportunities, and the predicted value of m_{ij} changes only as D_{ij} changes. An alternative model is one where, for two origins, h and k, even if D_{hj} and D_{kj} are equal, the predicted values of m_{hj} and m_{kj} are not necessarily equal, but depend on the distances of other possible destinations from h and k. The predictive weakness of the gravity model in this type of situation, which is also apparent in traditional gravity models of shopping behavior [31], prompts the suggestion that a model which explicitly considers the nature of the alternatives available as well as the one chosen might be more appropriate in explaining those movements that are thought to be the result of choice between alternatives.

THE SPATIAL CHOICE APPROACH

To date there have been relatively few analyses of spatial interaction couched in terms of spatial choice [5, 9, 10, 14, 15, 22, 25, 37], most of them in the field of shopping behavior. Moreover, they typically incorporate very few predictive variables, and these are normally assumed, rather than proved, to be the most important in explaining spatial choice. Two exceptions meriting attention are studies by Burnett [5] and Goodchild and Ross [15] that do not constrain the number of independent variables considered. The former uses a method that requires that several individuals or groups rank the same set of alternatives. However, to be able to consider a destination as the *same* alternative for two or more individuals or groups it must be the same distance from them. Hence the method successfully employed by Burnett where several similarly located subjects ranked alternative destinations is inappropriate in this case where few origin states are similarly located with respect to destination states, and census data on migrants from within the same state provide no information on individuals' ranking of destinations. By contrast, the method devised by Goodchild and Ross is able to handle differently located origins; but since it is designed to consider only cases where a more distant alternative is chosen in preference to a nearer one, spatial bias in the distribution of origins relative to destinations is liable to bias results.

The following discussion suggests a procedure that avoids the latter problem and does not restrict the number of variables considered. Beginning by assuming a particular spatial choice model, the proposed method of solution is argued for against a background of alternative, more direct, and traditional methods that might seem appropriate but are suggested to be unfeasible. This line of reasoning should also illustrate the considerable problems that have been encountered in trying to operationalize spatial choice models of multiorigin interaction data.

Spatial choice models may take many forms, but the one most commonly used in geography [5, 9, 14, 22, 25] and with its origins in psychology [2, 28] can be generalized as follows:

$$ip(j/T) = {}_iU_j \Big/ \sum_{\substack{g=1 \\ g \neq 1}}^{n} {}_iU_g \tag{2}$$

$$= \left[\sum_{k=1}^{r} a_k V_{jk} / D_{ij}{}^b \right] \Big/ \left[\sum_{\substack{g=1 \\ g \neq 1}}^{n} \left(\sum_{k=1}^{r} a_k V_{gk} / D_{ig}{}^b \right) \right]$$

where $_ip(j/T)$ is the probability of a subject located at i choosing alternative j from T, the total set of alternatives: $_iU_j$ is the utility of worth of alternative j as viewed from location i; and n is the number of alternatives in the total set, T. Equation (2) is in fact the probabilistic allocation component of what Wilson defines as the production-constrained gravity model [42, p. 171] in his "family of spatial interaction models." Unlike the traditional gravity model, which predicts the absolute rate of flow between all pairs of origins and destinations, the allocation model assumes the rate of departure from an origin to be given, and predicts only the probability that a departure from i will terminate at j, $_ip(j/T)$, where for any origin i, $\sum\limits_{\substack{j=i \\ j\neq i}}^{n} _ip(j/T) = 1$. In other words, for each origin it predicts the relative rates of movement from it to all destinations, not absolute rates from all origins to all destinations. Spatial choice models do *not* predict whether a trip will take place, but rather assume a trip as given and predict its destination deterministically or probabilistically. In order to predict absolute rates of interregional migration for all origin-destination pairs, a separate model of the emigration rate from any origin, i, would be required. The choice model coupled with the emigration model would enable the interregional migration rate from i to j to be predicted as:

$$m_{ij} = _ip(j/T)em_i \qquad (3)$$

where em_i is the emigration rate from i. Since no emigration model is defined here, no attempt is made to compare a choice model with a gravity model in terms of predictive capability. Rather, the following discussion will concentrate on demonstrating that it is possible to empirically determine estimates of the constants in the spatial choice model in equation (2).

The data analysed are interstate migration flows between the conterminous states as defined in the 1960 United States population census [41] and interprovincial flows based on data in the 1961 Canadian census [6]. Both sets of statistics are based on a 25 percent sample in which the number of migrants from i to j is defined as those residents of j in 1960 or 1961 who were domiciled in i in 1955 or 1956, for the United States and Canada respectively.

DIFFICULTIES IN SOLVING THE SPATIAL CHOICE EQUATION

Almost invariably, studies of migration and of other interaction data that use a traditional gravity model such as equation (1), solve for the parameter values in the gravity equation that minimize

$$\sum_{\substack{i=1 \\ }}^{n} \sum_{\substack{j=1 \\ j \neq i}}^{n} (m_{ij} - m^*_{ij})^2,$$

where m^*_{ij} is calculated in equation (1). This is usually accomplished by rewriting the model as a linear equation. Thus, equation (1) would be rewritten as:

$$\log m_{ij} = \log c + a_1 \log V_{j1} + a_2 \log V_{j2} + \ldots \qquad (4)$$
$$+ a_r \log V_{jr} - b D_{ij}$$

and provided the number of observations, $n(n-1)$, at least equals the number of parameters to be empirically determined, least-squares linear regression can be used to estimate parameter values.

In contrast, a choice model such as equation (2) cannot be transformed to a linear equation in which the weighting factors become regression coefficients. The alternative method of solution which the form of equation (2) might suggest, nonlinear regression, is only suitable if the number of unknown parameter values is not large. But, if one of the objectives is to include many variables in the model and determine empirically which are significant, then non-linear regression, which typically uses an iterative heuristic to solve for parameter values, is infeasible due to the vast computation time required as the number of parameters to be estimated gets large.

An alternative approach is to try to solve initially for values of $_iu_j$ for all i and j. Given estimates of these, it would then be possible to determine the relative influences of V_k, $k = 1, 2, \ldots, r$ and D_{ij} on $_ip(j/T)$ by solving the equation

$$_iU_j = c \sum_{k=1}^{r} a_k V_{jk} D_{ij}{}^b. \qquad (5)$$

One possible means of estimating all $_iU_j$'s is to solve the equation

$$_ip(j/T) = \sum_{k=1}^{n} (_kU_jx_k / \sum_{\substack{g=1 \\ g \neq k}}^{n} {}_kU_gx_k) \tag{6}$$

for values of $_kU_j$, where x_k is a dummy variable, such that $x_k=1$ if $k=i$, and $x_k=0$ otherwise. Although it is in principle soluble, since there are no more unknowns than observations, it is in practice insoluble because the number of unknowns is very large, specifically $n(n-1)$, i.e., 48×47 in the U.S. case and 10×9 in the Canadian.

An alternative to the above analytic method of solving for $_iU_j$ values would be a scaling procedure. Each $_iU_j$ refers to the utility of place j at a particular distance, D_{ij}, which will be referred to as a place/distance combination. If a matrix could be constructed in which the probability of

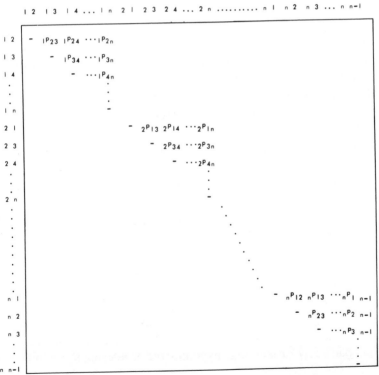

FIG. 1. Matrix of preferences between place/distance combinations

any one place/distance combination being chosen in preference to any other combination was known from migration data, then scaling techniques would enable an interval scale value ($_iU_j$) to be estimated for each place/distance combination. The order of the matrix would be $n(n-1)$, which is the number of place/distance combinations, given that there are $n-1$ possible destinations for each of n origins, and no destination is equidistant from two or more origins. But, as shown in Figure 1, only 1/nth part of the matrix could contain information on the probability of one place/distance combination being chosen in preference over another, since by definition it is only if the origin is common that two alternative destinations can be considered to be chosen between by any individual or group. In addition the 1/nth of the matrix would consist entirely of unconnected submatrices, making it impossible to determine an interval or even an ordinal scale of $_iU_j$ values.

A related procedure designed to produce a smaller but more complete matrix of preference probabilities, involves assigning each place/distance combination to one of a small set of categories, or "location types" that are defined in terms of a few variables, for example, distance, unemployment rate, and urbanized percentage. For example, California as seen from North Carolina might belong to the location type defined by the limits 3,000–4,000 miles, 5–7 percent unemployment, and 60–70 percent urbanized. As long as there are relatively few location types (which in turn implies relatively few variables hypothesized as relevant, as well as relatively few categories for each variable), then a fairly large percentage of all possible pairs of these location types may actually exist as alternatives for choice. But as soon as there are a large number of variables each with two or more categories, the product of these categories defines such a large set of location types that only a small percentage of all possible pairs of them would exist as actual pairs of destinations. The resultant highly incomplete matrix of preference probabilities would therefore be unscalable. Thus, although this method has been used [9, 10, 37], it is typically very restrictive as to the number of variables that can be handled and permits only fairly gross distinctions between destinations in terms of their scores on any one variable. This approach is therefore unsuitable where more than a few variables are hypothesized as relevant to the interaction data.

A METHOD OF SOLVING THE SPATIAL CHOICE EQUATION

The crux of the problem, in trying to solve either analytically or by scaling for values of $_iU_j$, is the fact that destinations are at different distances from different origins. In other respects any one destination can be considered as the same combination of variables, or "commodity bundle," irrespective of the origin it is viewed from. But, given that the distances to each of $n-1$ destinations are different for each of n origins, there is a total of $n(n-1)$ alternatives, only a small percentage of which are compared by subjects (see Fig. 1). But if it were possible to hold distance constant, the number of alternatives would be reduced to n, enabling a much larger percentage of them to be compared. The resultant preference matrix of order n where the cell in row i, column j contains the probability of alternative i being chosen in preference to j, would enable an interval scale of these places' attractiveness to be estimated, where "attractiveness" is defined as the utility of a place when distance from origin is ignored.

The basis of a solution, then, depends on somehow holding the effect of distance constant. One way is to consider only migration to pairs of destinations that are equidistant from an origin and therefore to ignore all migration figures for destinations that are at different distances from an origin. Since choice between only pairs of equidistant destinations is involved now, rather than choice from the total set, T, the choice probability model in equation (2) can be simplified to

$$p_{jk} = A_j D_{ij}^{-b}/(A_j D_{ij}^{-b} + A_k D_{ik}^{-b})$$

$$= A_j D_{ij}^{-b}/D_{ij}^{-b} (A_j + A_k), \quad \text{given that} \quad D_{ij} = D_{ik}$$

$$= A_j/(A_j + A_k) \tag{7}$$

where p_{jk} is the probability that j is chosen in preference to the equidistant alternative k; and A_j is the attractiveness of destinations j, defined as

$$A_j = c + \sum_{k=1}^{r} a_k V_{kj}. \tag{8}$$

If interval scale estimates of $A_j, j = 1, 2, \ldots, n$ are obtained, the relative influence of the attributes of a destination on its attractiveness can then be found by solving equation (8). In addition, given estimates of A_j, $j=1, 2, \ldots, n$ and the equality in equation (8), an estimate of b in equation (2) can be found. Thus, the ability to estimate p_{jk} values, where j and k are equidistant destinations, provides the basis of a complete solution of equation (2), the spatial choice model.

An empirical estimate of p_{jk} is defined as

$$p^*_{jk}=m_{ij}/(m_{ij}+m_{ik})$$

where m_{ij} is the migration rate from i to j, defined as M_{ij}/P_iP_j; and i is an origin from which destinations j and k are equidistant. Although this equidistance criterion for including data in the analysis inevitably reduces the amount of migration data that is usable, the problem is still soluble.

One other situation where the effect of distance is the same for two destinations, and can therefore be considered constant, is shown in Figure 2. Considering j and k as destinations and g and h as origins, any additional size in the migration rate m_{gj} over m_{gk} due to g's proximity to j is compensated for by a larger m_{hk} compared to m_{hj} due to h's proximity to k. Thus, with the effect of distance constant the following estimate is valid:

$$p'_{jk}=(m_{gj}/m_{gj} + m_{gk})/[(m_{gj}/m_{gj} + m_{gk}) + (m_{hk}/m_{hk} + m_{hj})]. \quad (10)$$

Of the estimates obtained by equations (9) and (10), less than 5 percent are p'_{jk} values. The overall estimate of p_{jk} used is the weighted average of all p^*_{jk} and p'_{jk}. Specifically, the estimate is

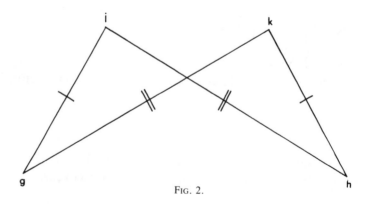

Fig. 2.

$$\hat{p}_{jk} = \left[\sum_{i=1}^{s} p^*_{jk} \min \{M_{ij}, M_{ik}\} \right.$$

$$\left. + \sum_{g,h=1}^{t} p'_{jk} \min \{M_{gj}, M_{gk}, M_{hj}, M_{hk}\} \right] \bigg/$$

$$\left[\sum_{i=1}^{s} \min \{M_{ij}, M_{ik}\} + \sum_{g,h=1}^{t} \min \{M_{gj}, M_{gk}, M_{gj}, M_{h}\} \right] \quad (11)$$

where s is the number of origins, i, that are equidistant from j and k and therefore satisfy equation (9); and t is the number of pairs of origins, g and h, that satisfy the equidistance criterion for using equation (10).

Estimates of p_{jk} for most pairs of destinations were obtained. But in order to maximize the amount of information so obtained without doing violence to the notion of equidistance, all distances where the larger was less than 10 percent greater than the smaller, are assumed to be equal. The resultant probabilities form a lower[1] off-diagonal triangular matrix of order n, with the row and column objects being destination states. From equation (7), the greater the probability of one destination being chosen over another, the more one can be said to exceed the other in attractiveness, that is, the larger is p_{jk}, the greater the size of A_j relative to A_k.

Given estimates of p_{jk}, A_j values for all states can be estimated using a nonmetric multidimensional scaling algorithm, in this instance Guttman-Lingoes Smallest Space Analysis (SSA−I) [26]. In one respect this application differs from normal usage. An algorithm such as SSA-I is typically used to analyze a matrix of coefficients of stimulus dissimilarity (d_{jk}) with the aim of determining the number of dimensions of space necessary to configure the stimuli such that the inter-stimulus distances (d'_{jk}) are as nearly as possible monotonic with the d_{jk} values. In the ideal solution the least dissimilar pair of stimuli should be the closest pair of points in the space; the second least dissimilar pair, the second closest; and so on. But in this application the data are measures of dominance, not dissimilarity; specifically they measure the extent to which one stimulus exceeds another in terms of attractiveness. As a consequence the solution should be, by definition, a unidimensional scale of attractiveness. In fact, the solution is necessarily unidimensional, since only a scale, and not a space, can convey dominance information.

Since SSA-I, like related algorithms, requires data in the form of dissimilarity measures, an appropriate transformation of the dominance coefficient, p_{jk}, is required. And, since this involves a transformation of the left-hand side of equation (7), the same transformation of the right-hand side must yield a measure that can be interpreted as a measure of the difference in j and k's attractiveness. The following shows a transformation satisfying this requirement.

It is clear from equation (7) that

$$p_{jk}/p_{kj} = [A_j/A_j + A_k)]/[A_k/(A_j + A_k)]$$
$$= A_j/A_k. \tag{12}$$

Hence,

$$|\log p_{jk} - \log p_{kj}| = |\log A_j - \log A_k|. \tag{13}$$

Equation (13) provides a measure of the difference in j and k's attractivenesses on a logarithmic scale ($\log A$). It is assumed that the empirical estimate, $|\log \hat{p}_{jk} - \log \hat{p}_{kj}|$ is a monotonic function of $|\log p_{jk} - \log p_{kj}|$, and therefore of $|\log A_j - \log A_k|$, and it is this estimate that serves as the dissimilarity measure analysed. The SSA-I algorithm seeks those values of $\log A_j$, for $j = 1, 2, \ldots, n$, such that the attractiveness differences $|\log A_j - \log A_k|$, for all pairs of j and k, are as closely as possible a monotonic function of the input dissimilarity estimates, $|\log \hat{p}_{jk} - \log \hat{p}_{kj}|$, $j, k = 1, 2, \ldots, n$. The resultant interval scale of $\log A_j$ values is shown in Figure 3. Since the scale is unique up to only a linear transformation, that linear transformation is sought which maximizes the correlation between A_j/A_k and $\hat{p}_{jk}/\hat{p}_{kj}$, for all pairs of j and k. The limits of the scale shown in Figure 3 are the result of that transformation. Though an indication of the scale's orientation is not provided by the algorithm, inspection of the original $\hat{p}_{jk}$ matrix clearly indicates Nevada to be at the top and West Virginia to be at the bottom.

The first striking feature of the scale is the similarity in the attractiveness of states belonging to the same geographic area, and the correspondence of these areas to readily identifiable geographic regions. The regional labels, based on a subjective grouping, are provided solely as a visual aid. The second feature to note is that the intrinsic attractiveness of areas that either have relatively low absolute immigration due to their small population or lower migration rates than might otherwise exist,

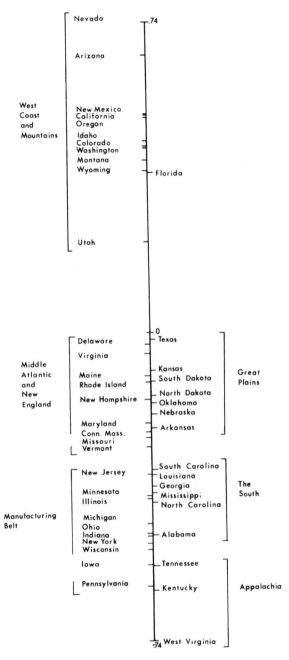

FIG. 3. Attractiveness scale of states

due to less central locations, is revealed by this method, in which effects of size and distance are held constant.

Spatial variation in the attractiveness of states and its strong regional trend are more clearly illustrated in Figure 4. Contour interpolation is based on values of log A_j assigned to the major center of the jth state. The dominance of the West Coast and mountain states, and the striking resemblance between the area of lowest attractiveness and the manufacturing belt and Appalachia is suggestive of explanatory variables, which are considered below. As might be expected Florida ranks close behind most western states, and one might speculate as to whether an image of a staid Utah compared to other western states explains its lower scale position. The higher rating of areas with relatively small populations such as the mountain states, and most of the Great Plains might be treated as evidence that, if the capacity of these states grew, they would experience significant immigration, assuming continuation of this attractiveness structure. Though the stress value of .34 indicates an imperfect monotonic fit of $|\log \hat{p}_{jk} - \log \hat{p}_{kj}|$ and $|\log A_j - \log A_k|$, the very definite regional structure in the scale suggests that at least the general pattern is valid, if not the precise location of each state. In any case, the remaining analysis serves in part as a test of the validity of the scale values.

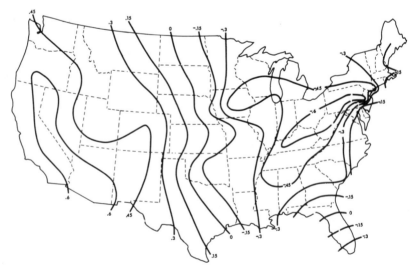

Fig. 4. Attractiveness surface of states

In general, the scale not only reveals interesting evidence of decidedly regional preferences, as revealed by actual migration behavior, but it also suggests variables that might explain scale positions. Before referring to these variables, a comparison with results of the Canadian interprovincial migration analysis is provided.

AN ATTRACTIVENESS RANKING OF CANADIAN PROVINCES

Given that there are only ten provinces and that they are arranged linearly, significant gaps result in the $\hat{p}_{jk}$ matrix, so that at best a ranking algorithm can be used to provide an ordinal scale of provinces (see Table 1); and even then the scale is not wholly reliable since many $\hat{p}_{jk}$ are based on only one or two equidistant origins. Certain similarities to the U.S. picture are nevertheless evident. Excepting Nova Scotia and Prince Edward Island, the general pattern, similar to that in the United States, is for the new west to dominate the industrialized, "crowded," or economically depressed east. Also, just as New England states are rated as attractive as Great Plains states, the Canadian equivalents of the former, Nova Scotia and Prince Edward Island, rate about equal to the prairie provinces.

Insofar as the two more economically depressed Maritime Provinces, Newfoundland and New Brunswick, are perhaps more comparable to the Appalachian states than New England, their low rank is again comparable to the U.S. picture. The one province that has no U.S. counterpart, namely Quebec, ranks lowest, attributable in part to its being predominantly French-speaking and therefore unattractive to

TABLE 1

ATTRACTIVENESS RANKING OF CANADIAN PROVINCES

Nova Scotia
Alberta
British Columbia
Prince Edward Island
Manitoba
Saskatchewan
Ontario
New Brunswick
Newfoundland
Quebec

many migrants from the virtually unilingual English-speaking provinces.

A REGRESSION OF ATTRACTIVENESS SCORES
AGAINST STATE CHARACTERISTICS

Having determined an interval scale of log A, a least-squares solution to equation (8) is sought in terms of the following social, economic, and physical variables describing the jth state:

V_{1j} = total state population in thousands, 1960

V_{2j} = nonwhite population in thousands, 1960

V_{3j} = percentage of the state population that is urbanized, based on the 1960 U.S. Census definition of an urban place as any town with a population above 30,000

V_{4j} = average annual per capita dollar expenditure by manufacturing industries on new plant and equipment between 1954 and 1960

V_{5j} = percentage change in manufacturing industry's expenditures on new plant and equipment between 1954 and 1960

V_{6j} = average male weekly wage in manufacturing between 1956 and 1960

V_{7j} = average annual percentage of unemployed in the civilian labour force, 1956–60

V_{8j} = a social welfare index[2]

V_{9j} = black percentage of population, 1960

V_{10j} = living cost in a selected city based on average annual budget of a four-person family living at an intermediate level, as defined by the U.S. Department of Labor for fall, 1971[3]

V_{11j} = an estimate of real living costs defined as V_{10j}/V_{6j}

V_{12j} = population density per square mile, 1960

V_{13j} = mean annual number of hours of sunshine in a major city

V_{14j} = mean annual precipitation in a major city, in inches

V_{15j} = mean annual snowfall in a major city

V_{16j} = sum of departures of daily average temperature above 65°F. in degrees Fahrenheit in a major city

V_{17j} = sum of departures of daily average temperature below 65°F. in degrees Fahrenheit in a major city

V_{18j} = average annual sulphur dioxide emission in SMSA's in the jth state between 1961[4] and 1965 in tons per square mile

V_{19j} = average annual suspended particulates in SMSA's in the jth state between 1961 and 1965 in micrograms per cubic meter.

Since the distribution of A_j is highly skewed, the dependent variable is defined as log A. Stepwise linear regression yields the results shown in Table 2. On the basis of F-statistics, only the first six variables entered contribute significantly to an increase in the multiple correlation coefficient. The fact that six variables account for 63 percent of the variance in attractiveness scores suggests the procedure used to determine state attractiveness scores has some value. Although causal interpretation of the equation can be misleading, the results are suggestive of general factors affecting state attractiveness to migrants. Significantly, the three

TABLE 2

STEPWISE LINEAR REGRESSION RESULTS

Variable	Regression Coefficient	Standard error of estimate	Cumulative R²	F
V_{14} (precipitation)	−0.01066	.00420	.30	19.36
V_{17} (day degree departures below 65°F)	−0.00005	.00003	.38	6.90
V_2 (non-white population)	−0.00026	.00013	.47	6.62
V_3 (percentage urban)	0.01454	.00395	.51	3.25
V_{18} (sulphur dioxide)	−0.00191	.00061	.60	9.92
V_{12} (population density)	−0.00051	.00030	.63	2.91

$F_j = SS_{regj}/(SS_{res}/N\text{-}m_j)$

where SS_{regj} = the contribution of the variable entered at the jth step to the regression sum of squares;

SS_{res} = residual sum of squares;

N = number of observations; and

m_j = number of variables included in the equation at the jth step.

variables contributing most to the model all relate to the physical environment (precipitation, day degrees below 65° F. and sulphur dioxide in SMSA's), leading to the obvious interpretation that interstate migrants prefer locations with a dry, warm climate and low urban pollution levels. The negative regression coefficient on the fourth most significant variable, nonwhite population, indicates that areas with large nonwhite populations, specifically the South and the industrialized northeastern states, are less attractive. A conclusion as to whether this is directly attributable to the number of nonwhites or to a large variety of possible correlates of that variable, not considered in this study, cannot be drawn from the data available here.

Finally, the positive coefficient on the "percentage urban" variable combined with a negative coefficient on population density suggests that urbanized states with a low overall population density are more attractive than others. States with a sizable percentage of their population in urban centers but surrounded by large sparsely populated areas such as much of the western United States typify this combination and presumably are more attractive because they provide an unparalleled combination of employment opportunity in the urban centers and outdoor leisure facilities in the nearby sparsely populated areas. The most unattractive states in terms of these two variables would be relatively densely populated rural states. The states coming closest to that description are in Appalachia, and do in fact rate lowest on the attractiveness scale.

ESTIMATION OF THE DISTANCE EXPONENT
IN THE SPATIAL CHOICE EQUATION

Having determined values of A_j, it is possible to solve equation (2) using nonlinear regression, assuming that A_j is an estimate of $\sum_{k=1}^{r} a_k V_{jk}$. However, since the A_j values have interval properties and are therefore only unique up to any linear transformation, equation (2) can be rewritten as

$$p(j/T) = [(c + d\ A_j)/D_{ij}^{b}]/[\sum_{\substack{j=1 \\ j \neq 1}}^{n} (c + d\ A_j)/D_{ij}^{b}], \qquad (14)$$

with c, d, and b the parameters to be solved for. Initial investigation showed the function to be insensitive to changes in values of c and d over a wide range, but very sensitive to relatively small changes in b. Thus, it is assumed that $c = 0$ and $d = 1$. A value of b equal to .97 gives maximum correlation ($r = .62$) between the 2,256 observed and predicted values of $_ip(j/T)$. Although this means only 39 percent of variance in $_ip(j/T)$ is explained by the choice model in equation (14), at least some of the unexplained variance is due to the distorting effect of high $_ip(j/T)$'s associated with large short-distance, trans-border movements between adjacent states whose D_{ij}'s are defined in terms of the distance between the major city of each state. A degree of error in the A_j estimates is another possible source of unexplained variance. However, it is noteworthy that such a simple one-parameter model is capable of explaining even 39 percent of variance.

CONCLUSION

Since considerable variance of $_ip(j/T)$ remains unexplained, it is reasonable to speculate about general reasons, beside the two already mentioned. Three in particular are apparent. First, the particular choice model assumed here, based on a place's utility as a ratio of the sum of all places' utilities, is but one of many possible formulations of a choice model. For example, one reasonable and soluble alternative is a utility difference model of the form

$$_ip(j/T) = c + d(_iU_j - \sum_{\substack{g=1 \\ g \neq i,j}}^{n} {_iU_g}). \tag{15}$$

Second, the assumption that the attractiveness of a state is the same for migrants from all states, which forms the basis of the p_{jk} estimates, and therefore the A_j estimates, is open to question. But to date, analyses seeking to test this assumption [9, 24] have been very restrictive in the independent variables considered and lacking in test for statistically significant differences in regression coefficients. If the above assumption were abandoned, separate predictive models would be required for different origin states or groups of them. Third, the possibility exists that involuntary migration distorts the $\hat{p}_{jk}$ values estimated and the $_ip(j/T)$ values predicted. But for this to be so it requires a sizable percentage of such migrants and significant variation in that percentage for different states. This would seem the least restrictive of the three assumptions. Irrespective of reservations about the predictive ability of the choice model, the attractiveness scale and the independent variables explaining the scale contain interesting evidence as to the motive forces behind long-distance migration in the United States.

1. By definition, $p_{jk} = 1 - p_{kj}$. Hence half the matrix is redundant.
2. Attributable to J. O. Wilson [43].
3. For states where no city was used to estimate living costs, an interpolated estimate is used. The absence of data for the migration period necessitated the use of available recent data. It is likely, however, that the spatial pattern of living costs, as distinct from its absolute level, did not alter much between 1960 and 1971.
4. 1961 is the earliest year for which these data are available.

LITERATURE CITED

1. Anderson, T. R. "Intermetropolitan Migration: A Comparison of the Hypotheses of Zipf and Stouffer." *American Sociological Review,* 20 (1955), 287–91.
2. Atkinson, R. C., G. G. Bower and E. J. Crothers. *An Introduction to Mathematical Learning Theory.* New York: Wiley, 1965.
3. Blanco, C. "The Determinants of Interstate Population Movements." *Journal of Regional Science,* 5 (1963), 77–84.
4. Bright, M. L., and D. S. Thomas. "Interstate Migration and Intervening Opportunities." *American Sociological Review,* 6 (1941), 773–83.
5. Burnett, P. "The Dimensions of Alternatives in Spatial Choice Processes." *Geographical Analysis,* 5 (1973), 181–204.
6. Canadian Dominion Bureau of Statistics. *Census of Canda, 1961, Series 4. 1–9, General Characteristics of the Migrant and Non-migrant Population.* Ottawa, 1963.
7. Celuba, R. J., and R. K. Vedder, "A Note on Migration, Economic Opportunity, and the Quality of Life." *Journal of Regional Science,* 13 (1973), 205–12.
8. Clark, C., and G. R. Peters, "The 'Intervening Opportunities' Methods of Traffic Analyses." *Traffic Quarterly,* 19 (1965), 104–15.
9. De Temple, D. J. "A Space Preference Approach to the Diffusion of Innovations." Geographic Monograph No. 3, Department of Geography, Indiana University, Bloomington, 1971.
10. Ewing, G. "An Analysis of Consumer Space Preference Using the Method of Paired Comparison." Ph.D. dissertation, McMaster University, Hamilton, 1970.
11. ———. "Gravity and Linear Regression Models of Spatial Interaction: A Cautionary Note." *Economic Geography,* 50 (1974), 83–87.
12. Fabricant, R. A. "An Expectational Model of Migration." *Journal of Regional Science,* 10 (1970), 13–24.

13. Galle, O. R., and K. E. Taeuber. "Metropolitan Migration and Intervening Opportunities." *American Sociological Review*, 31 (1966), 5–13.

14. Girt, L. "A Constant Utility Model of Spatial Choice." *Proceedings, Canadian Association of Geographers*, 2 (1971), 63–70.

15. Goodchild, M. F., and J. H. Ross. "Methodological Explorations within the Preference Model of Consumer Spatial Behavior." Multilith, University of Western Ontario, 1971.

16. Greenwood, M. J. "The Determinants of Labor Migration in Egypt." *Journal of Regional Science*, 9 (1969), 283–90.

17. ———. "Lagged Response in the Decision to Migrate." *Journal of Regional Science*, 10 (1970), 375–84.

18. ———. "A Regression Analysis of Migration to Urban Areas of a Less-Developed Country: The Case of India." *Journal of Regional Science*, 11 (1971), 253–64.

19. Greenwood, M. J., and P. J. Gormerly. "A Comparison of the Determinants of White and Nonwhite Interstate Migration." *Demography*, 18 (1971), 141–55.

20. Greenwood, M. J., and D. Sweetland. "The Determinants of Migration between Standard Metropolitan Statistical Areas." *Demography*, 9 (1972), 665–81.

21. Haynes, K. E., D. L. Poston, Jr., and P. Schnirring. "Intermetropolitan Migration in High and Low Opportunity Areas: Indirect Tests of the Distance and Intervening Opportunties Hypotheses." *Economic Geography*, 49 (1973), 68–73.

22. Huff, D. L. "A Probabilistic Analysis of Consumer Spatial Behavior." In *Emerging Concepts in Marketing*, ed. W. S. Decker. Proceedings of the Winter Conference of the American Marketing Association, Chicago, 1962.

23. Isbell, E. C. "Internal Migration in Sweden and Intervening Opportunities." *American Sociological Review*, 9 (1944), 627–39.

24. Laber, G., and R. X. Chase. "Interprovincial Migration in Canada As a Human Capital Decision." *Journal of Political Economy*, 79 (1971), 795–804.

25. Lakshmanan, T. R., and W. G. Hansen. "A Retail Market Potential Model." *Journal, American Institute of Planners*, 31 (1965), 134–43.

26. Lingoes, J. C. *The Guttman-Lingoes Nonmetric Program Series*. Ann Arbor: Mathesis Press, 1973.

27. Lowry, I. S. *Migration and Metropolitan Growth: Two Analytical Models*. Institute of Government and Public Affairs Series, UCLA. San Francisco: Chandler Publishing Co., 1966.

28. Luce, R. *Individual Choice Behavior: A Theoretical Analysis*. New York: Wiley, 1959.

29. Lycan, R. "Interprovincial Migration in Canada: The Role of Spatial and Economic Factors." *Canadian Geographer*, 13 (1969), 237–54.

30. Miller, E. "A Note on the Role of Distance in Migration: Costs of Mobility versus Intervening Opportunties." *Journal of Regional Science*, 12 (1972), 475–78.

31. Mitchell, R. A. "An Explanation of the Expenditure Pattern of a Dispersed Population." Ph.D. dissertation, State University of Iowa, Iowa City, 1964.

32. Okun, B. "Interstate Population Migration and Income Inequality." *Economic Development and Cultural Change*, 16 (1968), 297–313.

33. Oliver, H. "Inter-regional Migration and Unemployment, 1951–61." *Journal of the Royal Statistical Society, Series A*, 127 (1964), 42–75.

34. Pack, J. R. "Determinants of Migration to Central Cities." *Journal of Regional Science*, 13 (1973), 249–60.

35. Roger, A. "A Regression Analysis of Interregional Migration in California." *The Review of Economics and Statistics*, 49 (1967), 262–67.

36. ————. *Matrix Analysis of Interregional Population Growth and Distribution.* Los Angeles: University of California Press, 1968.

37. Rushton, G. "The Scaling of Locational Preferences." In *Behavioral Problems in Geography: A Symposium,* ed. K. R. Cox and R. G. Golledge. Northwestern University Studies in Geography No. 17, Department of Geography, Northwestern University, 1969.

38. Stouffer, S. A. "Intervening Opportunities: A Theory Relating Mobility and Distance." *American Sociological Review,* 5 (1940), 845–67.

39. ————. "Intervening Opportunities and Competing Migrants." *Journal of Regional Science,* 2(1960), 813–27.

40. Strodtbeck, F. L. "Equal Opportunity Intervals: A Contribution to the Method of Intervening Opportunity Analysis." *American Sociological Review,* 14 (1949), 490–97.

41. United States Bureau of Census. *1960 Census of Population, Subject Report PC (2) 2B.* Washington: GPO, 1964.

42. Wilson, A. G. *Papers in Urban and Regional Analysis.* London: Pion, 1972.

43. Wilson, J.O. "Regional Differences in Social Welfare." Multilith, University of Kansas, Kansas City, 1967.

CHAPTER 14

VAUGHN M. LUECK

Cognitive and Affective Components of Residential Preferences for Cities: A Pilot Study

This research explores the utility of a multidimensional scaling approach as an actor-oriented procedure for inferring the place utility and action space concepts outlined in Wolpert's [53] model of the migration decision process. During the decade since Wolpert noted the declining prediction ability of regression models employing distance and economic opportunity variables, predictions of a coming era of "telemobility," when migration will be partially "absorbed" by electronic communications [5, 54], and of the possible emergence of cultural changes deemphasizing traditional economic concerns [37, 38, 45, 46] imply that the R^2's obtained in such models may approach zero at an accelerating rate. Meanwhile, the stream of regression studies continues unabated [24, 28, 32, 42, 50]. In large measure, this atavistic tendency has resulted from the limitations of Wolpert's model as an alternative behavioral formulation. As Wolpert himself admitted [53, p. 161], his framework was "of doubtful usefulness as an exact predictive tool," because it did not specify the measurements and observations needed to infer its central concepts, and later investigators [7, 8, 29] have had only partial success in specifying them. Wolpert's concept of action space was also ambiguous about whether action spaces were subjectively perceived entities or external ex post facto designations of the objective locational coordinates of places contained in the migrant's cognitive image. His satisficing concept of place utility, an additive composite of positive and negative utilities referred to a "threshold reference point" of neutral affect, carried the disturbing implication that migrants seek to avoid negative utilities but fail to be much attracted by positive utilities. Harvey [26] strongly criticized this aspect of the satisficing concept as theoretically barren unless given a multivariate optimizing interpretation, where deviations from optimality, rather than neutrality, serve to predict the preference ordering of spatial opportunities.

Despite its limitations, Wolpert's framework provides the germ of a viable model of the migration decision in its actor-oriented emphasis and in its analytical distinction between the cognitive (action space) and affective (place utility) components of the migration decision process. To produce a useful predictive tool one must give the action space concept a totally subjective interpretation, replace the assumption of satisficing behavior with an optimizing assumption, and specify a set of actor-oriented measurement procedures for inferring the cognitive and affective parameters included in the model. Recent suggestions that multidimensional scaling (MDS) models can form the basis of an integrated conceptual framework for describing spatial choice processes [13, 14, 15, 41] suggest that they may be precisely what is needed to accomplish this task. Strictly speaking, MDS algorithms are merely measurement models, but in their applications to similarities and preference data they can also be regarded as models for a low-level substantive theory of decision processes. Such a theory, while low level, nevertheless can be complete, since MDS models explicitly specify both the cognitive and affective components of decision processes and implicitly suggest transformation and combination rules for deriving preference rankings from underlying cognitive structures. Since these models both imply an underlying choice theory and provide an established repertoire of measurement procedures, they offer much hope for eliminating what Downs [15, p. 92] called "the most formidable obstacle in the development of theory in geographic space perception," namely, "the fundamental problem of integrating conceptual framework and measurement procedures."

Any choice theory based on MDS will be essentially synchronic, and questions concerning the origins of cognitive images and preferences in terms of learning, diffusion, information searching, personal influence, cognitive-affective consistency, and other processes are beyond the scope of such a theory. With repeated samplings of subjects, it is possible, in principle, to use MDS predictions to produce cross-temporal generalizations that can be used to test predictions derived from social and psychological process theories; but such generalizations do not provide a model for a process theory. Given the current state of the behavioral geographer's art, this is more a virtue than a defect of the approach. Until satisfactory empirical generalizations are formulated about the kinds of place and opportunity images and preferences that migrants possess, attempts to relate the migration decision to a larger system of behavioral processes and environmental influences (e.g. [33]) are apt to drift into the teleological fallacy of inferring the characteristics of system elements from the operating characteristics of the whole [26]. Successful prediction of the functioning of these elements (migrants) within a system structure depends on hard data on the "operating parameters" of the elements. An MDS-based framework can raise the questions that process theories and systems approaches must answer— a function of inestimable value— but it cannot provide the theories to answer them.

REFORMULATING WOLPERT

The Cognitive Component

In borrowing MDS concepts to reformulate Wolpert's framework, one may begin by replacing its ambiguous notion of action space with a subjective entity, the *cognitive map*.[1] Each spatial opportunity known to an individual may be represented by an n-dimensional vector defining its location in an n-dimensional cognitive space, with each of the n dimensions representing an attribute the individual perceives as independently contributing to the dissimilarity or discriminability of the opportunities. All of these dimensions are presumably commensurable, that is, an individual would judge two opportunities located a given distance apart along one dimension (all other dimensions being held constant) as unlike as another pair the same distance apart along another dimension. Cognitive maps thus correspond to the latent structures revealed by "simple space MDS" [20], which constructs a multidimensional configuration of stimulus objects from a dissimilarities matrix, in this case a matrix of individual or collective dissimilarities judgments collected by the method of paired comparisons or by one of the "pick k/n" techniques. [12].

The dimensionality of cognitive maps for particular kinds of spatial opportunities, the interpretation of cognitive scales, the typical position of given opportunities or opportunity types within the maps, and interpersonal and intergroup variations in these parameters are all empirical matters beyond the scope of this discussion. However, a few negative caveats concerning the contents of cognitive maps should be entered. First, cognitive scales derived from MDS analyses are not isomorphic with the semantic structures underlying the dissimilarities judgments used to construct the cognitive space. Rather they are composite scales somewhat akin to those constructed by Osgood, Suchi, and Tannenbaum [34], who used factor analysis to determine the basic dimensions of word meaning, and the nuances of meaning associated with individual descriptors of spatial opportunities would therefore be expressed by the angles between descriptions and the cognitive scales and by projections of the descriptors into additional dimensions represented by residual stress or unexplained variance. Therefore, one should not conclude that a given dimensionality represents the use of a corresponding number of descriptors, or that two individuals with identical cognitive maps would necessarily provide the same verbal description of opportunities whose dissimilarities they have judged.

Second, although the present use of the term "cognitive map" may suggest a parallel with the traditional geographic use of the term "mental map," which has connoted a kind of mental cartography in which the attributes represented are strictly locational, or at best preference scores hung on conventional geographical coordinates [22, 23], nothing of the sort is intended here. Migrants *may* employ geographical location, distance, or some similar variable in judging the dissimilarity of opportunities, but it is more reasonable to assume that they would more frequently employ other phenomenal attributes, such as attainable income, urban amenities, or climate [31]. A migrant's cognitive map may therefore contain either phenomenal or geographical scales, or both. Of course, many scales have a mixed character in that certain locational and phenomenal characteristics are perceived as strongly associated (climate and latitude, for example) and "load" on the same scale. Indeed, location itself may be a multidimensional construct.

Third, whereas most preference studies that have elicited responses on residential desirability [13, 22, 31] have concerned themselves solely with aggregate place attributes, the concept of cognitive map employed here is somewhat broader in scope. Many migrants are more concerned with evaluating particular opportunities, such as jobs, college openings, or retirement housing than they are with the environmental characteristics of the places in which those opportunities are located. For this reason the stimuli represented in the cognitive space must comprise a class or opportunity relevant to the goals for which an individual would undertake a migration, and the cognitive scales associated with these opportunities must represent both the specific characteristics of opportunities and the characteristics of locations offering opportunities. However, amenity and opportunity descriptors may not necessarily load on disjunct sets of cognitive scales. A migrant may, for example, infer the probability of encountering a satisfactory opportunity from the cognized place characteristics of potential destinations, and opportunity-specific scales may only be employed after a migration has been undertaken.

The Affective Component

Wolpert's concept of a threshold reference point of neutral affect can be replaced with the optimizing ideal point assumption embodied in a number of MDS algorithms that have been devised to scale preference data. The ideal point represents the combination of the attributes that the migrant associates with an optimal opportunity, and disutility or dissatisfaction is presumed to increase as some monotonic function of the cognitive distance between stimuli and the ideal along each of the scales. In some cases, it is conceivable that no optimal value exists, since the migrant may either prefer an infinite quantity of an attribute (for example, income) or prefer infinitely extreme quantities to intermediate amounts (for example, an individual who prefers either cold or hot climates to moderate ones). It is then more convenient to define a minimally preferred value for that dimension, away from which utility increases rather than declines [10, p. 121]. The ideal point for such a scale is thus really an anti-ideal. Multidimensional cases may contain some dimensions that have ideal points and others that have anti-ideals, in which case the location of the composite ideal within the cognitive space defines what Shepard [10, p. 122] has termed a "saddle point," a point "that is optimal with respect to some dimensions and 'pessimal' with respect to others."

Since the distances between the ideal and individual stimuli in such a joint space [20, p. 60] merely express dissimilarities between stimuli and the ideal, rather than disutilities or affective distances, one also needs a function that will transform cognitive distances into affective distances. Rushton's [39] revealed space preference technique, which estimates the location of indifference (isopreference) contours within a two-dimensional objective space, offers one partial solution to this problem, assuming that it could be generalized to multidimensional situations and that cognitive, rather than objective, spaces are used as reference coordinates. However, this approach provides no basis for generating prediction equations by which preference scores may be derived from cognitive scale values, and this impairs our ability to draw comparisons among individuals, locations, and demographic groups. Linear-quadratic unfolding models, as employed in the PREFMAP [23, pp. 108–32] algorithm escape this limitation, since they provide a means of estimating cognitive-to-affective prediction equations having parameters comparable across subjects and samples. The underlying assumption is that subjects or sample aggregates assign linear weights (here called *utility functions*) to each of the cognitive scales expressing its decision-making salience. In effect, these functions stretch or compress the cognitive scales to produce another space whose ideal-to-stimulus distances represent disutilities.

Given such a transformed space, it is then possible to derive "place disutilities" representing the aggregate amount of dissatisfaction associated with each opportunity, and to adopt a choice rule stating that the opportunity offering the smallest aggregate dissatisfaction would be selected. This requires a definition of affective distance, that is, a combination rule for combining the part-worths associated with each dimension of the transformed affective space into an aggregate measure of disutility. The definition of distance adopted in the linear-quadratic model differs from the conventional practice of employing either a Euclidean [41] or "city-block" [4, 14, 15] definition of distance, and rather assumes that preference scale values are linearly related to the *squares* of the Euclidean affective distances between stimuli and the ideal.

Given a cognitive map (a group space assumed to be identical for all subjects) expressed as a matrix,

$$C = c_{ij}, i = 1, 2, \ldots, m, j = 1, 2, \ldots, n, \tag{1}$$

representing the coordinates of m stimuli in a cognitive space of n dimensions, and a vector of ideal point coordinates for the kth subject or subsample mean

$$Y = y_{jk}, \qquad j = 1, 2, \ldots, n \tag{2}$$

and a vector of utility functions

$$U = u_{jk}, \qquad j = 1, 2, \ldots, n \tag{3}$$

expressing the affective salience of each of the n dimensions of C, then the distances between the ith stimulus and Y would be defined by

$$d_{iy} = \sum_{j=1}^{n} u_{jk} \, (c_{ij} - y_{jk})^2, \tag{4}$$

the square of the Euclidean interpoint distances. Y and U may be estimated by standard regression procedures. Given a matrix of preference scores for mm subjects or subsamples

$$S = s_{ik}, \qquad i = 1, 2, \ldots, m, k = 1, 2, \ldots, mm \tag{5}$$

for each of the m stimuli,[2] and assuming that the d_{iy} are least-squares estimates of the s_{ik}, it follows from (4) that

$$s_{ik} \approx \sum_{j=1}^{n} u_{jk} \, (c_{ij} - y_{jk})^2. \tag{6}$$

Expansion of (6) yields

$$s_{ik} \approx \sum_{j=1}^{n} u_{jk} c_{ij}^2 - 2u_{jk} c_{ij} y_{jk} + u_{jk} y_{jk}^2. \tag{7}$$

If it is assumed that

$$y_{jk} = -.5b_{jk}/u_{jk},\qquad(8)$$

substitution of (8) into (7) yields

$$s_{ik} \approx \sum_{j=1}^{n} u_{jk}c_{ij}^{2} + b_{jk}c_{ij} + .25b_{jk}^{2}/u_{jk}.\qquad(9)$$

This clearly implies a quadratic regression equation of the form

$$s_{ik} \approx \sum_{j=1}^{n} u_{jk}c_{ij}^{2} + b_{jk}c_{ij} + a_{i}\qquad(10)$$

where a_i is a constant.

Thus, by regressing k's preference scores on the cognitive coordinates of the stimuli and their squares, a direct estimate of his (its) utility functions may be obtained, and the coordinates of the ideal may be obtained from the b_{jk} and u_{jk} according to (8). In cases where Y is a saddle point, negative u_{jk} will be obtained for dimensions having anti-ideals. As Radner [36] has suggested, it is also conceivable that utility functions may be nonlinear, possibly quadratic, polynomial, or even polygonal, in form. Such functions could be esitmated by substituting various transformation of the c_{ij} in (10), but this would be a trial-and-error exercise in curve-fitting in the absence of any theories of utility function formation, and the assumption of linearity is probably the best point of departure at present.

Research Strategies

The proposed approach will not provide a viable alternative to traditional regression, unless a number of potential obstacles to its successful implementation are overcome. Probably the most serious one is the massive number of subjects that may have to be interviewed to produce a reasonable level of spatial precision in forecasts. This problem is directly posed by the data collection designs required to generate the similarity matrices used to infer the contents of cognitive maps. Even the simplest of these, the method of paired comparisons, requires subjects to make a number of judgments that increases as the square of the number of stimuli presented, and the limits of subject fatigue are quickly reached. The similarities of a large number of stimuli can only be obtained by presenting subjects with selected stimulus pairs (or triads and so forth in a pick k/n design). At a minimum, this implies that the number of subjects that must be interviewed increases as the square of the number of stimuli if judgments on more than about fifteen stimuli are required. However, this difficulty may not be too serious if one is able to construct reliable cognition functions relating the positions of stimuli on objective scales to their subjective positions. In that case, the probable locations of a large number of stimuli could be inferred from the locations of a few without resorting to complex questionnnaire designs.

The magnitude of the data collection task also depends on the amount of spatial variation in the cognitive maps and preference structures of potential migrants. If these variations are substantial, separate estimates of the aggregate cognitive maps and distributions of affective parameters of every origin region and/or pertinent sociodemographic stratum within a migration system may be required to avoid excessively noisy forecasts. Gould [22] and Rushton [40] have observed relatively little spatial variation in aggregate preference ordering of American states and midwestern rural shopping alternatives and offer hope that such fine stratification may be unnecessary, but Demko's [14] MDS study of the cognition of southern Ontario cities suggests that this stability may only characterize the affective component of choice, and a spatially stable mean does not necessarily imply a stable variance.

Even if the means and variances of all relevant parameters were absolutely stable, finely stratified samples may still be required if one contemplates construction of a probabilistic simulation model based on MDS results. Ideally, a probability density function would have to be specified for each relevant choice parameter—the positions of opportunities along each cognitive scale, ideal point locations, and utility functions. Unfortunately, such a task is beyond the capabilities of existing MDS procedures, and all that is currently feasible is estimation of the distributions of one or two parameters while holding the mean or group aggregate of another constant. For example, the INDSCAL [11, 52] model permits estimates of the across-subjects variance of cognitive dimension saliences, or the linear-quadratic models permit estimates of variances in utility functions and ideal point locations, but both models require one to assume the existence of a constant group cognitive space. Given these limitations, the only way in which an appropriate degree of realism can be introduced into forecasts is by using a hybrid approach in which some parameters, preferably the cognitive, are treated deterministically, but in which a kind of pseudoprobabilism is introduced by estimating group maps for finely divided strata, then referring the probability distributions of affective parameters to the subaggregates.

Considering the potential roadblocks, the data requirements for successful predictive application of the model may be so severe that a virtual census would be required to obtain the appropriate data. Obviously, data are needed on the magnitudes and sources of individual differences in cognitions and preferences and on spatial stability before a conclusive answer can be given.

Another potential obstacle is the problem of conjointly measuring the cognition and evaluation of amenity and opportunity characteristics. Migrants vary in their motives for migration, and while they may employ a common set of amenity scales describing the environmental characteristics of potential destinations, they also probably employ a set of goal-specific opportunity scales that vary according to the reason for migrating. Therefore, one is faced with the task of constructing goal-specific maps and affective structures whose amenity and opportunity scales are commensurable. This could be accomplished in principle by asking subjects to make similarity and preference judgments about hypothetical members of an opportunity class that simultaneously vary in location, as Hansen [25] has attempted to do, but such an experimental design may not produce valid results. Because of "man's demonstrable inability to take proper account, simultaneously, of the various component parts of . . . alternatives," when judgment tasks become excessively complex, "there seems to be an overwhelming tendency to collapse all dimensions into a single 'good versus bad' dimension with an attendant loss in detailed information about the configuration or pattern of attributes unique to any one object" [43, p. 257]. Thus, experimental designs that force subjects to make rapid-fire judgments about complex alternatives normally evaluated with greater deliberation are unlikely to yield data expressing the full complexity and subtlety of the migration decision process.

Probably the best means of avoiding this pitfall is to perform initially separate experiments on the environmental characteristics of locational alternatives and on each relevant opportunity class (occupations having certain incomes, retirement housing, colleges and universities, and so forth), in order to obtain reliable estimates of the parameters associated with each stimulus category. Once these benchmarks were well established, one could then carry out carefully designed factorial experiments eliciting preference and similarity judgments of location-opportunity combinations. Integration of the two substructures would not be too difficult for affective parameters, since if one assumes orthogonality of the two subspaces, a combined affective structure is easily described by the linear-quadratic models. Unfortunately, it would be difficult to determine whether the spaces are cognitively independent and, consequently, whether an orthogonality assumption is justified, since if a common space generated from location-opportunity similarities is of lower dimensionality than the summed dimensionalities of the corresponding subspaces, one can either infer interaction between the two sets of scales or attribute the results to the complexity of the judgment task. Perhaps one way out of this dilemma would be to systematically vary the complexity of the factorial designs and observe the effects on dimensionality. If the lower dimensionality of the common space is independent of complexity, then one would have to assume interaction, but if it approached the combined dimensionality of the subspaces as complexity was reduced, then an orthogonality assumption would be justified.

Some effort must also be devoted to determining the magnitude of differences between the preferences and cognitive structures of the general population and those of groups of potential migrants. The decision to migrate stimulates information-searching [53], and even in the absence of new information the mere act of thinking about something is apt to produce changes in the structure of preference and belief through the resolution of latent inconsistencies [2]. Thus, samples taken from the general population may not properly represent the characteristics of the soon-to-migrate. On the other hand, if it could be demonstrated that differences between the two populations were small, at least for some relevant parameters, then economies could be gained by sampling the general population instead of seeking out target groups of potential migrants.

Ultimately, we cannot avoid the issue of the validity of the parameters obtained from MDS analyses of similarities and preference judgments as predictors of spatial behavior. Do cognitive maps, ideal points, and utility functions obtained from data collected in contrived experimental situations really predict what people will do when confronted by real-world alternatives? Here the experience of investigators in the closely related domain of attitude research is instructive. Triandis [49, p. 15], summarizing research on the relationship between attitudes and behavior, concludes that "attitudes are neither necessary nor sufficient causes of behavior," and that they are rather "facilitative causes," which merely "predispose a class of actions to a particular class of social situations" [49, p. 2]. Attitudes do not completely predict behavior because other variables often intervene at the time behavior occurs, especially when the behavior is habitual or governed by social norms [49, p. 14]. While most migration behavior is probably not habitual,[3] conformity to family and community norms may frequently predispose potential migrants to define the decision-making situation in "should" terms rather than the "would like to" context of preference-judging experiments. The importance of such intervening variables can only be evaluated by follow-up studies that compare the predicted distribution of choices derived from scaling experiments with a later distribution of actual choices.

Thus, even though the proposed model provides a useful exploratory tool which can provide increased understanding about the virtually unexplored domain of the behavioral determinants of migration, increased understanding does not necessarily mean that we will soon be able to advance beyond the predictive ability of regression models. That depends on a demonstration of the predictive validity of an MDS-based approach and on the resolution of a number of potentially serious data collection problems.

THE PILOT STUDY

In May 1971, a pilot study was carried out to explore some of the unanswered questions just raised and to develop a survey questionnaire that could be administered en masse in the manner of a personal psychological inventory in future larger-scale investigations. Interest centered on the formulation of preliminary hypotheses about the dimensionality of the typical cognitive map, the subjective meaning and salience of its cognitive scales, and the values of the affective parameters associated with the scales. The study also investigated the degree of demographic and locational variation in the cognitive characteristics of the survey population, in order to formulate an intuitive estimate of the probable magnitude of the data collection problems outlined in the preceding section. The inquiry was restricted to responses concerning residential amenity characteristics of potential destination in the interests of reducing the complexity of the judgment tasks required of survey participants. Thus, the results of this survey cannot serve as a prediction of the future migration behavior of the survey population, even if it be assumed that the measures obtained properly represent the characteristics of a decision-making population.

The questionnaire elicited judgments on the dissimilarities and residential desirabilities of a group of American metropolitan areas from a sample of sixty-nine Michigan State University faculty members and students. It contained three batteries of items: an eleven-point rating scale on the residential desirability of thirty-two cities (Table 1), a five-point ordinal scale on information availability ranging from "no information" to "once lived in the city" for the same thirty-two cities (Table 2), and an eleven-point rating scale of paired comparison of dissimilarity for a subset of nine cities selected from the larger set of thirty-two. The nine cities selected were Ann Arbor, Atlanta, Cleveland, Flint, Gary, Milwaukee, Nashville, New York, and San Francisco; and the pairs were presented in random order (although the order was necessarily constant across subjects). The questionnaire also collected data on the age, sex, academic status, and longest exposure residence of the subjects.

Cognitive Characteristics

The dissimilarities judgments obtained from the questionnaire were normalized for each subject, and group means were then calculated for each judgment. The resulting mean dissimilarities matrix was scaled by Torgerson's [48] metric procedure, and experimentation with spaces of varying dimensionality indicated that a three-dimensional solution accounted for most of the variance in the input mean dissimilarities. The

TABLE 1

MEAN PREFERENCE RATINGS AND ASSOCIATED T-VALUES

City	Mean Rating			T-Statistic, for Cross-Group Comparisons		
	Group 1 (N=31)	Group 2 (N=22)	Group 3 (N=16)	1 vs. 2	1 vs. 3	2 vs. 3
Ann Arbor	1.52	1.59	2.13	.12	.86	.75
Atlanta	1.16	1.55	1.69	.54	.76	.17
Cleveland	−1.58	−1.45	−1.25	.22	.43	.26
Flint	−1.35	−2.82	−0.88	2.79[a]	.82	3.21[a]
Gary	−3.26	−3.95	−2.32	1.10	1.30	2.29[b]
Milwaukee	1.10	0.18	0.19	2.25[b]	1.68	.58
Nashville	−0.19	−1.95	0.00	2.83[b]	.34	3.34[b]
New York	−0.77	−0.32	0.81	.51	1.71	1.09
San Francisco	2.84	2.95	3.07	.21	.40	.17

[a]Significant at the .01 level.

[b]Significant at the .05 level for a two-tailed test under assumptions of unequal variances.

Item wording: "Listed below are some American Cities. Rate each one according to your conception of an ideal urban living environment. Consider the entire metropolitan area including both central city and suburbs in formulating your rating. If you think a city is an extremely desirable place to live, rate it a plus 5; if you think it extremely undesirable, rate it a minus 5; if your rating is neutral or indifferent, rate it a zero, and so on for intermediate ratings." Preference data for twenty-three other cities, not given here, were also collected.

TABLE 2

MEAN INFORMATION LEVELS AND ASSOCIATED T-VALUES

City	Mean Rating			T-statistic, for cross-group comparisons		
	Group 1	Group 2	Group 3	1 vs. 2	1 vs. 3	2 vs. 3
Ann Arbor	2.74	2.86	2.75	.68	.04	.48
Atlanta	2.10	2.36	1.88	1.01	.66	1.50
Cleveland	2.10	2.09	2.25	.02	.55	.51
Flint	1.87	2.64	2.00	2.41	.36	1.80
Gary	2.32	2.36	1.63	.14	2.28[a]	2.13[a]
Milwaukee	2.10	1.82	1.63	.94	1.57	1.26
Nashville	1.71	1.95	1.63	.78	.25	.20
New York	2.77	2.82	2.82	.19	.16	.03
San Francisco	2.13	2.32	2.25	.86	.56	.32

[a]Significant at the .05 level for a two-tailed test under assumptions of unequal variances.

Item wording: "Check the number that best describes the kind of information you have about the cities listed below; 0=no information, 1=only information gained from mass media TV, radio, newspapers, magazines, 2=letter from or conversations with friends or relatives, 3=have personally visited the city, 4=have once lived in the city."

three dimensions accounted for 45, 27, and 18 percent of the total variance, respectively, for a combined total of 89 percent. The cognitive map obtained by plotting the eigenvectors from the scaling solution (Fig. 1) is difficult to associate with external objective descriptors of city characteristics. In fact, experimentation indicated that most of the indicators that urban geographers have traditionally regarded as primary

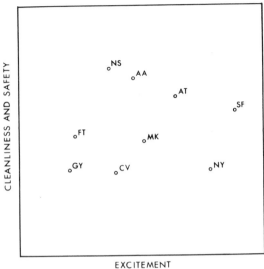

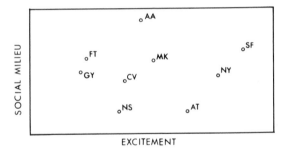

FIG. 1. Cognitive map for total sample

descriptors [6], such as functional importance, social rank, or economic specialization, display small and statistically insignificant correlations with all three of the subjective scales.[4] Nevertheless, it is possible to make a provisional assessment of the cognitive meaning of the scales, based on subsequent interviews with subjects and a lot of intuitive guesswork.

The first dimension appears to represent an "excitement" scale describing the physical amenities of the cities. It contrasts the primate metropolises New York and San Francisco, which have a wide range of entertainment, cultural activities, fine restaurants, quality shops, and visually exciting skylines and physical sites, with the perceived industrial drabness and "shot-and-a-beer" life styles available in Flint and Gary. The second dimension seems to be a "cleanliness and safety" scale describing the perceived quantity of threats to personal health and safety: crime, air pollution, substandard housing, and general filth and decay. New York, Cleveland, and Gary are perceived as slum-infested, crime-ridden, and polluted, in contrast with small, nonindustrial Ann Arbor and Nashville, seen as clean, safe, and tidy. The third dimension

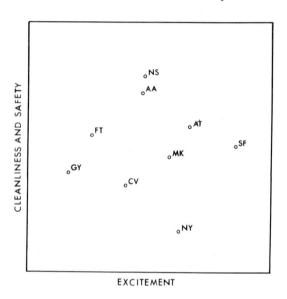

Fig. 2. Cognitive map for group 1

appears to be a ''social milieu'' scale describing the social or cultural characterisitics of the cities' populations, especially the degree of intellectual sophistication, and political-social liberalism. The scale contrasts the academic and counterculture-oriented atmosphere of Ann Arbor with what, from a Yankee viewpoint, appears to be the ''hillbilly'' or ''redneck'' qualities of the two southern cities, Atlanta and Nashville.

In order to examine intergroup variation in cognitive viewpoint, the subjects were classified into cognitively homogeneous groups using the

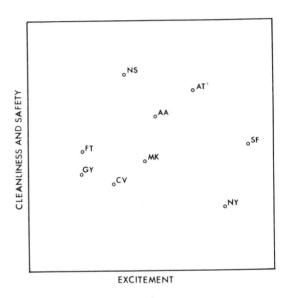

Fig. 3. Cognitive map for group 2

H-group [51] cluster analysis routine, which sequentially aggregates according to a criterion of minimum contribution to within-group variance. Normalized subject vectors of dissimilarity judgments were used as the *H*- group input. The results indicated a large increase in within-group variance after three groups were defined, and the three-group classification was selected for further analysis. Mean dissimilarities judgments were then calculated for each group, and the resulting matrices were separately scaled for three-dimensional solutions. Although the obtained configuration (Figs. 2, 3, and 4) display considerable

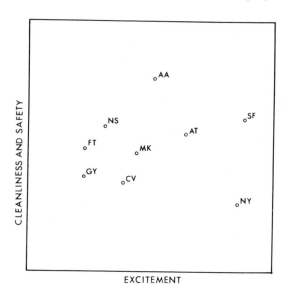

Fig. 4. Cognitive map for group 3

TABLE 3

ASSOCIATIONS BETWEEN GROUP MEMBERSHIP AND
DEMOGRAPHIC CHARACTERISTICS

	Group 1	Group 2	Group 3	Total
Place of longest *exposure residence*				
Detroit SMSA	4 (8.1)[a]	2 (5.7)	10 (4.2)	16
Other Michigan	10 (10.3)	10 (7.2)	3 (5.3)	23
Outside Michigan	17 (13.5)	10 (9.4)	3 (7.0)	30
Total	31	22	16	69
Chi-square = 17.96; df = 4; p = <.01				
Age				
20 and under	10 (9.4)	5 (6.6)	6 (4.9)	21
21 to 24	9 (12.6)	10 (8.9)	9 (6.5)	28
25 and over	12 (9.0)	7 (6.3)	1 (4.3)	20
Total	31	22	16	69
Chi-square = 6.45; df = 4; p = >.05				
Sex				
Male	27 (23.5)	15 (16.3)	10 (12.0)	52
Female	4 (7.6)	7 (5.3)	6 (3.9)	17
Total	31	22	16	69
Chi-square =4.37; df = 2; p = >.05				
Academic status				
Undergraduate	20 (21.6)	17 (15.1)	13 (11.1)	50
Geography graduate students and faculty	11 (8.5)	5 (6.0)	3 (4.4)	19
Total	31	22	16	69
Chi-square = 2.02; df = 2; p = >.05				

[a]Values in parentheses are expected frequencies.

mutual similarity, the minor differences that can be observed stimulate a provocative hypothesis.

Examination of the relationships between the demographic characteristics of the subjects and their group membership indicated that only the place of longest exposure residence was significantly related at the .01 level to group membership according to a chi-square criterion (Table 3). Group 1, with thirty-one cases, had a greater-than-expected frequency of non-Michigan exposure residences; Group 2, with twenty-two, had a modest bias toward outstate Michigan exposure residences; while group 3, containing sixteen cases, had a substantially greater-than-expected frequency of longest exposure residence in the Detroit metropolitan area. The association with residential experience suggests an explanation of the cognitive differences in terms of the ''milieu effects'' of long-term exposure to the particular set of information channels present in the places of previous residence. However, this expectation is denied when the mean familiarity scores (Table 2) for each city are compared between groups. No significant differences at the .05 level emerge, except for a relatively high familiarity with Flint for group 2, the group with many outstate Michiganders, and a relatively low familiarity with Gary for group 3, composed mainly of Detroiters. This probably reflects differences in the frequency of representation of these nearby cities within the direct contact spaces of group members [9]. Furthermore, the cognitive positions of these two cities vary little between groups. The observed cognitive differences thus cannot be explained by differences in information availability. The "milieu effect" must rather be described as residence-related variations in the way in which available information was processed and interpreted.

One possible explanation of the differences may be provided by the Sherif-Hovland social judgment theory [44], which suggests that an individual's reaction to information or opinions depends on his previous experience with the domain to which the items pertain. The theory states that an individual will develop an adaptation level along an affective continuum as a consequence of previous exposure that represents his most-preferred position. The most-preferred position will serve as an "anchor" against which new opinions are compared and distorted in a process of assimilation and contrast. Stimuli located near the reference point will be assimilated and pulled toward the most-preferred position, while those that are farther away will be contrasted and pushed even farther away. While social judgment theory has largely been used to explain the development of affectively laden attitudes, its generalization to the formation of cognitive images is perfectly reasonable, since the Sherif-Hovland theory itself was generalized from theories describing the perception of psychophysical, and presumably affectively neutral, stimuli such as weight or temperature. Thus, one can hypothesize that perhaps personal experience, interpersonal contacts, and media exposure in a person's home community generate a *cognitive* adaptation point, which is analogous to the most-preferred position but describes a "most-normal" reference anchor against which information about places outside the home community is assimilated and contrasted.

Several of the notable displacements of the cities within the group maps support an assimilation-contrast interpretation. For example, group 2 displaces Ann Arbor downward to a more dangerous and dirty location, while group 3 assigns it a very clean and safe position; yet both groups, because of their Michigan origins, would have been heavily exposed to news about a series of murders that afflicted the Ann Arbor–Ypsilanti area during the preceding year. The Detroiters, apparently adapted to more extensive violence in their own area, see nothing dramatic about a dozen homicides in a satellite center, whereas the outstaters, originating in more placid rural and small-city milieus, see their safety as threatened. Similarly, the Detroiters seem to be adapted to a higher level of cultural sophistication in their home city than are the outstaters, and have assimilated Ann Arbor to a more neutral position, while Atlanta and Nashville are contrasted with a more "hickish" image. However, there are other displacements that are difficult to explain in this way—for example, the downward displacement along dimension II of Atlanta and Nashville by group 3, or group 2's "unsophisticated" image of Cleveland. The deviant location of New York along dimensions I and II for group 1 is also difficult to explain with an adaptation hypothesis, given the heterogeneous residential experience of the group.

Affective Characteristics

In order to explore the affective differences among the three groups, the linear-quadratic unfolding model was applied to the mean preference scores of each group and its cognitive map (Table 4 and Fig. 5). The model provided a seemingly excellent fit of the preference scores to the cognitive spaces with R^2's of .994, .996, and .989 for groups 1, 2, and 3, respectively. However, with only six and two degrees of freedom, the associated F-ratios were significant only at the .05 level, and the error terms on the utility weights were very large, with only those for group 2 significantly different from zero at the .05 level. The regression coefficients for the raw coordinates are considerably more reliable, suggesting that the derived ideal point coordinates may have a reasonable stability despite higher errors on the denominator side of the ratio (see equation (8)). However, since the standard error of a ratio of two random variables is undefined, having a Cauchy distribution of infinite variance [30], standard inferential procedures could not be applied to the ideal

TABLE 4

SUMMARY OF RESULTS OF REGRESSION ANALYSIS OF
PREFERENCE SCORES ON COORDINATES OF COGNITIVE MAPS

	Group 1	Group 2	Group 3
Utility weights and standard errors[a]			
Dimension 1	50.05 ± 25.81	45.26 ± 16.56	18.34 ± 25.92
Dimension 2	50.11 ± 18.56	247.72 ± 37.00	20.61 ± 38.58
Dimension 3	12.41 ± 71.40	−329.34 ± 85.81	−17.01 ± 156.11
Coordinates of ideal point[b]			
Dimension 1	.216	.253	.409
Dimension 2	.092	.018	.407
Dimension 3	.444	.011	.017
Regression coefficients and standard errors for raw cognitive coordinates			
Dimension 1	−21.80 ± 1.76	−22.83 ± 1.16	−15.01 ± 2.21
Dimension 2	9.22 ± 2.63	− 8.96 ± 1.71	−16.76 ± 2.76
Dimension 3	−11.03 ± 2.35	− 7.01 ± 1.77	0.58 ± 4.40
Multiple R	.997	.998	.994
R^2	.994	.996	.989
F-ratio	56.41	86.25	29.15

[a]The utility weights are the $b_i x_i^2$ in the multiple regression equation

$$P = a + b_1 x_1^2 + b_2 x_2^2 + b_3 x_3^2 + c_1 x_1 + c_2 x_2 + c_3 x_3$$

where P is the preference scores multiplied by minus one, and the x_i are the coordinates of the cities in the cognitive dimensions.

[b]The coordinates of the ideal point are defined by $-.5 C_i x_i / B_i X^2_i$ (see Carroll, 1972).

coordinates. The most that could be done, given the limited goals of the present study, was to adopt provisionally the assumption that the ideal point locations are reasonable approximations of the locations that would be obtained with a sufficiently large number of stimuli. The comments that follow are therefore highly speculative and are merely intended to raise some questions that need to be explored in future investigations.

The most striking thing about the intergroup differences in ideal point locations is that these differences apparently are much greater than the intergroup differences in the positions of the stimuli in the cognitive spaces, even though the groups were defined according to cognitive similarity. Group 1's ideal is located a little beyond San Francisco on the excitement scale, at the midpoint of the cleanliness-safety scale— indicating that cities can apparently be too clean and too safe—and far beyond Ann Arbor on the social milieu scale. Groups 2's ideal has a similar location for excitement and cleanliness and safety, but its ideal on the social milieu dimension has moved down to a mid-scale location.

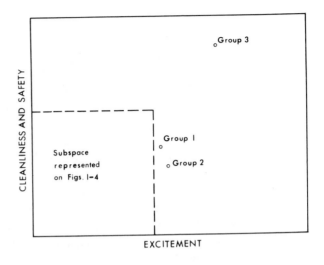

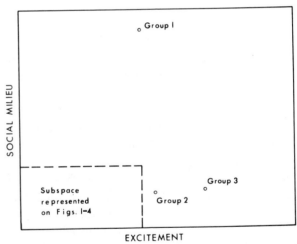

FIG. 5. Inferred locations of group saddle points referred to cognitive coordinates

The statistically significant negative utility function for this dimension indicates that the location is actually a saddle point representing the worst conceivable social milieu. Group 3 shares 2's social milieu saddle point, but prefers an extreme amount of cleanliness and safety, along with more excitement than the other two groups.

The ideal point locations prompt a number of questions. The greater degree of affective, as opposed to cognitive, variation between groups suggests the operation of cognitive-affective consistency processes, which may have systematically distorted the cognitive images to make them consistent with more salient underlying attitudes. This effect may simply be an artifact of questionnaire design, since the preference items were presented first, or it may reflect real exposure-related differences in attitude-formation processes, which, in turn, may have created the previously described distortions of information received from the national information pool.

Inferences about the sources of affective differences are complicated by the peculiar exposure history of the sample population. Most subjects had lived in East Lansing only a short time, which suggests that the ideal points obtained may well reflect a mixture of adaptation at the place of longest-exposure residence and the dissonance effects of moving to East Lansing. Affective adaptation effects (in this case involving ideal rather than most-normal anchors) from long-term exposure at the place of previous residence to attitude positions concerning the desirability of various characterisitics in one's living environment should have an influence on ideal point locations. On the other hand, cognitive dissonance theory [16, 17], which holds that affect and cognition are made consistent with past behavior, suggests that any adaptation effects may have been greatly disturbed by the necessity to rationalize the move to East Lansing. The combined effect of these two processes is difficult to specify, but the ideal point locations suggest that the dissonance effect is operating along dimensions where East Lansing compares favorably with the place of former residence; but where East Lansing compares unfavorably, the lingering adaptation from the former residence remains. In other words, the subjects seem to have concentrated their dissonance reduction efforts on increasing the salience of the negative features of the former place of residence, rather than by minimizing the importance of positive features.

Thus, group 1, with heterogeneous residential experience, much of it concentrated in the East Coast or California, locates the ideal in the "normal" position on the excitement and the cleanliness-safety scales, but on social milieu, where East Lansing is more likely to appear lacking, the effect of previous adaptation takes over and the ideal is moved upward. Likewise, the outward displacement for the ideal along the excitement scale for group 3, composed mainly of ex-Detroiters, may reflect lingering adaptation from the metropolitan milieu, whereas the extreme location along the cleanliness-safety scale may reflect a dissonance-reducing tendency to seize upon the crime and pollution of the metropolis as a reason for leaving it. The imposition of an anti-ideal on the social milieu dimension by groups 2 and 3 may also be accounted for by this hypothesis. Moving from urban working-class and middle-class Michigan environments into the student culture of East Lansing may have created a strong dissonance effect, in which any midwestern city became rejected as "too much like home," and either extreme of the social milieu scale became attractive by contrast.

CONCLUSIONS

The results of the pilot study suggest that cognitive images of residential amenity are relatively simple and locationally and demographically invariant. If this be the case, then the data-collection problems associated with an MDS-based approach to migration forecasting may not be as serious as one might fear. But since the survey population was demographically homogeneous, and the entire sample was drawn from the population of a single city (albeit a population of short-term residents), and since judgments were elicited about a very small number of stimuli (limiting the number of dimensions obtained) about which information is nationally available, firm conclusions about cognitive simplicity and locational and demographic variations require additional research.

As far as affective characteristics are concerned, future surveys clearly must collect data on a larger number of stimuli before the suggested linear-quadratic approach will give reliable results. The inferences that can be drawn from the affective characteristics of the sample do suggest, however, that affective structures are subject to more variation than the associated cognitive structures, that affective variations may even be the most important source of cognitive variations, and that the past migration experience of an individual may have a substantial influence on his current affective structure. If these inferences are correct, then samples drawn from the general population probably would not properly represent the images and preferences of migrants, since a substantial proportion of migrations are undertaken by repeat migrants [18, 19]. It also appears that theories of attitude formation and change, such as the assimilation-contrast or dissonance theories, may ultimately provide process explanations of the sources of cognitive and affective variations. If nothing else, the pilot study demonstrates that MDS analyses of cognitions and preferences can stimulate some provocative questions.

1. The original use of the term "cognitive map" [47] referred to mental images of spatial relationships, but the term later broadened in meaning to embrace any sort of cognitive image, whether spatial or phenomenal [1]. Demko [14] has recently used the term to specifically denote an MDS-derived cognitive space.

Since any spatial choice decision is derived from a perceived rather than objective environment, knowledge of cognitive structures is essential for a complete understanding of preference and choice. Nevertheless, few studies of spatial preferences have attempted simultaneous measurement of preferences and cognitive structures, and have instead preferred to relate preferences either directly to the objective characteristics of opportunities [39] or to cognitive structures inferred from factor analyses of individual differences in preference scores [22, 35]. The latter approach is especially likely to give misleading results, since many of the obtained scales may have been "folded" about an ideal point [12], and therefore may not necessarily be monotonic functions of the corresponding stimulus locations along cognitive scales.

2. The s_{ik} should be measured in such a way that scale values are *inversely* related to the degree of liking for the stimulus. However, this may easily be accomplished by multiplying preference judgments by minus one in cases where scores are positively related to preferability.

3. Other forms of spatial behavior, such as shopping behavior, do have a habitual repetitive character [21], and this may impair the predictive validity of MDS approaches for such classes of stimuli.

4. A later experiment (as yet unpublished), which employed a larger number of stimuli, obtained significant correlations between stimulus coordinates and objective variables. The results confirm the tentative interpretation of cleanliness-safety and social milieu scales, but suggest that the excitement scale is probably a compression of three dimensions not revealed here because of the limited number of stimuli employed.

LITERATURE CITED

1. Abelson, R. P. "A Technique and a Model for Multidimensional Attitude Scaling." *Public Opinion Quarterly*, 28 (1955), 414.

2. Abelson, R. P., and M. J. Rosenberg. "Symbolic Psycho-logic: A Model of Attitudinal Cognition." *Behavioral Science*, 3 (1958), 1–13.

3. Adams, R. B. "U. S. Metropolitan Migration: Dimensions and Predictability." *Proceedings, Association of American Geographers*, 1 (1969), 1–6.

4. Attneave, F. "Dimensions of Similarity." *American Journal of Psychology*, 63 (1950), 516–56.

5. Berry, B. J. L. "The Geography of the U. S. in the Year 2000." *Transactions, Institute of British Geographers*, 51 (1970), 21–43.

6. ———, ed. *City Classification Handbook: Methods and Applications*. New York: Wiley-Interscience, 1972.

7. Brown, L. A., F. A. Horton, and R. I. Wittick. "Place Utility and the Normative Allocation of Intra-Urban Migrants." *Demography*, 7 (1970), 175–83.

8. Brown, L. A., and D. B. Longbrake. "Migration Flows in Intra-Urban Space: Place Utility Considerations." *Annals, Association of American Geographers*, 60 (1970), 368–84.

9. Brown, L. A., and E. G. Moore. "The Intra-Urban Migration Process: A Perspective." *Geografiska Annaler*, 52B (1970), 1–13.

10. Carroll, J. D. "Individual Differences and Multidimensional Scaling." In *Multidimensional Scaling: Theory and Applications in the Behavorial Sciences*, ed. R. N. Shepard et al., pp. 105–55. New York: Academic Press, 1972.

11. Carroll, J. D., and J. J. Chang. "Analysis of Individual Differences in Multidimensional Scaling via an N-way Generalization of Eckart-Young Decomposition." *Psychometrika*, 35 (1970), 283–319.

12. Coombs, C. H. *A Theory of Data*. New York: John Wiley and Sons, 1964.

13. Demko, D. "Cognition of Southern Ontario Cities in a Potential Migration Context." *Economic Geography*, 50 (1974) 20–33.

14. Demko, D., and R. Briggs. "A Model of Spatial Choice and Related Operational Considerations." *Proceedings, Association of American Geographers*, 3 (1971), 49–52.

15. Downs, R. M. "Geographic Space Perception: Past Approaches and Future Prospects." In *Progress in Geography: International Review of Current Research*, vol. 2, ed. C. Board et al., pp. 65–108. New York: St. Martin's, 1970.

16. Festinger, L. *A Theory of Cognitive Dissonance*. Stanford: Stanford University Press, 1957.

17. ———. *Conflict, Decision, and Dissonance*. Stanford: Stanford University Press, 1964.

18. Goldstein, S. "Repeated Migration as a Factor in High Mobility Rates." *American Sociological Review*, 19 (1954), 536–51.

19. ———. "The Extent of Repeated Migration: An Anlysis Based on the Danish Population Register." *Journal of the American Statistical Association*, 57 (1964), 1121–32.

20. Golledge, R. G., and G. Rushton. *Multidimensional Scaling: Review and Geographical Applications*. Technical Paper No. 10., Commission on College Geography, Association of American Geographers, Washington, D.C., 1972.

21. Golledge, R. G., and G. Zannaras. "Cognitive Approaches to Spatial Behavior." In *Environment and Cognition*, ed. W. H. Ittelson, pp. 59–94. New York: Academic Press, 1973.

22. Gould, P. R. "On Mental Maps." In *Man, Space, and Environment*, ed. P. W. English and R. C. Mayfield, pp. 260–81. New York: Oxford University Press, 1972.

23. Green, P. E., and V. R. Rao. *Applied Multidimensional Scaling*. New York: Holt, Rinehart & Winston, 1972.

24. Greenwood, M. J. "An Analysis of the Determinants of Geographic Labor Mobility in the United States." *Review of Economics and Statistics*, 151 (1969).

25. Hansen, N. M. *Rural Poverty and the Urban Crisis*. Bloomington: Indiana University Press, 1970.

26. Harvey, D. W. "Conceptual and Measurement Problems in the Cognitive-Behavioral Approach to Location Theory." In *Behavioral Problems in Geography: A Symposium*, ed. K. R. Cox and R. G. Golledge. Northwestern University Studies in Geography No. 17, Department of Geography, Northwestern University, 1969.

27. Hempel, C. G. "The Logic of Functional Analysis." In *Aspects of Scientific Explanation*, ed. C. G. Hempel, pp. 297–330. New York: Free Press, 1965.

28. Hirsch, F. *Geographical Patterns of Intermetropolitan Migration in the United States, 1955 to 1960*. Ph.D. dissertation, University of Washington, 1969.

29. Horton, F. E., and D. R. Reynolds. "Effects of Urban Spatial Structure on Individual Behavior." *Economic Geography,* 47 (1971), 36–48.

30. Kendall, M. G., and A. Stuart. *The Advanced Theory of Statistics,* vol. 1, *Distribution Theory.* London: Charles Griffin, 1967.

31. Lieber, S. "A Joint Space Analysis of Preference and Their Underlying Traits." Discussion Paper No. 19, Department of Geography, University of Iowa, July 1, 1971.

32. Lowry, I. S. *Migration and Metropolitan Growth: Two Analytical Models.* San Francisco: Chandler Publishing, 1966.

33. Mabogunje, A. K. "Systems Approach to a Theory of Rural-Urban Migration." *Geographical Analysis,* 2 (1970), 1–18.

34. Osgood, C. E., G. J. Suchi, and P. H. Tannenbaum. *The Measurement of Meaning.* Urbana: University of Illinois Press, 1957.

35. Peterson, G. L. "A Model of Preference: Quantitative Analysis of the Perception of the Visual Appearance of Residential Neighborhoods." *Journal of Regional Science,* 7 (1967), 19–32.

36. Radner, R. "Mathematical Specification of Goals for Decision Problems." In *Human Judgments and Optimality,* ed. M. W. Shelly and G. L. Bryan, pp. 178–216. New York: Wiley, 1964.

37. Reich, C. A. *The Greening of America.* New York: Random House, 1970.

38. Roszak, T. *Where the Wasteland Ends: Politics and Transcendance in Postindustrial Society.* Garden City: Doubleday, 1972.

39. Rushton, G. "Analysis of Spatial Behavior by Revealed Space Preference." *Annals, Association of American Geographers,* 59 (1969), 391–400.

40. ———. "Preference and Choice in Different Environments." *Proceedings, Association of American Geographers,* 3 (1971), 146–50.

41. Sack, R. D. *Geographic Location and Human Behavior.* Ph.D. dissertation, University of Minnesota, 1970.

42. Schwind, P. J. *Migration and Regional Development in the United States, 1950–60.* Research Paper No. 133, Department of Geography, University of Chicago, 1971.

43. Shepard, R. N. "On Subjectively Optimum Selections among Multiattribute Alternatives." *Human Judgments and Optimality,* ed. M. W. Shelly and G. L. Bryan, pp. 257–81. New York: Wiley, 1964.

44. Sherif, M., and C. I. Hovland. *Social Judgment.* New Haven: Yale University Press, 1961.

45. Slater, P. *The Pursuit of Loneliness: American Culture at the Breaking Point.* Boston: Beacon Press, 1970.

46. Theobald, R. *An Alternative Future for America II.* Chicago: Swallow Press, 1971.

47. Tolman, E. C. "Cognitive Maps in Rats and Men." *Psychological Review,* 55 (1948), 189–208.

48. Torgerson, W. S. *Theory and Methods of Scaling.* New York: Wiley, 1958.

49. Triandis, H. C. *Attitude and Attitude Change.* New York: Wiley, 1971.

50. Vanderkamp, J. "Migration Flows, Their Determinants, and the Effects of Return Migration." *Journal of Political Economy,* 79 (1971), 1012–31.

51. Veldman, D. J. *FORTRAN Programming for the Behavioral Sciences.* New York: Holt, Rinehart and Winston, 1967.

52. Wish, M., M. Deutsch, and L. Biener. "Differences in Conceptual Structures of Nations: An Exploratory Study." *Journal of Personality and Social Psychology,* 16 (1970), 361–73.

53. Wolpert, J. "Behavioral Aspects of the Decision to Migrate." *Papers and Proceedings of the Regional Science Association,* 15, (1965), 159–69.

54. Zelinsky, W. "Hypothesis of the Mobility Transition." *Geographical Review,* 61 (1971), 219–49.

CHAPTER 15

W. A. V. CLARK

Technical and Substantive Approaches to Spatial Behavior: A Commentary

The quest for better explanatory models in geography has been a major element of geographic research in the 1960s and 1970s and an especially important reason for the development of behavioral research in geography. As Cox and Golledge [4, p. 1] point out, the examination of the behavioral basis of spatial activity is not new, "for many existing theories and models in geography have at least an implicit behavioral element in their structure." However, research using the behavioral approach in geography focuses on the explicit attempt to build geographic theory using postulates of human behavior. From this focus the emphasis on psychology as a source of models, methods, and meaning was a logical end. The four papers in this section are examples of the attempts to build models or to develop measurement techniques for the investigation of spatial phenomena.

While the early studies using a spatial behavioral approach drew on the allied fields of economics, sociology, and psychology, the more recent studies, including most papers in this volume, are more dependent on the use of models and techniques drawn exclusively from psychology. This concern with psychology has emphasized the investigations that focus on *why* certain activities take place, rather than simply on the actual spatial patterns [9]. The direct concern with explanation leads to an important distinction between explanation and predictions, and this dichotomy is one of the fundamental issues in the papers in this section and in the behavioral approach in general.

A central issue of consideration in the behavioral approach is the relationship between form and process. A classical geographical investigative framework is one in which we conceive of an individual operating within a given structure and we uncover inferences about behavior from an analysis of the spatial patterns. Indeed, the inferences about behavior may be drawn from the pattern of settlements or shopping centers, or there may be inferences about the reasons for a particular observed and existing behavior such as a change of residence. The directional bias work in intraurban migration is a good example of inferences about behavior from the knowledge of spatial patterns. On the other hand, the behavioral approach is directed to deriving spatial patterns from assumptions about individual or group behavior. The papers presently under analysis are attempts at an initial specification of the behavioral postulates [7, 13, 14, 15].

Harvey sums up the reason for the strong appeal of the behavioral approach—that we will understand "the real reasons why people behave with respect to their environment in the way that they do" [12, p. 37]. As Burnett notes, this view suggests that the interest is in a general theory of human spatial choice [2, p. 181]. But, such a sweeping aim is unlikely to be easily satisfied, and more importantly, as Burnett notes, it may be premature to develop or adapt sophisticated mathematical models of real-world spatial learning and choice until some largely qualitative empirical work on the appropriate forms for theory has been accomplished [2, p. 183]. Indeed, as we will discover, a critical issue in these and other papers is the need to develop "definitive answers about what properties of alternatives really condition spatial choices" [2, p. 183].

In that the discussion that follows draws only selectively from the articles for observations on various aspects of the behavioral approach in geography, it is important to see the four papers in a more general context. Two of the papers, those by Lieber and Louviere [13, 14], are essentially technical works concerned with the use of models borrowed or adapted from psychology. Although they use these models on spatial data, the substantive nature of the investigation is (seemingly) less important than the technical questions that are raised and answered. Both studies are dependent on data derived from sets of hypothetical situations. While Louviere has introduced the valuable theory and methodology of human information-processing, Lieber stresses that we need further knowledge not just about scaling the stimuli but also about the form of the scaling models. Thus, a principal aim of Lieber's paper is to specify the functional form of the preference function. But lest it be thought that the papers are narrowly technical, we can note Louviere's important reformulation of Rushton's [18] "spatial behavior" and "behavior in space" concepts to include the distinction among "a spatial variable being considered by an individual in the judgment process, the response [which may be spatial], or . . . the consequences of the response [which] are spatial sets." This division of the stimulus and the behavior shows clearly the close links to the approach of the psychologist.

Although the second pair of studies are also very much involved with the use of models drawn from psychology and their usefulness in geographical research, it seems appropriate to classify them as substantive investigations of the behavior of interstate and potential intercity migrants. While Ewing [7] focuses on uncovering the preference structure of interstate migrants, particularly emphasizing choice between alternative destinations, Lueck [15] analyzes a questionnaire of "responses concerning residential amenity characteristics of potential destinations." Thus, the Lueck study is of potential migration in contrast to the Ewing study of actual migration.

Underlying all the papers is the theme of attitude and behavior, although the authors in general do not spell out or discuss the assumptions of this problem. The first pair of papers are directly involved also with all the difficulties of adapting psychological models for spatial research, and the nature of the modeling procedures and their influence on substantive results. Whether the problems they choose to study are important for further understanding of spatial behavior is an important issue too. The Ewing and Lueck papers [7, 15] outline several criticisms of the regression approaches to spatial behavior, and migration in particular, and set up a dichotomy between economic regression approaches and cognitive behavioral models.

These general comments on the papers set the scene for a more detailed discussion of the several themes just outlined—all of them important in the realm of cognitive behavioral research. The remainder of the review will focus on the relationships between attitude and behavior, regression versus cognitive modeling, the technical difficulties of adapting psychological models for geographical investigations, and the analysis of substantive versus trivial problems. A separate but important problem that has already been emphasized generally in the geographical literature, but which is less relevant in the present studies, is the inadequacy of aggregate data bases.

One of the most important, and often unspecified, issues in the behavioral approach is related to the links between attitudes and behavior. We can think of a two-part paradigm in which first we assume that we can meaningfully separate attitudes (or cognition) and behavior and second, having separated attitude and behavior, we can either assume that attitudes cause behavior or behavior causes attitudes. The assumption often implicit in geographical behavioral studies is that attitude is a *good* predictor of behavior. However, Festinger [8] has noted that it is at least as likely that behavior determines attitudes, and it is this result that led him to emphasize in psychology the importance of an approach in which the investigator first measures attitude, then behavior, and finally attitude again (preferably several times). In fact, Wicker is more critical of attitude and behavior studies. In a review of attitude versus actions, he argues against the existence of stable underlying attitudes, and more explicitly he writes, "researchers who believe that assessing attitudes is an easy way to study overt social behaviors should provide evidence that their verbal measures correspond to relevant behaviors" [20, p. 75]. Lieber [13] uses a hypothetical situation of choices of gas prices and distances to gas stations as the basis for uncovering the consumer behavioral choice processes. Had he also investigated actual behavior, he would have been closer to the type of study suggested by Festinger, in which the relationships could be more specifically enunciated [8]. Lieber notes that the subjects' preference patterns remained essentially the same, despite the two-month lag *and whatever* changes might have occurred in their purchasing environment. However, it is their actual behavior that would bring further understanding to the cognitive-behavioral modeling strategies. Such an approach in geographical investigations has been missing; and until investigations that extend the Lieber approach are forthcoming, it is likely that we will leave unsolved the true relationships between attitude and behavior.

In attempting to investigate the links between attitude and behavior, there is not just a problem of which determines which, but also a problem of selecting variables as inputs to the choice models. Thus, in the Lieber study two variables, price and distance, were used to develop attitude structures [13]. Therefore, we are not only concerned with the problem of attitude as a good predictor of behavior, but also with the problem of whether attitude on the basis of *these two variables* is a good predictor of behavior. Even if we agree that attitude is a good predictor of behavior, we may not find that we can agree that price and distance are good predictors of the behavior related to buying gasoline, or indeed that these are a good operational definition of the attitude in question. In another context Burnett [2] argues convincingly against the "traditional" objective attributes in shopping center patronage. Even in an initial study it is important that we make an attempt to identify the real components of the attitude system, rather than assume away all complexity in order to employ a particular psychological model. Thus, the fact that the behavior remained stable over a two-month period in Lieber's research could be a reflection of the fact that the study assumed away the important attitude dimensions.

An equally important problem is that of regression versus cognitive modeling of behavior. Indeed, there is some evidence that a major dichotomy of regression economic models versus behavioral psychogeographical models is developing in the literature. Such a division is of more than temporary interest. Both Lueck and Ewing [7, 15] are severely critical of regression modeling for behavioral investigations, and Lueck in particular suggests that the R^2 obtained in models using distance and economic opportunity variables might soon approach zero. Ewing in this paper and in an earlier paper [6] emphasizes that there is the problem of the variation in results from the use of the gravity model formulation for either all origins and destinations, or some selected subset of origins and a destination. He argues that there is need for a "model which explicitly considers the nature of the alternatives available as well as the one chosen" [7]. But are these criticisms sufficiently documented so that we must shun regression models in investigations of behavior, particularly in migrational studies? Although there is no straightforward answer, it is important to recognize that substantive work is continuing within economics *and* that there is an important difference between prediction and explanation.

Both Lueck and Ewing reject the economic-regression work as exemplified by Greenwood [11] but without fully recognizing (*a*) that further developments within the economic-regression approach are emphasizing both noneconomic variables and the human capital investment concept [1, 5, 19] and (*b*) that the end aim of the economists is a predictive model that will yield serviceable results with respect to migration streams. Without further defending the economic-regression approach, suffice it to say that the end aim of the research is a prediction of migration flows, particularly with respect to policy decision-making [5]. Moreover, Lueck notes that presently his approach will not provide a viable alternative to traditional regression models, and Ewing skirts the problem of combining the choice model he develops with an emigration model in order to predict the interregional migration rate between regions. This may be the most important future development if the cognitive behavioral model (in this instance) is to supplant the economic-regression model.

Only Louviere (who in fact does not deal with migration) takes up the important prediction-versus-explanation discussion, even though both Olsson and Harvey have emphasized its importance in geographical research [12, 17]. Louviere notes that "where the emphasis is on theory construction rather than practical prediction . . . designs other than the regression model are more appropriate" [14]. Harvey [12, p. 37] developed an appealing set of strategies with respect to models of spatial phenomena. He suggested that we can seek to extend classical location theory, build a stochastic location theory, or develop cognitive behavioral models. But the approaches are not mutually exclusive, and normative-economic modeling may well be an important and continuing component of understanding spatial behavioral problems. Furthermore, the "general aggregative characteristics of migration, journey to work, journey to shop" will probably be usefully handled in models that have elements of the economic normative approach *and* stochastic variables [12, p. 39].

On a general philosophical level, the debate is between a model that yields "useful" parameter estimates and a "good" prediction and a model that is a good explanation. As Olsson notes, "since explanation requires the use of general law statements, it follows that successful prediction is not the same as successful explanation" [16, p. 230]. The quest for explanation in the cognitive behavioral mode may have led to the rejection of perfectly adequate predictive models.

A more serious difficulty is specific to the Ewing article. Although his development of a preference structure of states from the flows of migrants seems sound and yields a set of results that are consistent with our intuitive notions of the perception surface for states (*and,* interestingly, are not too different from the results of the much earlier and less structured perception study reported by Gould [10]), his use of this unidimensional scale of attractiveness is more difficult to accept. The concluding section of the paper regresses attractiveness scores by state, against some nineteen variables representing a variety of population, socioeconomic, and amenity measures by state. He cautions against a causal interpretation, but in fact a more important caveat is in order. Ewing seems to be implying that behavior of the migrants is affected by the variables that are significantly related to state attractiveness. In fact the attractiveness of a state for an individual might well be a variety of variables from job opportunities to the existence of family ties. It is important to recognize that *the reason* for migration has not been uncovered, not only because we do not have measures of attitudes, but also because we are dealing with aggregate migrational streams; and as Ewing recognizes, the attractiveness of a state is not the same for all residents. It seems unlikely that we can in fact say any more about migrational behavior from this model than we can from the preference maps of Gould [10] or Clark and Cadwallader [3].

The ways in which the psychological models have been adapted for use in geography and their relative ease of adaptation suggest that it is possible that the experimental paradigm will be an important contribution to further theory construction in geography. Louviere and Lieber make different but important points with respect to the use of psychological models in geography. The former emphasizes the usefulness of the laboratory to ''hold constant'' the myriad complex forces in the real world. The important conclusion is that consistent results from the laboratory will enable geographers to ''proceed from observed regularities, to model building, to empirical testing.'' Lieber in contrast introduces two models, one of which is suitable for the laboratory situation and the other suitable for survey situations. Naturally, he argues for the complementary use of the models. If, however, the models are going to be adapted for the analysis of spatial problems, it is important that they be used in important spatial contexts, with variables that are meaningful in terms of the attitudes and behavior being evaluated. The gas price-distance model is unlikely to yield significant output on spatial problems, but the bus-mode choice model is more promising. When Harvey raised the problem of whether only trivial behavioral formulations might be developed after enormous research effort, he was raising a very real problem for cognitive behavioral research—which has only partly been answered [12].

Finally, we might look briefly at the last theme, which is an explicit element of three of the papers. It is one of the strengths of the cognitive behavioral approach that the investigations of attitudes and behavior have forced our attention back to the individual and his spatial responses in the environment. Even if we cannot easily obtain the highly disaggregated data necessary for many of the cognitive behavioral models, the impetus towards more realistic data bases and away from aggregate census data is an important one.

The MDS approaches do accomplish more than "stimulate some provocative questions" (Lueck [15]). They have already yielded some important insights on the make-up of the cognitive map, and the ways in which we might reformulate the variables entering our general normative economic models. However, the actual substantive interpretations of spatial behavior based on cognitive behavioral modeling are still missing. The next important step is the presentation of substantive results that offer new insights into spatial structure and spatial behavior.

ACKNOWLEDGMENT

I would like to thank David Stea of the School of Architecture and Urban Planning, University of California, Los Angeles, for an enlightening discussion of the problems of relating attitudes and behavior.

LITERATURE CITED

1. Bowles, S. "Migration as Investment: Empirical Tests of the Human Investment Approach to Geographic Mobility." *Review of Economics and Statistics,* 52 (1970), 356–62.
2. Burnett, P. "The Dimensions of Alternatives in Spatial Choice Processes." *Geographical Analysis,* 5 (1973), 181–204.
3. Clark, W. A. V., and M. Cadwallader. "Residential Preferences: An Alternate View of Intraurban Space." *Environment and Planning,* 5 (1973), 693–703.

4. Cox, K. R., and R. G. Golledge, eds. *Behavioral Problems in Geography: A Symposium."* Northwestern University Studies in Geography No. 17, Department of Geography, Northwestern University, 1969.

5. DaVanzo, J. *An Analytical Framework for Studying the Potential Effects of an Income Maintenance Program on U.S. Interregional Migration.* The Rand Corporation, 1972.

6. Ewing, G. O. "Gravity and Linear Regression Models of Spatial Interaction: A Cautionary Note." *Economic Geography,* 50 (1974), 83–87.

7. Ewing, G. O. "Environmental and Spatial Preferences of Interstate Migrants in the United States." This volume.

8. Festinger, L. *A Theory of Cognitive Dissonance.* Stanford: Stanford University Press, 1957.

9. Golledge, R. G., L. A. Brown, and F. Williamson. "Behavioral Approaches in Geography: An Overview." *The Australian Geographer,* 12 (1972), 59–79.

10. Gould, P. "Structuring Information on Spacio Temporal Preferences." *Journal of Regional Science,* 7 (Supplement, 1967), 259–74.

11. Greenwood, M. J. "An Analysis of the Determinants of Geographic Labor Mobility in the United States." *Review of Economics and Statistics,* 51 (1969), 189–94.

12. Harvey, D. "Conceptual and Measurement Problems in the Cognitive-Behavioral Approach to Location Theory." In *Behavioral Problems in Geography: A Symposium,* ed. K. R. Cox and R. G. Golledge, pp. 35–68. Northwestern University Studies in Geography No. 17, Department of Geography, Northwestern University, 1969.

13. Lieber, S. R. "A Comparison of Metric and Nonmetric Scaling Models in Preference Research." This volume.

14. Louviere, J. J. "Information-processing Theory and Functional Form in Spatial Behavior." This volume.

15. Lueck, V. M. "Cognitive and Affective Components of Residential Preferences for Cities: A Pilot Study." This volume.

16. Olsson, G. "Explanation, Prediction, and Meaning Variance: An Assessment of Distance Interaction Models." *Economic Geography,* 46 (1970), 223–33.

17. ———. "Inference Problems in Locational Analysis." In *Behavioral Problems in Geography: A Symposium,* ed. K. R. Cox and R. G. Golledge, pp. 14–34. Northwestern University Studies in Geography No. 17, Department of Geography, Northwestern University, 1969.

18. Rushton, G. "Analysis of Spatial Behavior by Revealed Preference." *Annals, Association of American Geographers,* 59 (1969), 391–400.

19. Sjaastad, L. A. "The Costs and Returns of Human Migration." *Journal of Political Economy,* 70 (Supplement, 1969), 80–93.

20. Wicker, A. W. "Attitudes versus Actions: The Relationship of Verbal and Overt Behavioral Responses to Attitude Objects." *Journal of Social Issues,* 28, no. 4 (1969), 41–78.

NOTES ON THE CONTRIBUTORS

John F. Betak is assistant director of the Division of Research, Council for Advanced Transportation Studies, University of Texas at Austin.

Pat Burnett is assistant professor of geography at the University of Texas at Austin.

William A. V. Clark is professor of geography at the University of California—Los Angeles.

Gordon O. Ewing is assistant professor of geography at McGill University.

Reginald G. Golledge is professor of geography at Ohio State University.

Michael F. Goodchild is associate professor of geography at the University of Western Ontario.

Peter Gould is professor of geography at Pennsylvania State University.

Susan Hanson is assistant professor in the Department of Geography and the Department of Sociology at the State University of New York at Buffalo.

Elizabeth J. Harman is a policy analyst in the Canadian Department of Regional Economic Expansion, Ottawa.

Robert L. Knight is associated with DeLeu, Cather & Company, San Francisco.

Stanley R. Lieber is lecturer in geography at the University of Haifa.

Jordan J. Louviere is assistant professor of geography at the University of Wyoming.

Vaughn M. Lueck is instructor in geography at the University of Pittsburgh.

Mark D. Menchik is associated with the Rand Institute, Los Angeles.

Victoria L. Rivizzigno is graduate teaching associate in the Department of Geography at Ohio State University.

Gerard Rushton is professor of geography at the University of Iowa.

Joseph Sonnenfeld is professor of geography at Texas A & M University.

Aron Spector is graduate teaching associate in the Department of Geography at Ohio State University.

Waldo R. Tobler is professor of geography at the University of Michigan.

INDEX

316